Winners Without Losers

Winners Without Losers

Structures and Strategies for Increasing Student Motivation to Learn

JAMES P. RAFFINI
University of Wisconsin–Whitewater

ALLYN AND BACON
Boston   London   Toronto   Sydney   Tokyo   Singapore

Copyright © 1993 by Allyn and Bacon
A Division of Simon & Schuster, Inc.
160 Gould Street
Needham Heights, Massachusetts 02194

Library of Congress Cataloging-in-Publication Data

Raffini, James P.
  Winners without losers : structures and strategies for increasing
student motivation to learn / James P. Raffini.
     p.   cm.
  Includes bibliographical references and index.
  ISBN 0-205-16707-1
  1. Motivation in education.   2. Achievement motivation in
children.   3. Learning, Psychology of.   4. Teaching.   I. Title.
LB1065.R324   1992
370.15′4–dc20   92-19529
                                                         CIP

Printed in the United States of America
10 9 8 7 6 5 4 3 2   98 97

To the students and teachers who have suggested or field-tested the enclosed motivational strategies—without your contributions this book would have remained half finished.

CONTENTS

Preface   **xi**

1 Introduction   **1**
Goals for Education—Excellence *and* Effort?   2
This Book's Approach—Research-Based Recommendations
and Strategies for Motivation   5

2 Psychological Needs of Students   **11**
Maslow's Hierarchy of Needs   11
A Perceptual View of Student Behavior   13
The Need for Self-Worth   15
The Need fo. Autonomy and Self-Determination   17
The Need for Competence   20
The Need for Belonging and Relatedness   23

3 Student Apathy in the Classroom   **31**
Apathy—The Student's Point of View   36
Academic Ability: Fixed or Malleable?   39
Norm-Referenced Evaluation: For Every Winner, a Loser   46
The Threat to Self-Worth: Forced Competition   50
Failure-Avoiding Behavior   56

4 Fostering and Undermining Intrinsic Motivation   **63**
Characteristics of Intrinsically Motivating Behavior   64
Suggestions for Fostering Intrinsic Motivation in the
Classroom   67

Sources of Intrinsic Motivation   69
The Effects of External Rewards on Intrinsic Motivation   72
How Rewards Affect Motivation   74
Implications of Using Rewards in the Classroom   76
When Learning Is *Not* Intrinsically Motivating   81
Fostering Self-Control and Internal Motivation in the
Classroom   87
Minimally Sufficient Control   92

5 Developing a Motivating Classroom Personality   95
Teachers' Beliefs about Learners, Learning, and Teaching   96
Organizational Patterns   111
Organizing to Develop Unity   119
Goal Orientation   129
Target Structures   132

6 Enhancing Student Self-Esteem   141
Security   144
Selfhood   146
Mission   147
Recommendations for Enhancing Student Self-Esteem   147
Strategies for Enhancing Self-Esteem   149

7 Enhancing Student Autonomy   163
Goal-Setting Conferences   165
Recommendations for Enhancing Student Autonomy   167
Strategies for Fostering Student Autonomy   169

8 Enhancing Competence in All Students   181
Goal Setting and Competence   182
Outcome-Based Education   185
Recommendations for Enhancing Competence in All Students   190
Strategies for Fostering Competence in All Students   193

9 Facilitating Students' Need for Relatedness   **207**

Cooperative Learning   208

Recommendations for Building Student Relatedness   217

Strategies for Building Student Relatedness   220

10 Stimulating Student Involvement and Enjoyment in Learning   **239**

Recommendations for Stimulating Student Interest and Involvement   245

Strategies for Stimulating Student Involvement and Enjoyment in Learning   248

References   **263**

Appendix A: Motivational Strategies Classified by TARGET Areas and Grade Level   **273**

Index   **279**

─── PREFACE ───────────────

LARGE NUMBERS OF STUDENTS are rejecting schools as a means for improving their lives. Many start by becoming truant at the age of 13 or 14, and then dropping out officially at their first opportunity. Others endure their school years with sullen, glassy-eyed looks on their faces as they slouch in their desks without books, pens, or paper. With two or three notable exceptions, few books are written to help teachers understand these students or deal with the problems of student apathy. Undergraduate educational psychology texts usually devote one chapter to student motivation, and most books about human motivation are written for graduate psychology students, offering few suggestions for elementary, middle, and secondary school teachers.

While competent and highly skilled teachers will always be capable of igniting academic sparks, their job has become more difficult as politicians and administrators increase the emphasis they place on academic competition in schools. While these "reformers" extol the need for national assessment tests to determine students' relative achievement, they often fail to consider the ramifications of forcing up to half of our student population to accept an inferior or loser identity. After all, for every student whose performance is labelled "above average" on these assessments, they must label one "below average." As Martin Covington and Richard Beery have so clearly described in their book *Self-Worth and School Learning*, the threat created by this compulsory and often unfair academic competition forces large numbers of students to withhold effort and involvement with learning as a defense to protect their vulnerable senses of self-worth.

As reformers seek to "restructure" schools and classrooms, it is imperative that they have a clear understanding of the effects of their structural changes on the psychological and academic needs of students. This is an important key to understanding student motivation to learn, since it is the frustration of these needs that has forced many students to reject school as a valued activity.

Meeting the needs of students within the context of education's academic, social, and economic mandates is no easy task; it requires an understanding of schooling and the process of learning from the student's point of view. While some may advocate an increased use of bribes or punishments to produce short-term gains in student learning, in the long run such external controls will likely continue to extinguish students' desire to learn.

This book has two major purposes: first, to help teachers gain a firm understanding of the theory and research that identifies the factors that have made it difficult for many students to meet their psychological and academic needs within traditional classrooms and, second, to provide teachers with over a hundred suggestions for structural changes and motivational strategies designed to help satisfy these needs and thereby increase student motivation to learn.

The ideas contained in this book are the result of the contributions of many people. I am especially grateful to Richard Larson for his significant contributions to Chapter 5 and for sharing his poetry, to Robert Berglund, Donna Rae Clasen, and George Mischio for their valuable suggestions and comments when reviewing chapters of the manuscript, and to Dianne Paley for her perceptive editorial suggestions. Finally, I would like to thank the many teachers who, as graduate students, shared their beliefs and observations and worked together to help each other develop strategies for meeting their students' needs and thereby increasing their motivation to learn. I have tried to give credit to the individuals who have suggested each strategy, and I apologize if I have missed anyone.

Winners Without Losers

_1

Introduction

"AMERICAN SCHOOLS ARE IN TROUBLE. In fact, the problems of schooling are of such crippling proportions that many schools may not survive. It is possible that our entire public education system is nearing collapse." These apocalyptic words open chapter 1 of John Goodlad's 1984 book, *A Place Called School.* His monumental study of schooling in the United States, based on data provided by over 27,000 individuals, indicated that large numbers of students are rejecting school as a valued activity. Statistics on annual dropout rates support Goodlad's conclusions, in 1985, for example, 4.3 million youth between the ages of 16 and 24 left school without completing graduation requirements (Hahn, 1987). Currently, more than one in four students who enter first grade leave before graduating, and many of those who do continue avoid making a personal commitment to the learning process.

As Jonathan Kozol poignantly describes in his book *Savage Inequalities: Children in American Schools* (1991), the statistics are much worse for the poor and minorities living in large cities. In Chicago, for example, it is estimated that 10 percent of students stop attending classes after seventh or eighth grade and never make it to high school.

> *This would put the city's actual dropout rate, the* Chicago Tribune *estimates, at "close to 60 percent."* . . . *[G]oing by official school board numbers[s] the attrition rates in certain of the poorest neighborhoods are quite remarkable. For children who begin their school career at Anderson Elementary School, for instance, the high school dropout rate is 76 percent . . . at the McKinley School, it is 81 percent. For those who start at Woodson Elementary School, the high school dropout rate is 86 percent. (Kozol, 1991, p. 58)*

Kozol reports that the figures are just as bad in Detroit, a school system that is 89 percent black and "so poorly funded that three classes have to share a single set of books in elementary school. . . . Of an entering ninth grade class of 20,000 students in Detroit, only 7,000 graduate from high school, and, of these, only 500 have the preparation to go on to college" (p. 198).

In addition to dropout rates, Kozol reports:

> *Nationwide, black children are three times as likely as white children to be placed in classes for the mentally retarded but only half as likely to be placed in classes for the gifted: a well-known statistic that should long since have aroused a sense of utter shame in our society. (p. 119)*

These observations, of course, are not new. National dropout rates have not changed drastically in the past fifteen or twenty years, nor is academic apathy a recent discovery. What is new is the growing realization by politicians that when students fail to achieve academic competence they create a serious threat to the economic well-being of our country. By the year 2000, for the first time in history, more than half of all new jobs will require education beyond high school, and almost a third will require a college degree (Johnson, 1987). Furthermore, a ranking of new areas of employment according to skill requirements indicates that the fastest growing job categories require much higher math, language, and reasoning capabilities than do current job categories. While it is generally expected that the greatest job growth will occur in the service industries, only recently have we realized that even the least skilled of these jobs will require a mastery of reading, computing, and thinking that was once expected only of professionals.

Goals for Education—Excellence *and* Effort?

Fear of losing our competitive edge in the international economic community spurred President Bush and the fifty state governors to establish two major goals for educators to attain by the year 2000. First, the United States should rank number one in the world in the fields of math and science, and, second, high school graduation rates should reach 90 percent. Considering the issue of student motivation, it seems clear that if we continue to rely on current educational practices to reach the first goal, it is highly unlikely that we will achieve the second. Without major changes in how politicians view student motivation to learn, schools will be forced to continually endure simultaneous cases of lockjaw and seasickness.

Our educational system, it appears, is currently producing academic winners and losers in about equal numbers. According to William Glasser (1986), 50 percent of students in school recognize knowledge as power, and 50 percent do not. Few politicians or educational commissions have identified this dichotomy within the school population, and even fewer have been willing to consider the motivational factors that have contributed to it. Yet, at some point during their school experience, most students are forced to choose between the paths of academic apathy or academic competence as the route to follow through the daily routine of school life.

Schools have traditionally been confronted with two apparently contradictory challenges. First, they must identify and reward those students who excel academically; second, they must foster and reinforce reasonable effort from students, regardless of ability, so that all will acquire the basic skills necessary for lifelong learning. The first challenge has been the easier to achieve since it depends largely on the straightforward use of academic competition and norm-referenced testing to differentiate achievement among students and to reward those who excel. This competition for excellence, however, demands that educators systematically stratify the school population. As a result, many of those who are consistently forced to the bottom strata choose to withdraw from the competition. "If I don't have a chance to be a winner," they reason, "I don't want to participate." Given this loser perception and sense of hopelessness—a direct byproduct of forced, zero-sum competition—many reject involvement in academic activities and withhold effort toward learning. The result, of course, is that it is difficult, if not impossible, for schools to accomplish the second challenge of fostering and maintaining reasonable effort from all students.

Historian Michael Katz in his book *Reconstructing American Education* observed that public schools have exhibited an amazing ability to secure the loyalty of citizens to a competitive system in which, by and large, they have been losers (Katz, 1987). (Given the current apathy in our schools, it appears that many of the children of these citizens are not quite so loyal.) Katz also believes that by indoctrinating children to the belief that the unequal distribution of rewards in school mirrors the unequal distribution of ability, schools have legitimized inequality by teaching students to blame themselves for failure.

When schools label children "learning problems" or "at risk" and then blame them for their failures, they seem to be inadvertently using a reasoning process similar to that used by former Georgia governor Lester Maddox when he was asked at a press conference if there was any way to improve the mess in Georgia's prisons. The governor is said to have replied, "What we really need is a better class of prisoner."

The effective schools movement of the late 1970s and early 1980s, according to Katz, challenged the "blame the victim" reasoning so prevalent since the nineteenth century. Founded on research that indicated that even in the worst systems some schools are able to develop students who thrive and succeed, the movement began to shift the burden of responsibility for academic failure from students to educational policy makers, administrators, and teachers. It also challenged the traditional belief that those who achieve deserve their success and those who fail are less worthy.

In 1983 the well-known report from President Reagan's National

Commission on Educational Excellence, *A Nation at Risk,* clouded the effective schools movement with a new educational imperative—excellence. Unfortunately, according to Katz, the report substituted the mixed metaphor "a rising tide of mediocrity" for a clear analysis of why large numbers of students have rejected schooling. The commission's recommendations for longer school days, increased academic requirements, and a stronger emphasis on academic excellence did little to achieve its goals. Avoiding such specifics, President Bush and the governors called for a "restructuring" of the public schools in order to make them "more competitive." While many educational reformers find hope in the call for restructuring, not all agree that it should be designed to render public education more competitive.

Restructuring to attain "excellence" requires a stratification of the student population into a hierarchy based on meritorious academic performance. After all, if we want to rank number one in the world in math and science, we need to know how each state, school, and student ranks in our own country. In short, excellence based on increased competition appears to be a reasonable attempt to substitute a meritocracy for the mediocrity in American schools. Yet, as Kozol (1991) clearly warns, unless all children are given the "means of competition," the poor in our society will become increasingly more hopeless and desperate. When states like Illinois, for example, spend $2,100 per year to educate a child in the poorest districts to over $10,000 per child in the richest districts, or when district spending in Texas ranges from $2,112 to $19,333 per child, the call for competition for excellence has a hollow ring.

According to Katz:

> *For many reasons, meritocracies usually serve best those who enter them with a favored position, and it's not hard to predict who will appear most excellent and garner most rewards. A policy stressing excellence, therefore, is another way of redistributing resources upward. As has usually happened in the past, a new educational policy proposed in the interests of everyone would serve best those already privileged. (1987, p. 131)*

There are, however, alternatives to an educational reform that is based on an exclusionary view of achievement. Rather than focusing on excellence, Katz suggests that educators need to concentrate on the development of *competence* in all students. Such a goal makes it possible for all students to succeed, and it reflects the genuine core of democratic educational ideals. It will also allow President Bush and the governors to achieve their second goal.

This book is based on the assumption that the path to excellence and the path to competence do not have to diverge in different directions— excellence and competence need not be exclusionary. If we are willing to understand the motivational factors that contribute to student apathy and are willing to alter the educational practices that undermine student desire to expend effort toward academic competence, it may be possible to excel in math and science *and* to increase the graduation levels of all students. Indeed, the path to competence *is* the path to excellence when it fosters motivation to learn in all students.

School apathy is not caused by a genetic deficiency, nor do students choose ignorance over competence when they have an equal choice. Many students reject school because they find the academic practices in their classrooms threatening to their sense of self-worth. They have learned that withdrawing from academic effort is less painful than experiencing the feelings of failure and hopelessness created by the systematic exclusion of forced academic competition.

Transforming schools into places where all students can hope that reasonable effort will lead to success will be difficult, at best. In some ways it is a task similar to that identified in the story of an eastern European economist and an American economist discussing the changes required in the new eastern European democracies. When asked by the American economist how these countries would make the difficult but necessary changes in moving from communistic to capitalistic economies, the eastern European thought for a moment and then said he believed there were two possible approaches. The first would be to use the naturalistic method, and the second would be to rely on the miraculous method.

"With the naturalistic method," he explained, "the heavens will open and bands of angels will descend on eastern Europe and diligently make all of the necessary economic changes."

"If that is the naturalistic method," replied the surprised American economist, "what could possibly be the miraculous method?"

In answer to the question the eastern European quietly responded, "We will make the changes by ourselves."

If educators are to work miracles—to recognize the reforms that are needed and to take the initiative to put them in place—they must first understand the factors that contribute to academic apathy and those that foster student motivation to learn in school. Only when these factors are identified and analyzed will it be possible to design educational procedures and strategies that nurture and strengthen student willingness to expend effort to master learning goals.

This Book's Approach—Research-Based Recommendations and Strategies for Motivation

Former Secretary of Education Terrell Bell is quoted as saying, "There are three things to remember about education. The first is motivation. The second is motivation. The third is motivation." The following chapters examine motivation to learn from the student's point of view. They are based on the assumption that teachers cannot motivate students directly. In fact, as Wlodkowski (1978) suggests, no one can directly motivate anyone to learn. "Between what we do as teachers and what students do as learners are the student's perceptions, values, personalities, and judgments. These elements decide the final outcome of student motivation" (p. 14). Yet as educators we are not helpless in this process. While one may be tempted to invoke the old adage, "You can lead a horse to water, but you can't make him drink," Madeline Hunter is fond of pointing out that we certainly can increase the likelihood of the horse drinking if we feed it large amounts of salt before bringing it to the trough. By arranging conditions that attract, invite, and stimulate interest and that help students meet their psychological and academic needs within the classroom, teachers can have a powerful influence over the academic motivation of their students.

With this assumption in mind, Chapter 2 discusses the psychological needs of students from several perspectives. Awareness of these needs—and of how traditional educational practices have often served to stifle them—is the first step toward an understanding of why large numbers of students have chosen to reject school as a valued activity. Starting with a discussion of Maslow's hierarchy of human needs, this chapter goes on to focus on the three fundamental psychological needs of autonomy, competence, and relatedness that have provided the foundation for recent research and theory development in student motivation conducted by Edward Deci and his colleagues at the University of Rochester (Connell, 1990; Connell & Wellborn, 1990; Deci, 1975; Deci & Ryan, 1985b; Ryan, 1991). Although these psychologists subsume the need for a positive sense of self-esteem or self-worth within the need for relatedness, this chapter will consider the need for a positive self-worth as a separate, fundamental psychological need.

Adults often equate student apathy with laziness, weakness of character, or shortsighted self-gratification. Chapter 3 views apathy as a rational, albeit self-defeating, defense mechanism that many students believe will help them fend off threats to their feelings of self-worth. These threats usually emerge after fourth or fifth grade and are the byproducts of educational practices that rely on zero-sum evaluation procedures. Such practices systematically limit the number of students who can feel good about their academic performance in school. After all, for every child labelled "above average" in reading or math, our educational system demands that another be labelled "below average." Few adults who have never been branded with the "below label" label can appreciate the impact of the label on the self-worth of those forced to accept it. Even the label "average" can be devastating to many students.

In 1963 psychologist John Carroll hypothesized that differences in student ability are primarily the result of differences in the speed at which one acquires knowledge (Carroll, 1963). This hypothesis contradicts the traditionally held belief that aptitude or innate ability determines the level at which a student can be expected to learn a given subject–those with high ability can master the complexities, while those with low ability are destined to rudimentary memorization. Research results presented in Chapter 3 compel us to reconsider our conceptions of student ability and student effort.

Chapter 4 explores the characteristics of intrinsic motivation and how a student's intrinsic motivation to learn can be fostered or stifled in the classroom. A major purpose of this chapter is to examine the growing body of research that indicates that the unquestioned use of stickers, candy, happy faces, free pizzas, and hundreds of other external rewards may actually serve to undermine and extinguish the intrinsic motivation of students. While such tokens–or bribes–often temporarily increase performance and achievement, there is a considerable amount of evidence that they can also kill intrinsic motivation by undermining a student's perception of self-determination. As research discussed in this chapter will indicate, rewards themselves are not the culprit; it is the way that they are used by the teacher that makes the difference.

Chapter 4 will also examine the developmental process whereby students learn to develop self-control. Although most students may not be intrinsically motivated to do math problems or to walk quietly in hallways, this section will examine ways that teachers can help students internalize or regulate these academic and social behaviors without the continued use of threats or bribes.

Chapter 5 explores the characteristics of classrooms that generate motivating personalities. It is based on the assumption that the group of students within a classroom, under the direction of the teacher, develops a unique personality during the course of the time spent together. This personality is influenced by the students and by the beliefs and goals of the teacher who leads them. This chapter analyzes three components of classroom personality that can influence student motivation: (1) teachers' perceptions of their unifying purpose, (2) the organizational pattern selected by teachers, and (3) the goal orientation fostered within students.

Chapter 5 discusses how teacher beliefs affect student expectations for success. Expectancy theory proposes that students' decisions to expend effort on tasks is the product of their judgment regarding the probability or expectancy for success and the value they ascribe to the task. Both variables are important to an understanding of student academic motivation since educators can influence a student's judgment in both arenas.

Chapter 5 also examines how classroom personality can influence the causes to which students attribute their successes or failures. With an understanding of attribution theory, it is possible for teachers to help students attribute their failures to lack of effort, rather than to external factors beyond their control. Genuine involvement with learning requires that students accept the risks of failure as they strive for success. If, however, students attribute small but inevitable failures to deficiencies in their own level of ability rather than to the learning process, they will avoid involvement or will quickly give up when confronted with a learning challenge. This chapter discusses attribution retraining as a method for helping students attribute their failure to lack of productive effort rather than to lack of ability. Research on the effects of attribution training is discussed, and recommendations for implementing attribution retraining are presented.

In addition, this chapter also studies the organizational patterns of most classrooms and how these patterns can influence student motivation through the communication, sense of belonging, and norms for expected behavior that develop. It also discusses the motivational differences between classrooms that encourage students to develop mastery-oriented rather than performance-oriented learning goals.

The last five chapters of the book explore instructional procedures and motivational strategies that can help overcome the factors identified in the first five chapters that contribute to student apathy in the classroom. Each of these chapters includes a summary of major ideas formulated into ten specific recommendations followed by ten classroom-tested strategies designed to help students meet their psychological and academic needs, discussed in Chapter 2. These recommendations and strategies avoid the negative effects of norm-referenced evaluation identified in Chapter 3, eliminate the negative effects of external rewards identified in Chapter 4, and enhance effort/outcome dependence and the perceptions of self-efficacy identified in Chapter 5.

Chapter 6 deals with the definitions and uses of the words *self-concept, self-esteem,* and *self-worth.* Although students' self-esteem is directly related to satisfaction of the needs for competence, autonomy, and relatedness (which are considered in later chapters), this chapter provides specific strategies that can help teachers improve students' self-concept. The purpose of these strategies is to help students clarify the beliefs they hold about themselves and to increase their self-esteem by experiencing activities that can contribute directly to positive self-judgments.

This chapter presents ten motivational strategies designed to increase student self-worth. Useful in a variety of classroom settings, each strategy is presented in a six-part format: (1) title; (2) statement of purpose and identification of appropriate TARGET category (discussed in Chapter 5); (3) applicable grade level; (4) list of required material, if any; (5) step-by-step procedures for implementing the strategy; and (6) possible variations for use in different settings.

Chapter 7 offers strategies and procedures for enhancing student perceptions of autonomy and self-determination. If it is the teacher's goal to help students discover that reasonable effort can lead to success, then it is necessary for the teacher to provide opportunities for students to define their own goals and standards for success. When students experience feelings of autonomy and self-determination, their level of aspiration can operate as a governing mechanism that provides protection against repeated failure, on the one hand, and against easy achievements that do not provide gratification, on the other. In addition to reviewing research on the effects of using goal-setting strategies in the classroom, this chapter examines procedures for implementing goal-setting paradigms and explores possible problems that may be associated with the use of individual goal-setting procedures. Chapter 7 ends with a summary of ten recommendations and ten motivational strategies designed to enhance student autonomy and self-determination.

Chapter 8 provides strategies and recommendations designed to enable all students to experience academic competence in school. These recommendations presume that replacing norm-referenced standards with standards of absolute performance based on clearly stated instructional objectives will allow for greater numbers of students to achieve success from reasonable effort. The mastery-based instructional model presented in this chapter is based on research that indicates that primary differences in student ability are often demonstrated in the amount of time required to master instructional tasks. Quicker-learning students learn from five to seven times faster than their slower-learning peers. Thus, when classroom instruction is designed to allow students differential amounts of time on task, about 80 percent of the students can attain the same level of achievement as the top 20 percent under traditional instruction (Bloom, 1981). It is difficult to imagine another instructional approach that would have more potential for reducing student apathy.

Chapter 8 includes ten specific motivational strategies and ten instructional recommendations that have as their major purpose the enhancement of perceptions of competence for *all* students. Each motivational strategy is presented in the six-part format established in Chapter 6.

Chapter 9 discusses ways to help students develop feelings of group relatedness and identity. A major focus of this chapter is the examination of strategies for inviting apathetic students back into the learning process through the use of cooperative learning activities. The term *cooperative learning* refers to a variety of instructional methods through which students of different achievement levels work together in groups of three to five members. Many apathetic students feel isolated and alone when competitive contingents within the classroom are emphasized. While acknowledging that competition, in itself, is not debilitating, this chapter focuses on the use of cooperative learning strategies to foster feelings of relatedness and group identity.

Chapter 9 also discusses both the Slavin and the Johnson and Johnson models as well as specific procedures for implementing each approach. Research on the effectiveness of cooperative learning is presented, and several difficulties with implementing cooperative learning in the classroom are identified. This chapter also includes ten recommendations and ten motivational strategies useful in a variety of classroom settings that have as their major purpose the enhancement of student relatedness.

Chapter 10 discusses strategies for stimulating student interest, enjoyment, and active involvement in the learning process. It includes specific recommendations and motivational strategies useful in a variety of classroom settings that have as their major purpose the stimulation of student involvement, interest, and enjoyment in learning tasks.

The fifty motivational strategies presented in the book's last five chapters are referenced to the six manipulatable TARGET classroom structures discussed in Chapter 5. Research by Ames (1990a) has found that these structures significantly influence student motivation to learn. The strategies have been derived from a variety of sources, and acknowledgment is given where possible; each has been used successfully in a variety of classroom settings. When a source is not indicated, it is either unknown or the strategy was developed by the author. Most of the strategies are derived from the contributions of teachers who were graduate students in courses taught by the author. Without their suggestions and their contributions to class discussions that examined the foundations on which the strategies are based, this book would not have been possible.

__2__
Psychological Needs of Students

IN 1983 THE NATIONAL Commission on Educational Excellence concluded in its well-known report, *A Nation at Risk,* that while most students have the potential to achieve excellence, many accept mediocrity. Ironically, a major cause of student apathy may be that many students in fact are *not* willing to accept mediocrity and choose apathy instead. To understand the factors involved in this choice, it will be useful to examine some of the fundamental psychological needs of students. The reason for this examination is the assumption that many students reject academic education because they find it impossible to meet their basic psychological needs in school.

The list of student psychological needs discussed in this chapter is not exhaustive, but research indicates that students' needs for positive self-worth, autonomy, competence, and group relatedness significantly influence their motivation to learn in the classroom. Starting with a discussion of Maslow's hierarchy of human needs, this chapter then examines student self-concept from a perceptual point of view. This is followed by a discussion of the fundamental psychological needs for positive self-worth, autonomy, competence, and relatedness. Chapters 6 through 9 provide structural recommendations and specific instructional strategies that teachers can use to help *all* students satisfy these important psychological needs in the classroom.

Maslow's Hierarchy of Needs

Any discussion of student psychological needs would be remiss if it did not mention Abraham Maslow's hierarchy of human needs. Most textbook discussions of student motivation start with a presentation of Maslow's theory, and some authors have provided detailed discussions of how teachers can draw upon the theory when designing instructional practices and motivational activities (Wlodkowski, 1986; Jones & Jones, 1990). This section briefly reviews Maslow's hierarchy since it serves as the foundation on which most discussions of psychological needs are based.

Maslow (1970) believed that individuals are driven to satisfy both their basic, or deficiency, needs and their meta-needs, or growth needs. He conceptualized these two need systems as organized into a hierarchy where satisfaction of basic needs generally takes precedence over satisfaction of growth needs. The elimination of deficiencies in basic *physiological needs* provides the foundation of Maslow's hierarchy. Unless students have adequately satisfied their biological needs for food, water, sleep, and temperature regulation, it is unlikely that they will become interested in the division of fractions or the rhyme scheme of a Shakespearean sonnet. The starving artist who continues to create in spite of physiological deprivation appears to be an exception to Maslow's hierarchy, but such an image probably draws more on fiction than fact. It appears that man *does* live by bread alone—when bread is scarce. This reality is portrayed in the words of a survivor of the 1933 eastern Ukraine famine in which over 4.5 million people starved:

> *All you think about is food. It's your one, your only, your all-consuming thought. You have no sympathy for anyone else. A sister feels nothing for her brother; a brother feels nothing for his sister; parents don't feel anything for their children. You become like a hungry animal. You will throw yourself on food like a hungry animal. That's what you're like when you're hungry. All human behavior, all moral behavior collapses. (Lefrancois, 1988, p. 269)*

Satisfying the *need for safety and security* is next in Maslow's hierarchy of basic needs. Students must feel safe from both physical and psychological harm or intimidation before they can focus their attentions on the work of school. Both dysfunctional families and dysfunctional classrooms can create a threat to the safety and security of many students. When parents resort to physical violence or emotional abuse, or when teachers resort to screaming, threatening, and ridiculing, children often respond by either withdrawing into themselves or lashing out with vengeance. Students also need to feel safe from threats of violence from peers. Increases in gangs in some environments have made this a real and frequently experienced fear. Regardless of the source, however, a lack of safety, orderliness, and predictability in a student's living or learning environment can sap the energy that might otherwise be channelled toward personal growth and academic learning.

The *need for love and belonging* is the next in Maslow's hierarchy of basic needs. To avoid feeling isolated or alone, students must develop reciprocal relationships, and they must be able to identify themselves as members of a larger group. This sense of caring and belonging is often threatened in classrooms where students are forced to compete against each other or where peers reject those who look or act differently.

The last of the deficiency needs is the *need for self-esteem,* or to hold a positive view of one's self. A sense of personal esteem is developed through countless experiences with significant others whose actions and reactions teach us who we are and whether we are worthwhile and valued human beings.

When the four deficiency needs are satisfied, students are free to focus their energies on meeting their personal growth needs. According to Maslow, these meta-needs include both the desire to acquire cognitive knowledge and truth and the urge to appreciate aesthetic beauty and symmetry. Finally, the growth toward *self-actualization* stands at the top of the Maslow hierarchy. This somewhat elusive desire for self-fulfillment refers to an individual's intrinsic drive to meet his or her full potential. Armed with a sense of curiosity and creativity and a belief in our own worth, each of us is inextricably involved in a lifelong process of striving to reach and understand all that exists in our world of experience. It is understandable that such a heady process demands the complete or at least partial satisfaction of our deficiency needs.

A Perceptual View of Student Behavior

Perceptual psychology is based on a phenomenological approach that seeks to understand how individuals act and react to the world as they perceive it, rather than as it may exist as an external reality. The word *phenomenological* is derived from a school of philosophy known as phenomenology, "which holds that reality lies not in the event but in the phenomenon, that is to say in the individual's experience of the event" (Combs & Syngg, 1959, p. 21). People behave according to their personal view of the world at any given moment; to understand another's behavior, we must see the world through his or her eyes. This approach does not reject the principle that behavior is influenced by past experience. Rather, it attempts to understand behavior by viewing it as a consequence of one's total field of personal meanings at the instant of behaving.

Perception and behavior are intractably linked, and one's perception of reality is constantly changing. In fact, it is the perceptional field's capacity to change that makes learning possible. These changes are directly related to the way people focus on certain images or thoughts, encounter new input, consider familiar ideas and beliefs, or experience emotions. At this moment, depending on how much you are concentrating on the meaning of this paragraph, you may or may not be aware of background distractions or be thinking about food, sleep, or other needs. Now, as you reflect on the last sentence, thoughts about food or your surroundings may begin to enter your field of awareness.

Our unique and personal interactions with the world generate thoughts and images. Some of these gain our undivided attention; others barely register their presence. As these perceptions flow in and out of our field of awareness, they may cause us to view the world differently than we viewed it at the instant we behaved. It is this kind of change in perception that causes us to regret some of our behaviors. Regret is a signal that the perceptual field has changed from what it was at the moment of the behavior. By helping students examine the broader implications of their behavior, we can help them weigh alternatives before they experience consequences.

At the core of the perceptual field are those perceptions one holds about one's self. Perceptual psychology is based on the assumption that all individuals are motivated toward the maintenance and enhancement of these self-perceptions (Combs & Snygg, 1959; Combs & Avila, 1985). The *self-concept* is a composition of thousands of self-perceptions that vary in importance and in clarity. One may see oneself, for example, as a poor banjo player, an effective teacher, a poor mathematician, a sensitive human being, a gifted singer, and so on. If one does not value mathematics or depend on mathematics for one's livelihood, it is possible to live happily with a self-concept that includes being lousy at math. On the other hand, if a person has invested years of his or her life to becoming a teacher, it is difficult to live with a self-concept that includes being ineffective in that role. Perceptions and judgments of physical appearance, competence, and intellectual prowess all have an important influence in defining the set of beliefs that we hold about ourselves.

Although the perceptual field changes from moment to moment, beliefs about the self are generally stable and usually present in awareness. They provide a frame of reference to evaluate such relative concepts as "old" or "smart," and they allow us to define "what is me" and "what is not me." Combs and Avila (1985) suggest that we feel at home with "what is me" and are likely to be indifferent or even repelled by "what is not me." They use an example mentioned by psychologist Gordon Allport to dramatize this point. When most people get a small cut in a finger, they usually do not hesitate to put the wounded finger in their mouth until the bleeding stops—thus, swallowing their own blood without the slightest concern. Drinking the same blood from a glass, or swallowing someone else's blood, however, would be quite a different matter. Thus, removing the blood from its source makes it "not me," and something abhorrent or repulsive.

Perceptions that relate to one's sense of identity command the greatest attention and significantly influence behavior. Based on personal perceptions of reality at any given moment, individuals strive to behave in ways that are consistent with the view they hold of themselves. Students who believe that they cannot understand math behave in ways that reinforce this perception. They may search for excuses to avoid math homework, or they may expend little effort at completing an assignment. As adults they may avoid balancing their checkbooks, pay others to calculate their taxes, or ask their dinner companions to just tell them how much they owe when it is time to divide up the check.

A vivid example of an individual behaving in ways consistent with his view of self is reported by Coach Darrel Mudra of Western Illinois University:

What a boy believes about himself is really important. We had a student at Greeley who scored in the 98 percentile on the entrance test, and he thought that he had a 98 IQ. And because he thought he was an average kid, he knew college would be hard for him. He almost failed in his first term. He went home and told his parents, "I don't believe I'm college caliber," and the parents took him back to school and talked with the college counselor. When he found out that 98 percentile score meant that he had a 140 IQ he was able to do "A" work before the year was over. (Combs, Avila, and Purkey, 1971, p. 43)

The Need for Self-Worth

We are all highly motivated to behave in ways that enhance our self-perceptions. When these perceptions are threatened, we struggle desperately to protect them. Martin Covington (1984) refers to this tendency of all individuals to enhance, maintain, and protect the perceptions they hold of their self-image as the *self-worth motive.* His theory is based on the assumption that all people have a need to seek experiences that generate feelings of success, accomplishment, and esteem and to avoid experiences that generate feelings of failure, worthlessness, and social disapproval.

Your own perceptions are useful for confirming the need for self-worth and self-enhancement identified by both Combs and Covington. It is easy, for example, to agree with someone who suggests that you are a lousy cook, singer, or banjo player if being an accomplished cook, singer, or musician is not an important part of your self-image. Some people are actually proud of being lousy cooks. This perception becomes integrated into their self-image, and they may enjoy finding opportunities to prove that they are deficient in culinary skills; it may, after all, relieve them of kitchen duties. If, on the other hand, someone suggests that you are a lousy teacher or an ineffective parent, you probably will respond quite negatively. Being an effective teacher or parent is likely to be integral to your self-image, and you will probably respond defensively to whatever threatens that image. "Who do you think you are, telling me I'm a lousy teacher! If your kid would only open a book once in a while, he wouldn't be getting an **F**," is a thought familiar to more than one teacher.

In addition to responding defensively when our self-worth is threatened, we often seek out and focus on examples that confirm the judgments we have of ourselves. It is a rare teacher who forgets the names of students who come back a year or two later to say how much they admired his or her teaching ability.

Soon after children begin school they discover that their personal worth as students is largely dependent on their classroom accomplishments—good students achieve; poor students do not (Covington & Beery, 1976). Although other educational goals may deserve equal priority, we are all aware of the value currently being placed on high levels of academic achievement. This close link between self-worth and school achievement provides a foundation for understanding why many students *choose* apathy and noninvolvement in school.

Figure 2-1 provides an analysis of a self-worth theory of achievement motivation. It indicates that three factors have a direct effect in influencing an individual's sense of self-worth. According to Covington (1984), an individual's level of performance and his or her self-estimate of personal ability and degree of effort expenditure have a direct influence on judgments of self-worth and adequacy. Since the direction of the arrows indicates causal relationships, the diagram emphasizes the important role that successful performance or accomplishment plays in determining an individual's judgments of self-worth. As the diagram indicates, whether pertinacity or brilliance is the primary factor in determining one's achievement appears not to matter; successful performance is valued no

FIGURE 2-1   Covington's Self-Worth Model

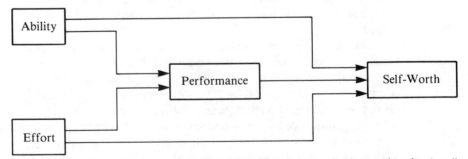

From M. V. Covington. (1984), "The Self-Worth Theory of Motivation: Findings and Implications," *The Elementary School Journal, 85*(1), p. 8, copyright 1984. Reprinted by permission of the publisher.

matter what its causes. There are, however, important exceptions to this general relationship. Successes resulting primarily from assistance from others, for example, are sometimes valued less than those achieved solely through one's own efforts (Covington & Omerlich, 1981). When parents assume the responsibility for completing their children's homework, for example, they undermine any feelings of success students may experience. In addition, feelings of inadequacy and fear that they may be unable to repeat successful performances may pressure some people to reject credit for their successes (Covington & Omerlich, 1979). "If I take pride in this accomplishment," a child may reason, "then I may be expected to continually perform at this level and I don't think I can.") With few exceptions, however, students continue to struggle to enhance their feelings of worth, and there is evidence to indicate that they typically discount information that might discredit their own evaluations or judgments of successful performances (Raffini, 1988).

The arrows in Figure 2-1 suggest that self-perceptions of ability and effort can also have a direct causal effect on judgments of self-worth, regardless of performance. For some students, belief in their own high ability is tantamount to a positive self-identity in school regardless of actual performance. The inverse is also true; believing one has been endowed with low ability, regardless of performance, causes judgments of negative self-worth. While students view effort, or trying hard, as a key ingredient in successful performance, the diagram indicates that some students, especially younger ones, value effort in its own right as a source of self-worth.

Chapter 6 offers structural suggestions and specific motivational strategies that teachers can use to help all students develop and maintain a positive sense of self-worth, and Chapter 8 offers structures and strategies to help all students believe that reasonable effort can lead to feelings of success.

The Need for Autonomy and Self-Determination

Deci and Ryan (1985b) have proposed a theory of human motivation based on the proposition that all individuals seek a quality of human functioning that has at its core the desire to determine for themselves what behaviors to adopt. At the foundation of their theory is the belief that all human beings have an innate need to feel autonomous and to have power over their own lives. This desire for self-determination is realized when individuals have the capacity to choose and to have choices as they interact with their environment; they choose to engage in activities because they want to, not because they have to. According to Maslow, "It is the strong, healthy, autonomous person who is most capable of withstanding loss of love and popularity" (1954, p. 106). Schooling at its finest empowers students to meet their need for self-determination as they engage in behaviors that support the acquisition of knowledge and skills.

When individuals satisfy their need for self-determination, it means that they are free to act of their own volition and are behaving autonomously. This is the opposite of heteronomous behavior, which means that one is being governed or coerced according to the desires of someone else. Autonomy and freedom of choice are inherent in behavior that is intrinsically motivated. The characteristics of intrinsic motivation will be examined in more detail in Chapter 4.

In the classroom, teachers often try to control the behavior of students with rewards or with punishments. While these two time-worn techniques are often quite effective for influencing and controlling behavior, they usually stifle self-determination. The famous Swiss psychologist Jean Piaget believed that adults undermine the development of autonomy in children when they rely on the use of rewards and punishments to influence a child's behavior (Kamali, 1984). Punishment, according to Piaget, is an heteronomous behavior management technique that often leads to blind conformity, deceit, or revolt in those being controlled. Punishment often creates conformity because with conformity comes security. Children who choose to become conformists need not make decisions; all they need do is obey. Other children practice deceit to avoid punishment. When parents or teachers say, "Don't let me catch you doing that again!" children respond by exerting every effort to not get caught. Despite these accommodations to the reward-punishment system, children's need for autonomy usually resurfaces as they begin to revolt against the conformity pressures of punishment.

Piaget, according to Kamali (1984), suggested the use of "sanctions by reciprocity" rather than punishment when dealing with inappropriate behavior. Similar to Rudolph Dreikurs's concept of logical consequences, sanctions by reciprocity encourage the child to examine other viewpoints of his or her inappropriate behavior. Through dialogue with an adult, the child can focus on the tangible effects and natural consequences of the behavior. The reader will find a more detailed analysis of alternatives to punishments in Albert (1990), Dreikurs, Gruenwald, and Pepper (1982), and Raffini (1980).

The use of external rewards to control behavior can also undermine self-determination and the need for autonomy. Richard deCharms (1977, 1983) has argued that when students lose their sense of self-determination in the classroom, they begin to operate like pawns in a game of chess; they have, in effect, relinquished control over the decisions as to what, how, and when behavior is to be performed. Chapter 4 examines how intrinsic motivation is often inadvertently undermined by the reward structures commonly used in classrooms.

It is obvious to most parents that babies are born heteronomous and in infancy require the constant care, supervision, and control of an adult.

Yet, even then, infants seem to have an insatiable curiosity about the objects around them, grasping everything in reach, shaking, smelling, chewing, and then throwing it aside in favor of a new item. It is during toddlerhood, about age 18 months to 3 years, that children begin to strongly affirm their desire for autonomy. It is in this stage, according to Erikson (1968), that children want to declare their independence from the constant control of adults. After having heard the word "no" countless times, little Jimmy begins to make it part of his vocabulary. As a defiant response from a 2-year-old, it shocks Jimmy's parents, who have become accustomed to routinely determining his every behavior. Unfortunately, they will also discover that the "terrible twos" and toilet training arrive together. If his parents are reasonable in their demands and don't overreact to Jimmy's assertions, he will begin to feel confident in himself and exercise self-control over his behavior. On the other hand, if he experiences too many demands and becomes completely dominated by his parents, Jimmy may lose his sense of autonomy and feel totally dependent on and controlled by his parents. If this happens he will begin to experience feelings of shame and doubt and will encounter later difficulties in acquiring self-esteem and control of his behavior (Erikson, 1968).

With the onset of adolescence, students again begin to assert their need for self-determination. As they begin to define their own sense of identity, they find it increasingly more difficult to accept adult direction. The more insistent parents become with imposing their will and decisions on these young adults, the more their adolescent children resist. Many conflicts between adults and teenagers have started with the statement "You can't order me around and tell me what to do!" followed immediately with an "Oh yes I can!" reply. Accepting adolescents' need for autonomy is the first step in helping them learn to assume the responsibility and consequences of their own behavior. Their desire to explore independently, undertake challenges, and solve problems provides the foundation for intrinsic motivation and will be examined in more detail in Chapter 4.

Psychiatrist and author William Glasser (1984, 1986) believes that all individuals have an intense desire to feel in control of the phenomena and interactions within their environment. According to Glasser (1984), "Our lives . . . are a continual struggle to gain control in a way that we satisfy our needs and not deprive those around us, especially those close to us, of satisfying theirs" (p. 44). Glasser believes that the need for power (he uses the terms *power, importance,* and *self-esteem* synonymously) is built into the genetic structure of all human beings and is a difficult need for students to satisfy in schools.

When I ask, as I very frequently do, students aged 11 to 15, "Where in school do you feel important?", they look at me as if to say, "That's ridiculous! Who listens to us?" . . . You can't have self-esteem, you don't feel important, unless you have some sort of power which means at a minimum somebody listens to you.

As I pursue this question . . . eventually, about half of them say they do feel important in school to some extent—but almost never in classrooms. (Brandt, 1988, p. 39)

Glasser proposes three levels of satisfying the need for power (Brandt, 1988). The first level is when someone whom we respect listens to us. The next level is when someone listens and says, "You're right." With the exception of tests, this level is seldom achieved by students in the classroom. The third level is when, ". . . not only does somebody listen to us, but once in a while he or she says, 'You know, your way is better than mine. I think we ought to do it your way.' That's the pinnacle for satisfying this need and students, especially, rarely have this experience in class" (Brandt, 1988, p. 40).

It appears that students' satisfaction of the need for autonomy is primarily a matter of gaining power and control over their own lives. This process suggests that all students have a natural resistance to orders like "Be quiet"; "Sit down"; "Stop talking"; "Get out your books"; "Pay attention"; or "Stop teasing the gerbil." Some students, recognizing the purpose of these commands, suppress the desire to resist and choose to conform. Others, who may also agree that the orders are necessary, bristle at the thought of being controlled by others; they often assert their desire for autonomy by resisting. One need only watch television in a room where another controls the remote channel changer to experience the acute frustration of being controlled by others.

Chapter 7 offers specific motivational strategies that teachers can use to help all students develop and maintain a sense of autonomy and self-determination.

The Need for Competence

Deci and Ryan (1985b) believe that in addition to the need for self-determination, individuals also have a need to feel successful in their attempts to understand and master their environments. This need for competence motivates people to behave in ways that allow them to feel capable and effective. According to Allport, "It would be wrong to say that 'need for competence' is the simple and sovereign motive of life. It does, however, come as close as any" (1961, p. 214).

This assertion seems to contradict many of the student behaviors observed in middle and high school classrooms. How can we ascribe a need for competence to Eric, for example, who has been absent from his English class twenty times this quarter, or to Leslie, who hasn't completed a single math homework assignment in four weeks? The following chapter will address this question in detail. For now, it is important to affirm that given a choice in a situation in which other factors are equal, students do not choose ignorance over competence. Further, it is often the desire to protect their sense of self-worth that prompts unsuccessful students to choose apathy over involvement; they believe that they will experience less threat to their self-worth if they withhold effort than if they were to expend effort and not be able to experience success.

Robert White (1959) was one of the first psychologists to assert that all human beings have an innate need for competence. His definition of competence referred to the broad desire of individuals to interact effectively with their environment. This desire for mastery, called "effectance motivation" by White, provides the driving force behind behaviors designed to explore, understand, and conquer one's surroundings. Effectance behaviors range from the irresistible impulse of infants to grasp and then transport to their mouth almost any object within reach, to the focused intensity of teachers who become so absorbed in preparing an instructional unit that they lose track of time, disregard other obligations, and occasionally forget the needs of their families. Stipek (1988) points out that people often persist in activities that satisfy their desire for competence even when the activity may be difficult and painful. Young children don't stop trying to walk because they fall, nor do adults stop struggling to grasp an unfamiliar concept because it is complex and challenging.

Harnessing the natural energy of a student's need for competence and channeling it into the achievement of classroom goals is one of the biggest challenges faced by teachers. It seems almost impossible to orchestrate an environment in which twenty to thirty-five individuals have the opportunity to pursue their personal and unique definitions of competence. Yet, if it is the mandate of teachers to persuade students to voluntarily do what is required of them, then enlisting students' intrinsic need for competence can be a beneficial step toward that end.

The need for competence is concerned with self-perceptions as well as the ability to perform. The concept of *perceived self-efficacy* was developed by Albert Bandura (1977, 1981, 1989) and is concerned with the personal beliefs and judgments people hold about their ability to execute the behaviors necessary to obtain their desired outcomes. These subjective judgments are instrumental in determining how much effort students will expend on a given assignment and how long they will persist in working on that assignment after they begin to have difficulty understanding it. According to Bandura, "People tend to avoid situations they believe exceed their capabilities, but they undertake and perform with assurance activities they judge themselves capable of handling" (1981, p. 201). Although Eric, for example, may value obtaining an A or a B in his English class, he also must make a subjective judgment about his chances of earning one. If he believes that even his best efforts would not produce the desired outcome, he may choose to avoid the situation by not attending class.

Yet perceptions of capability are not the only determinant of student motivation in the classroom. The *expectancy-value* model (addressed at length in Chapter 5) suggests that it is also necessary for students to *value* what it is they are being asked to do. The activity itself may provide its own value, or it may be valued as a prerequisite to another desired outcome. In either case, a perception of self-efficacy is a necessary but not sufficient factor to overcome student apathy.

Chapter 4 will review evidence indicating that the more students feel competent in understanding or performing an activity, the more intrinsically motivated they will be to persist in that activity. This assumes, of course, that performance of the activity occurs within a context that provides for self-determination and that the requirements of the activity provide the student with a continued challenge. If, for example, the student acquires a skill to the point at which increased mastery is no longer evident or possible, he or she will consider dropping the activity in favor of one that provides a new challenge. This is particularly evident in the discouragement experienced by musicians or athletes when they reach a seemingly insurmountable plateau in their skill level.

Teachers are often faced with a dilemma when they try to structure activities that offer challenges to their students while also ensuring a thorough mastery of the skill or concept being taught. Some students, for example, are capable of mastering the skill of adding two-digit numbers after doing three or four homework problems. Yet the teacher knows that most students require more practice for the skill to become firmly imbedded in their mind. A colleague observed an example of this while visiting a third-grade classroom a few years ago. As he sat in the back of the room, he noticed the student sitting next to him was staring out the window instead of working on the addition problems that the teacher had distributed. After watching the student for a few minutes, he quietly leaned over and asked, "Why have you decided to look out the window rather than work on your addition problems?"

"Because I already know how to add these problems," the student replied.

My colleague pointed to one of the more complicated problems and said, "Would you mind doing this one for me?"

"Sure," said the student, who proceeded to quickly calculate the correct answer.

"Thank you," was all that my colleague could think to say. Clearly, the student believed that there was no point in practicing a skill he already possessed.

Differences in student learning rates make the task of providing challenges to students a challenge for the teacher. Yet there is considerable research to show that when most students are free to choose an activity, they select one that provides a moderate challenge (see Deci & Ryan, 1985, for an extensive review). As we will see in Chapter 3, however, willingness to choose optimally difficult activities does not generally characterize students who have had a history of failure in school. Students who discover that they are deprived of a sense of competence after persistent and repeated efforts toward mastery are likely to avoid contact with the activity in the future or, when contact is unavoidable, to withhold effort toward learning.

The Need for Belonging and Relatedness

Having one's existence recognized and accepted by peers is a psychological need of all human beings. Students discover who they are, what they believe, and what behavior is acceptable through honest self-disclosure with others. The need to belong and to relate to others has a significant influence on a student's behavior in the classroom, and it is a need that is easily dismissed or overlooked as we restructure for the single-minded pursuit of excellence. Research viewed by Schmuck and Schmuck (1974) found that student academic achievement (and presumably motivation) were enhanced when children were willing to help and support one another and when friendships within the classroom were broadly dispersed among many peers. Often a student's "lack of motivation" can be traced to a real or imagined fear of being isolated or rejected by peers and being labelled a "brain," "nerd," or "retard" or derided for "acting white."

Adlerian psychology can be useful for understanding and reducing these fears. It is founded on the principle that human behavior is embedded in a social context, and the need to develop a sense of social and psychological belonging is a major challenge of childhood (Dewey, 1978). Adler used the term *social interest* to represent both an individual's capacity to develop a sense of belongingness with mankind and a willingness of the individual to contribute to the common good. Rudolph Dreikurs (1968) was instrumental in adding a democratic philosophy to Adlerian psychology and in translating its principles into practical suggestions that could be implemented by parents and teachers. He believed that all humans were social beings and that all had a basic desire to belong to a group. Indeed, there may be nothing more painful in the process of growing up than feeling isolated, rejected, and alone:

> *Because of the primacy of the desire to be an accepted, participating member of a group, the most painful experience for any child—as for any adult—is the feeling that he is inferior to others. Any hardship, tragedy, pain, and inconvenience is relatively tolerable as long as it does not imply a lowering of social status. Only then is the feeling of belonging to the group impaired. And not to belong is the greatest hardship for any human being. (Dreikurs, 1968, p. 20)*

Dreikurs also believed that since children grow up in a world of giant adults, they all experience feelings of social inferiority. Many students overcome these feelings as they become accepted and valued in their own right by parents, peers, and teachers. Such acceptance builds a base of personal security and confidence in their social position and provides the strength they need to unite with others for their mutual benefit. Other students are not so fortunate. Continued comparisons with brothers, sisters, and classmates add to their sense of social inferiority and force them to discover ways to compensate for these feelings—or to withdraw from social participation.

Some individuals try to compensate for inferiority feelings by striving for self-elevation, or a sense that they are better than others. Our competitive society seems to encourage this vertical striving, but the risk of such behavior is the loss of an even broader sense of social belongingness and security. Others forsake such competitive striving and give way to their feelings of hopelessness and despair.

The family is the initial group to which all children seek to belong. Dreikurs believed that the constellation of parents and siblings and the emotional atmosphere surrounding this constellation were significant determinants of a child's struggle for security and belonging. "Whether the parents are orderly or disorganized, cooperative or antagonistic, the family atmosphere will present its characteristic pattern to the children as a standard of life" (Dreikurs, 1968, p. 23). The countless number of interactions between family members builds a foundation for a child's concept of self and for a basic personal style for approaching new experiences. These interactions also add significant weight to the child's perception of his or her place in the group.

Adlerian psychologists believe that the birth sequence within a family provides each child with a different and unique point of view and has an important influence on how each perceives his or her place within the family organization. As children struggle to discover a place of security and belonging within the family, they often are met with sharp challenges from their siblings. Dreikurs believed that these challenges inevitably occurred between the first and second child. With an addition of another member to the family, the first-born feels dethroned as the newcomer becomes the focus of the parents' attention. "He tries," says Dreikurs, "to maintain his superiority over the intruder, who in turn constantly challenges the position of the older sibling and his advantage of age" (Dreikurs, 1968, p. 24).

The competition between first- and second-born often leads each child to develop opposing character traits, interests, and temperaments as each seeks to succeed where the other fails. If one child excels in music, the other will often choose sports or some other activity to pursue—after all, why compete with the person who has the bigger marbles? This competition for belonging and security within the family explains why in most families, according to Dreikurs, the first and second child are so different.

Additional children create new family constellations with different competitive relationships. "The position of middle child," according to Dreikurs, "is particularly precarious; having neither the rights of the older nor the privileges of the younger, he often feels unfairly treated" (Dreikurs, 1968, p. 24). The youngest child often solicits the service of others and gains special attention by being either helpless and weak or charming and brilliant. In any case, the early motivation of children is to seek a sense of belonging and security within the family structure.

Dreikurs warned that child rearing is particularly difficult in democratic societies, where bribes, threats, rewards, and punishments are often diametrically opposed to the democratic goals of equality and freedom of choice. While it may not be apparent in many homes and classrooms, democracy in fact requires that we treat all children and students with an equal measure of respect—a respect that Dreikurs believed is undermined when parents and teachers impose their personal power over children.

When dealing with unacceptable behavior, parents and teachers often make the mistake of either violating their own dignity or the dignity of the child. In the first instance, overprotection and overindulgence are common; both take a heavy toll on adult and child. By doing for children what they can do for themselves or by allowing children to terrorize the family or the classroom with inconsiderate, self-gratifying behavior, parents and teachers violate their own dignity and fail to establish responsibility in the child. Alternative approaches of screaming, humiliation, and inappropriate punishment may make some adults feel better, but they violate the dignity of the child. Overindulgence and humiliation represent opposite ends of a spectrum, but both demonstrate a lack of faith in children's abilities to take care of themselves; they also increase children's self-doubts and decrease their sense of belonging and relatedness.

Maladaptive Approaches to Gaining Acceptance

When students from a variety of economic, racial, and social backgrounds come together in the classroom, each is highly motivated to secure a place within the group. Many develop a sense of belonging and acceptance by conforming to the social and academic expectations of their teacher and peers and by making useful contributions to the group's solidarity. Others become discouraged by their attempts to gain acceptance. Being unsuccessful with what they perceive to be constructive means for obtaining social belonging, they are forced to seek alternative, antisocial methods for gaining status. The class clown, the angry and defiant rebel, the vicious bully, the hopelessly passive sleeper, and even the "teacher's pet" are all struggling in their own ways to gain status, acceptance, and social belonging.

Dreikurs believed that students who are unsuccessful with constructive efforts to gain a sense of belonging within the classroom often feel forced to seek acceptance through maladaptive approaches based upon either attention; power; or revenge-seeking behaviors or noninvolvement.

Attention Seeking

Some students believe that excelling in school work, being first in line, or being first finished with an assignment will gain them the recognition and approval they so desperately seek. These students will often trail the teacher around the classroom to show how nicely they have done their assignments. While this behavior may occasionally win praise from the teacher, the student is really quite vulnerable since such attention-seeking behavior doesn't increase the student's self-confidence or self-reliance; it only perpetuates the student's dependence on the approval of others. Some students use a more passive role to seek attention, relying on their charm and dependence to gain approval and service from others. While attention seeking may be either active or passive, the perceptive professional knows that although their apparently constructive behaviors may stroke the teacher's ego, these students have not developed confidence in their own self-worth, and they depend upon constant approval from others to reaffirm their sense of belonging.

When socially acceptable behaviors fail to achieve the status these students seek, they soon revert to disruptive behaviors such as talking out, making side comments, teasing others, and hundreds of other creative ways to gain attention. These behaviors may elicit threats, reprimands, and punishment from the teacher, but such consequences are preferable to being ignored. Dreikurs believed that students who exhibited active attention-seeking behaviors were less discouraged and maladjusted than those who were more passive in their responses to isolation and rejection. Nevertheless, the exasperating behaviors of active, destructive attention-seeking students can be a constant headache for a teacher who hasn't the time, inclination, or ability to help these students discover more positive ways to achieve self-reliance and belonging.

Power Seeking

Students' attention-seeking disruptions are likely to be met with a great deal of criticism and negative consequences from teachers. Some students succumb to these consequences and temporarily modify their behaviors. Others learn to fight power with power. "They expect and therefore provoke pressure," said Dreikurs, "and respond violently to the slightest pressure put on them" (1968, p. 42). These students often become aggressive and argumentative with the teacher and with their peers. Their insolent and belligerent protestations often are followed by stubborn refusals to do what they are told. Again, according to Dreikurs:

No final "victory" of parents or teachers is possible. In most instances the child will "win out," if only because he is not restricted in his fighting methods by any sense of responsibility or moral obligation. The few times that parents [and teachers] are able to score a "victory" and overpower the child make him only the more convinced of the value of power and the more determined to strike back, the next time with stronger methods. (1968, p. 29)

Another reason it is almost impossible to win power struggles with these students is that they feel no obligation to argue logically. As a result, their often illogical position further frustrates the teacher and reinforces the student's control over the situation. Many teachers have observed a student who has committed a transgression but who, when confronted about the behavior, vehemently denies the action. I recall seeing this happen in an elementary school classroom. An angry-looking student stood up in the middle of the math lesson and walked to the pencil sharpener. The teacher continued with the lesson. Rather than simply sharpen his pencil and return to his seat, the student continued cranking away. Finally, unable to control her frustration any longer, the teacher shouted, "Billy, get away from the pencil sharpener!"

Billy responded by looking the teacher directly in the eye, continuing his cranking and shouted back, "I'm not at the pencil sharpener!" I defy anyone to try to win an argument with a student who uses such logic. The teacher, of course, became even more frustrated; only by threatening a trip to the principal's office was she able to shout the student back to his seat. The whole class, of course, knew who had won the confrontation.

Students who have learned to fight power with power are a challenge to a teacher's control—the more insistent the teacher becomes, the more defiant the student becomes. Many new teachers have met their professional demise at the hands (or the mouths) of such students. It may be some consolation to know that the challenge of these students is not personal; it is usually directed at the authority that the teacher represents. Teachers require skill, confidence, and a clarity of purpose if they are to learn to take their sails out of this student's wind, while refusing to abdicate control. Although it is a difficult challenge, many of these students can be helped to channel their energies into more constructive behavior and to learn that they need not dominate others to achieve a sense of their own belonging.

Revenge Seeking
Teachers and parents are eventually able to overpower students. After all, they have the vice-principal and the city police on their side. Unfortunately, this kind of subjugation can drive some students to retaliate to revenge their hurt. It is as if they say to themselves, "You got me in school today, but I'll get your car tonight." The teacher's furious response to this

revengeful behavior often triggers further desire to retaliate, thereby continuing a vicious circle.

Revenge-seeking students have usually given up hope of finding acceptance and belonging in the classroom. Their behaviors evoke from teachers the type of treatment that further justifies their thirst for revenge, thereby forcing their teachers to retaliate again and again, which continues to justify their behaviors.

Revenge seekers often generalize their revenge to all teachers, adults, and even to society. An example of this was described by a teacher in one of my classes. It concerned a high school math teacher who was walking through the hall in a large urban school. A student whom the math teacher had never seen before punched the teacher squarely on the mouth, knocking him down and loosening three teeth. Later it was found that the student had been in a power struggle with his English teacher and was punished for his violence. As a result, he generalized his hate and revenge to all teachers, and the unfortunate math teacher suffered the consequences. The seemingly unbelievable wanton vandalism of art treasures, landscapes, or books is often traced to individuals motivated by this goal. "You hurt me, so I'm going to hurt you" is what this person is saying. The "you" is generalized to include all of society.

Although the only way to help revenge-seeking students, according to Dreikurs, is to convince them that they are acceptable and worthwhile human beings, they are often too filled with anger and hurt to believe that anyone within the conventional system can really care. Peer groups, close friends, and criminal gangs may provide the only sense of belonging experienced by these students. It is difficult for most adults to avoid viewing the sometimes criminal behaviors of these students as indications of meanness and juvenile delinquency, rather than an expression of the pain and anger these students feel after repeatedly unsuccessful attempts at finding socially acceptable ways to gain belonging and acceptance.

Noninvolvement

Some students simply give up trying to find a place in the group. They internalize feelings of complete discouragement and resign themselves to lives of isolation and school failure. The deep-seated apathy of these students is difficult to dislodge. It is as though they have been pounding their heads against a brick wall for several years and finally realize that it feels good to stop. Efforts to encourage these students to become reinvolved with the group and with learning are too often seen as requests that they start the pounding again.

Facilitating Belonging Needs

There are few influences in a student's life more powerful than the feeling of being rejected by others. The classroom, under the leadership of the teacher, can either provide support and approval for all of its members or it can become an arena for constant competitiveness that builds a crystallized dichotomy of acceptance and rejection. Satisfying the need for belonging and relatedness provides the security necessary for students to risk exploring and expanding the limits of their identities.

Dreikurs suggests that the first step in helping students find a legitimate place in the group is to encourage them to consciously examine the motives behind their maladaptive behaviors. I recall implementing Dreikurs's suggestion a few years ago when I took a short leave from my university to return to the public schools to teach junior high social studies. Jeff, an energetic student in my eighth-grade history class, seemed to suffer from a perpetual fear of being ignored by his classmates. It was obvious that his position in the group was a continuous concern to him, and his deep fear of rejection caused him to devise a variety of disruptive behaviors to remind the group of his presence. Although some of these behaviors were humorous and creative, they never seemed to provide him with the self-confidence and sense of belonging he so desperately sought; he required constant reassurance from his peers that they were aware of his presence.

When I occasionally took Jeff aside to discuss the consequences of his behavior, I was struck by how vulnerable he was to his need for belonging. His behaviors, however, were self-defeating; the more he strove for group acceptance, the more the group seemed to reject him. Yet, in the process of rejection they did acknowledge his existence, which Jeff seemed to prefer to being ignored. He seemed helpless to escape from this endless cycle of increased rejection caused by his ineffective attempts to belong.

Dreikurs suggested that with students like Jeff it is sometimes helpful to use a diagnostic question to help them reflect on the goal of their maladaptive behavior. With attention-seeking behavior a teacher might use a question like, "Could it be that you do (blank) because you like the attention you receive from me or from others in the class?" Most students will deny this motive for their behavior, but often a *recognition reflex*, or nonverbal response like a twinkle of an eye or a hint of a smile, will be an indication that the question has helped the student become consciously aware of the goal. Dreikurs believed that diagnostic questions can have the same effect as that experienced by a person who discovers that another has expectorated into the pot of soup from which that person was served. While the individual could continue to eat the soup, it will never taste the same again; new information has affected the individual's taste buds. Similarly, once the motives for students' inappropriate behaviors are brought into awareness, they can continue the behaviors, but they will never be as rewarding for them as they were when the motive was hidden.

Since Jeff and I seemed to be able to talk openly with each other, I called him in during an afternoon preparation period to see if a diagnostic question would help him examine the self-defeating nature of his behavior. After some general discussion about how he was doing, I said, "Jeff, do you have any ideas as to why you wander around the room and interrupt others with your comments?"

"No" he replied.

"I have an idea. Can I share it with you?"

"Sure," he said confidently.

"Could it be that you like the attention you get from me and from others in the class when you interrupt?"

Expecting a denial, I was prepared to look carefully for a recognition reflex. "Yup," he said, "I guess that's why I do it."

I was surprised by the frankness of Jeff's response. We continued to discuss the effects of his efforts to gain attention and belonging, and over a period of several weeks, he discovered that by making constructive contributions to class discussions and by participating in group projects he could begin to satisfy his need to belong. The use of a diagnostic question to help Jeff examine his attention-seeking motive caused him to acknowledge the disruptive consequences of his behavior and enabled me to help him find more positive ways to meet his need for attention. He still maintained his role as "class clown," but as his behavior became less disruptives others began to laugh with him rather than at him, and they started to accept and appreciate his constructive contributions to the class.

Relatedness Needs

A more recent, research-based view of student *relatedness* is provided by James Connell, Richard Ryan, and Edward Deci from the University of Rochester. Like Dreikurs, they perceive the desire for relatedness as a basic psychological need of students. In the context of school, Connell defines relatedness as the degree of emotional security that students feel with themselves and with the significant others involved in their lives as students—specifically parents, teachers, and peers. According to the model of student motivation proposed by Connell, Ryan, and Deci, "when students feel more connected to their schoolmates, teachers, and parents, and feel better about themselves, they will be more engaged in their learning than when they feel isolated or alienated from their social surround" (Vito, Crichlow & Johnson, 1989, p. 6).

Combining the need for relatedness with the needs for autonomy and competence, Connell, Ryan, and Deci have proposed a theoretical model of student motivation in which these three psychological needs interact with social contingencies and relationships to produce students' beliefs about themselves in relation to school. (The need for self-worth or self-esteem is subsumed within the need for relatedness.) These beliefs are referred to as "self-system processes" and are believed to be instrumental in influencing the degree to which students are actively involved or uninterested in academic tasks (Connell, 1990; Vito & Connell, 1989). Several aspects of this model and their classroom implications will be discussed in more detail in Chapter 4.

3

Student Apathy in the Classroom

Why Is a Wild Pig Called a Boar?*

Because pigs are pork
And pork is bacon
And bakin' makes bread
And horses are bred;
Horses wear reins
And rain brings tulips and
Two lips can lie,
And lye makes soap.
Some soap is ivory.
Ivory comes from elephants
And elephants have trunks
And trunks have locks
And lox are fish.
Fish have scales
And scales weigh.
Curds without whey
make cheese
And cheese has holes
And a whole is a unit.
You knit yarn,
A yarn is a story,
A bad story is a bore.
That's why a wild pig
Is called a boar.

RICHARD LARSON (1991)

Young children have an unlimited store of questions about the world around them, and, fortunately for parents, they do not always demand logical answers. Having once casually answered, "Chocolate cows" to the question, "Where does chocolate milk come from?", I was forced to retract my fabrication during a drive in the countryside a few weeks later when my daughter persisted in trying to distinguish the chocolate cows from the Holsteins and Guernseys.

While children's natural inquisitiveness accompanies them to elementary school, it is usually lost or suppressed by the time they reach middle or high school. In his extensive study of schools, Theodore Sizer concluded that "the American high school student, *as student,* is all too often docile, compliant, and without initiative" (1984, p. 54). This chapter will discuss some of the factors that have contributed to replacing the natural inquisitiveness of students with the pervasive academic apathy documented in Sizer's study.

The impact of this apathy on teachers and the teaching profession is far-reaching and disheartening. Quoting a 1980 NEA teacher opinion poll, the Carnegie Foundation reported that 73 percent of senior high school teachers believed that "student attitudes toward learning had a *negative* effect on their job satisfaction" (Boyer, 1983, p. 162). This frustration is summarized in a statement made by a teacher with twenty years experience: "When you accept the role of being a teacher, your satisfaction comes when you know you've helped and served. . . . My major problem is how to motivate students who don't care about themselves. And my biggest frustration is their "what's the difference" attitude" (Boyer, 1983, p. 163).

Rather than serving as catalysts and facilitators for their students' search for knowledge, many teachers find themselves struggling desperately to extract a glint of responsiveness and involvement from large numbers of students who find little meaning from their classes, are frustrated or bored from a lack of challenge, or are committed to avoiding the discomfort of failure.

Recent attempts at school reform, which have included greater accountability, increased academic requirements, and the infusion of computers and other technology into the classroom, have not appreciably reduced the teacher frustration and stress that result from student apathy toward learning. The 1990 Carnegie Foundation survey of more than 21,000 teachers found that 30 percent of all teachers (19 percent elementary, 46 percent secondary) rated student apathy toward school as a "serious" problem. In its 1987 survey, only 20 percent (13 percent elementary, 30 percent secondary) of the teachers rated it a serious problem (*Education Daily,* Sept. 4, 1990).

Yet, in spite of these gloomy statistics, there are many diligent students doing well in school, often working side by side with those who have given up. These students are actively committed to the pursuit of knowledge and to the full development of their academic potential; they dominate the laboratories, the libraries, and the keyboards. They are also conscientious and courteous, and, not surprisingly, are the recipients of their teachers' praise and smiles.

Many middle and high school teachers confirm the observation that schools seem to be producing academic winners and losers, in about equal numbers. New teachers first discover this when they examine the distribution of test scores in their heterogeneous classes. Anticipating the normal or bell-shaped curve they learned about in test and measurement courses, they are often surprised when they first observe the two-humped camel curve that inevitably emerges—the result of a moderate number of high scores, few average scores, and a moderate number of low scores. The Carnegie Foundation's report also identified a split in a student population:

> For a small percentage of students—10 to 15 percent perhaps—the American high school provides an outstanding education, perhaps the finest in the world. Their schooling combines a solid curriculum with good teaching. Students are not only expected to remember and recite, but also to explore, to think creatively, and to challenge.
>
> A larger percentage of students—perhaps 20 to 30 percent—mark time in school or drop out. For them, the high school experience occasionally may be socially supportive, but academically it's a failure. (Boyer, 1983, p. 39)

Although student apathy may have been as common as chalk dust in classrooms of the past, some believe that the increased use of computers in today's classrooms will help eradicate the problem. Classroom experience thus far, however, has failed to show that the availability of computers has had demonstrable impact on student attitudes toward learning. While teachers rate student apathy toward school as a more serious problem than they did just a few years ago, the ratio of students to computers during the same period fell from 125 students for each computer in 1984 to 22 students per computer in 1990 (ASCD, 1990). This is not an argument against the increased use of technology in schools. It is, however, a caveat that technology is not a panacea for student passivity and academic rejection. While computers have the potential to actively engage students in the learning process, they, like chalk and pencils, are no more than tools to be manipulated by students already committed to engaging in academic inquiry.

It has been observed that for every complex problem there is often a simple solution; the solution is just as often wrong. The complexity of interrelationships among students, teachers, parents, peers, administrators, and school policies makes it difficult to ferret out the reasons that a large number of students reject academic involvement while an equally large number pursue academic excellence. While the specific causes of a student's apathy can vary from community to community, school to school, and grade level to grade level, this chapter is concerned with identifying some of the key causes that are common to all.

Mackey and Appleman (1983) argue that the widespread increase in student apathy is caused by three major factors. The first is the economic and consumer pressures that force or encourage large numbers of students to hold down jobs while they are in school. They report that 40 percent of all high school sophomores and 63 percent of high school seniors are employed part time. They also found that 56 percent of the male students who work spend more than fourteen hours a week at their jobs. Although adolescents can learn responsibility and improve their communication skills while working at some jobs, Mackey and Appleman (1983) argue that a comprehensive study of student employment has found that work decreases student involvement in school and can lead to decreases in student achievement.

A second major contributor to student apathy, according to Mackey and Appleman (1983), is the increased use of drugs by a more diverse student population. In the past, drug use seemed to be confined to a specific subgroup of students, often labelled the "druggies" by their peers. It now appears that other social groups such as the "jocks" or "preppies" have incorporated drug use into their recreational activities. Mackey and Appleman (1983) believe that the increase in the amount of energy invested in secretive drug-centered activities by a broader spectrum of students has been accompanied by an increase in student academic apathy and a decrease in their motivation to learn.

Finally, Mackey and Appleman (1983) believe that although many students make it through school unaffected by drugs or employment, they often become apathetic due to their profound disinterest in and cynicism about all forms of political activity. This apoliticism contributes to feelings of powerlessness and futility in regard to the world beyond their own narrow adolescent personal and social interests.

Another opinion on the causes of student apathy is offered by John Bishop (1989) from the Center for Advanced Human Resources Studies at Cornell. Bishop argues that although everyone in the system recognizes the problem of student apathy and disinterest, each group fixes blame on someone else. The fundamental cause of student apathy, according to Bishop, is "our uncritical acceptance of institutional arrangements that do not adequately recognize and reinforce student effort and achievement" (1989, p. 7). While several factors have contributed to the belief held by many students that there is little incentive or value in working hard while in school, Bishop believes that the failure of the labor market to provide significant economic rewards for students who enter the job market with a record of high academic achievement is a major factor contributing to student docility. In his review of research dealing with the effect of academic achievement on the wage rates of high school graduates, he found that the school grades and test scores of non–college-bound students had a negligible influence on the wage rate of jobs obtained immediately after high school. Five years after graduation, however, the situation changes; a moderate relationship between high school grades and wages is observable. While this delay in reward is difficult to explain, it seems likely that management requires this long training period to ascertain worker qualities that are readily identified by teacher grades. Bishop believes that the shortsightedness of most teenagers makes these delayed labor market wage-rewards inconsequential to the decision of high school students to work hard in school.

For students seeking part-time employment while attending school, Bishop (1989) also reports that grades and standardized test scores had no effect on their chances of finding work or on the wage rate received once a job was obtained. Surprisingly, the category of "reading, writing, math, and reasoning ability" was ranked number five on a list of six factors that employers said they looked for when hiring job applicants (Bishop, 1989).

While effort toward academic achievement may not result in higher wages for students entering the work force after or during high school, it does benefit employers. According to Bishop, hundreds of studies over the past eighty years have found a strong relationship between scores on tests measuring competence in reading, mathematics, science, and problem solving and employer measures of job productivity. "Apparently, it is a youth's employer, not the youth, who benefits the most when a student who isn't college-bound works hard in school and improves his or her academic achievements" (Bishop, 1989, p. 8).

Kozol (1991) provides a convincing argument that large numbers of poor minorities give up on school because of the savage institutional inequalities they are forced to endure. Because of the way that we fund public education, many poor minority students are warehoused in overcrowded, rundown classrooms, often without textbooks, learning materials, or qualified teachers. The degradation and disillusionment they experience lead to feelings of hopelessness, cynicism, and despair. As Kozol so poignantly describes:

> *I look into the faces of these children. At this moment they seem full of hope and innocence and expectation. The little girls have tiny voices and they squirm about on little chairs and lean forward with their elbows on the table and their noses just above the table's surface and make faces at each other and seem mischievous and wise and beautiful. Two years from now, in junior high, there may be more toughness in their eyes, a look of lessened expectations and increased cynicism. By the time they are 14, a certain rawness and vulgarity sometimes set in. Many will be hostile and embittered by that time. Others may*

coarsen, partly the result of diet, partly self-neglect and self-dislike. Visitors who meet such girls in elementary school feel tenderness; by junior high, they feel more pity or alarm. (1991, pp. 182–83)

Arguing that the major causes of student apathy are part-time employment, drugs, apoliticism, grade/salary independence, or institutional funding inequalities places the major responsibility for the lack of student motivation outside of schools. Although this argument may be temporarily reassuring to educators, it leaves us helpless to significantly affect a solution. We can only hope that a new employment and salary program, a new drug czar, an equitable funding system, or a young charismatic politician will come along and transform our bleary-eyed, disinterested students into eager learners. Until these societal changes come about, teachers have little recourse but to focus on the variables for which they have control.

Most parents and educators agree that our student population has the potential to achieve at a level much higher than that currently demonstrated. In order to unlock this potential, it may be helpful to examine how traditional classroom practices may inadvertently contribute to the reasons that large numbers of students choose to reject academic achievement.

Apathy—The Student's Point of View

Psychologist Carol Dweck (1986) argues that a social-cognitive approach to student motivation can help educators understand why some students persist in their efforts to master learning challenges while others do not. This approach explores the ways in which students perceive, interpret, and process school-related experiences. As indicated in Figure 3-1, the beliefs and assumptions students hold about their ability and about the nature of intelligence are instrumental in determining whether they formulate adaptive or maladaptive motivational patterns and achievement goals.

Students demonstrating adaptive motivational patterns seek to conquer the intellectual challenges presented by their teachers. These academic winners work hard at trying to increase their competence in the skills being taught, and they have a strong desire to understand and find meaning in course content. In short, these students have acquired personally valued *learning goals*. Their curiosity and competence represent the best aspects of American education, and their presence in classrooms provides teachers with the optimism and reinforcement necessary to persist in the teaching profession.

Students who seek to avoid academic challenges or who abandon tasks as soon as they become difficult have adopted maladaptive motivational patterns and goals. Rather than establishing and working toward realistic goals, these students constantly look for the easy way out. They are more

FIGURE 3-1 Achievement Goals and Achievement Behavior

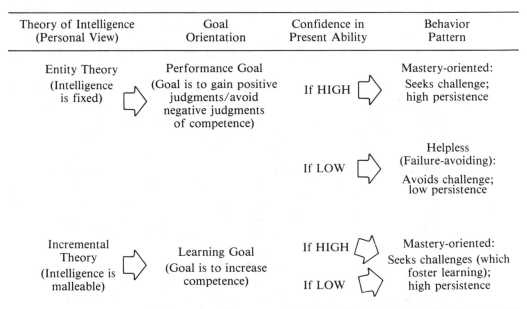

Theory of Intelligence (Personal View)	Goal Orientation	Confidence in Present Ability	Behavior Pattern
Entity Theory (Intelligence is fixed)	Performance Goal (Goal is to gain positive judgments/avoid negative judgments of competence)	If HIGH	Mastery-oriented: Seeks challenge; high persistence
		If LOW	Helpless (Failure-avoiding): Avoids challenge; low persistence
Incremental Theory (Intelligence is malleable)	Learning Goal (Goal is to increase competence)	If HIGH / If LOW	Mastery-oriented: Seeks challenges (which foster learning); high persistence

From C. S. Dweck (1986), "Motivational Processes Affecting Learning." *American Psychologist, 41,* p. 1041, copyright 1986 by the American Psychological Association. Reprinted by permission of the publisher and author.

concerned with gaining favorable judgments or avoiding negative judgments about their intelligence or ability than they are with mastering the course content. In short, they have acquired *performance goals.* Dweck concluded that while these two motivational patterns were not related to the intellectual ability of students, they did have profound effects on their academic behaviors.

Dweck hypothesized that when students believe that intelligence is a fixed trait from birth, similar to the color of their eyes, then the goal of their academic behavior centers around gaining favorable judgments and avoiding negative judgments about that trait. This *entity theory of intelligence* is closely aligned with Covington's theory of self-worth discussed in the previous chapter. If students view intelligence as a fixed entity, then judgments of this entity become equated with their sense of personal value. Since high levels of intelligence equal high levels of self-worth, these students try to avoid negative judgments about their innate ability.

Other students believe that intelligence is a malleable rather than a permanently fixed trait. This *incremental theory of intelligence* frees students from the maladaptive behavior patterns that develop from a fixed-entity view of ability. The belief that intelligence can be developed and expanded through personal effort orients these students toward goals that allow them to increase their academic competence. According to Dweck, "Research shows how a focus on ability judgments can result in a tendency to avoid and withdraw from challenge, whereas a focus on progress through effort creates a tendency to seek and be energized by challenge" (1986, p. 1041).

Figure 3-1 also indicates that if students believe that intelligence is a fixed entity, and if they have strong confidence in their ability, they will exhibit mastery-oriented behaviors toward challenging tasks. When students are driven by performance goals, therefore, confidence in high ability is a prerequisite for expending effort toward mastery. However, even when students have high confidence in their present abilities, research indicates that some individuals choose to sacrifice challenging learning opportunities in favor of defensive strategies that enable them to look smart in front of others (Dweck, 1986). Evidently, the fear of even a remote possibility of receiving a negative judgment about one's ability outweighs the desire for challenge and genuine competence.

With performance goals and low confidence in ability, students behave in ways that protect their perceived self-worth. They may try to prevent others from making judgments about their ability by choosing exceedingly difficult activities in which few would be expected to succeed, or they may select easy tasks that guarantee success. These failure-avoiding defensive strategies typically characterize students who are judged to be apathetic and nonmotivated, and they will be discussed in more detail later in this chapter.

Regardless of confidence in present ability, when students subscribe to an incremental view of intelligence, their behaviors are oriented toward task mastery and they are willing to risk failure or judgments of ignorance. Since self-worth is not at issue, they are free to choose challenging tasks that foster the development of skills and the acquisition of knowledge. They often doggedly persist at tasks when they become difficult since they believe that effort, not ability, is the key ingredient for mastery.

Dweck (1986) proposes two factors that foster maladaptive beliefs and motivational patterns in students. First, she suggests that our generous and injudicious use of "positive reinforcement," defined as frequent praise for short, easy tasks, undermines students' will to undertake difficult and challenging tasks that require persistence in the face of failure. We inadvertently teach students that "quick and clean" is the surest and safest road to approval.

The second factor contributing to maladaptive motivational patterns are teachers' beliefs about a student's ability and the way these often erroneous beliefs can actually affect student performance. The classic Rosenthal and Jacobson (1968) research on the "self-fulfilling prophecy" provides provoking, albeit controversial, evidence that educators can actually influence student performance by the beliefs they hold about the innate ability of each student. Rosenthal and Jacobson (1968) told teachers in the fall that newly developed tests had indicated that certain students would make huge achievement gains during the school year. Unknown to the teachers, these "spurters" were randomly selected from the teachers' class lists.

Retests in the following spring indicated that the spurters did, in fact, spurt; the randomly selected students demonstrated significantly greater IQ gains than their classmates. This research provides evidence that teachers' expectations can make a significant difference in student achievement.

Academic Ability: Fixed or Malleable?

As Dweck's social-cognitive approach to motivation suggests, students' assumptions about the nature of academic ability and assessments of their own abilities are significant factors in determining whether they will work hard on their assignments or give up and stare out the windows. Students have a need to feel competent as they interact with their environments, and their perceptions about their capabilities to master school tasks will strongly influence the amount of effort they are willing to expend to satisfy this need in the classroom.

As students progress through the grades, their conceptions about the nature of academic ability change. According to Rosenholtz and Simpson:

> [I]n the earliest elementary grades, students see ability as a malleable entity, which can be augmented or attenuated with the application of effort. As they progress through the elementary grades, children begin to conceive of ability as a stable, inherent trait. It no longer appears viable to change one's ability; the preoccupation instead is with continuous comparative measurement. (1984, p. 48)

In a thorough analysis of developmental changes in student cognition regarding the concept of ability, Nicholls (1989) avoids the duality of adaptive versus maladaptive behavior patterns by focusing on the nature of student involvement in achievement-oriented situations. His analysis indicates that although most early adolescents clearly differentiate ability from effort, this differentiation becomes irrelevant when the students are completely absorbed with problem solving or with trying to understand a concept thoroughly or completely. He refers to this absorption with learning goals as *task involvement*, as opposed to *ego involvement*, where students are more concerned with the enhancement and protection of judgments of their ability.

To overcome the problem of student apathy, Nicholls argues for a progressive approach to education in which classrooms set aside the ego orientations that foster norm-referenced competition, thereby forcing many students to opt out. For Nicholls, student withdrawal from learning is a predictable outcome of ego-oriented achievement structures:

> *A competitive, meritocratic society depends for its smooth functioning upon individuals' readiness to accept positions of varying status, power, and wealth without directly confronting all the others in combat or competition for those places. The normative conception of ability seems important for the functioning of such a society. Yet there is a price to pay for the individuals who discover that they are below average on valued skills. If one guiding principle of our society is that everyone be able to attain a sense of competence from developing and exercising his or her powers, the emergence of the normative conception of ability seems likely to make just classrooms and a just society a little harder to attain. (1989, pp. 46–47)*

Several additional cognitive theories and motivational models (attribution theory, Weiner, 1980; self-efficacy theory, Bandura, 1977; expectancy-value theory, Feather, 1982; socializing motivation to learn, Brophy, 1986; and the time-continuum model, Wlodkowski, 1986) imply that if we want to decrease students' apathy and increase their motivation on learning tasks, we must (1) help students attribute their low achievement and academic failure to insufficient effort rather than to insufficient ability, and (2) help students believe that reasonable amounts of effort toward mastering academic tasks will lead to feelings of competence and success.

These two recommendations require that educators challenge the firmly entrenched "fixed entity" view of academic ability. To argue that the ability to master learning tasks is a malleable trait does not deny obvious genetic differences to innate capacity among human beings; voluminous research centers on the inheritability of intelligence. But confusion arises when students begin to believe that norm-referenced IQ distributions represent inherent, insurmountable limits in their ability to succeed at academic tasks; such limits are, in fact, set by a student's experience and motivation rather than genetics.

According to psychologist Benjamin Bloom:

> *After forty years of intensive research on school learning in the United States as well as abroad, my major conclusion is: What any person in the world can learn, almost all persons can learn if provided with appropriate prior and current conditions of learning. This generalization does not appear to apply to the 2% or 3% of individuals who have severe emotional and physical difficulty that impairs their learning. At the other extreme there are about 1% or 2% of individuals who appear to learn in such unusually capable ways that they may be ex-*

ceptions to the theory. At this stage of the research it applies most clearly to the middle 95% of a school population. (1985b, p. 4)

It has always been the purpose of intelligence tests to determine how individuals rank among their peers on a variety of verbal and quantitative reasoning tasks. Adjusting for testing error, retesting over time has shown a reasonable degree of consistency in ranking; a student in the top quarter in third grade is likely to be in the top quarter in ninth grade. Although many factors affect classroom performance, IQ distributions tend to correlate somewhat with students' ranking on teachers' classroom tests and traditional grade distributions in academic courses covering a variety of content. In some schools, the combined ranking of these two distributions determines the academic "track" in which a student is placed.

Many students, parents, and educators believe that one's ranking on measures of intelligence or "scholastic aptitude" tests represents the limit of one's ability to master academic tasks. To the extent that students' performance on these tasks is also ranked relative to their peers, this conclusion seems somewhat justified. After all, Bloom reports that "the correlation between measures of school achievement at grade three and grade eleven is about .85, demonstrating that over this eight-year period the relative ranking of students in a class or school remains almost perfectly fixed" (Bloom, 1981, p. 133). While increased effort can sometimes make a difference in student ranking, assuming others do not increase their effort proportionately, most students discover early in their educational careers that +heir class ranking is a fixed entity. It is this relative immobility among one's peers that perpetuates a fixed rather than malleable assumption of the ability to achieve academically; it is also within this assumption that the seeds of student academic apathy are planted.

Yet, for the vast majority of individuals, the capability to reason, to problem solve, to acquire information about one's environment, and, as David Wechsler, one of the fathers of American intelligence testing might say, "to act purposefully, think rationally, and to deal effectively with one's environment" is not fixed at conception. A thirty-eight–year longitudinal study of IQ changes by Kangas and Bradway (1971) indicates that most individuals gained an average of about 25 IQ points over the course of a lifetime. McCall, Appelbaum, and Hogarty (1973), in an extensive study of IQ changes between the ages of 30 months and 17 years, reported that students from normal or high socioeconomic backgrounds tend to maintain or gain in IQ, while children from low-income families tend to show no gain or decline in IQ over time. Interestingly, they found an average IQ gain of 28.5 points for normal middle-class students, with about one-seventh of the students increasing their IQ scores by 40 points or more.

The findings of McCall, Appelbaum, and Hogarty in regard to the changability of IQ is not an argument against the heritability of IQ. They indicate, for example, that although one's height is an obvious hereditary attribute, the average height of individuals in the United States and Japan has increased by several inches over the last century. Clearly, the heritability of intelligence says nothing about our future ability to influence academic performance: "The important point is that an individual subject possesses a constant genotype throughout development; yet he changes almost as much in IQ during his childhood as different people vary in IQ at a single age as a function of contrasting between-family environments" (McCall, Applebaum & Hogarty, 1973, p. 74).

These somewhat conflicting conclusions regarding standardized intelligence test results are often overlooked by students and educators. The relative ranking of students by intelligence or aptitude tests remains more or less constant over time. Realistically, one's academic ranking among one's peers is a fixed entity. Yet intelligence tests do not measure innate capacity; they measure *relative* achievement. While one's ranking may be fixed, one's growth in IQ over the same period of time may change dramatically, indicating that academic achievement is a malleable trait influenced by one's experience and personal volition.

It seems reasonable to conclude from this discussion that although individuals differ in their genetically determined intellectual capacity, with proper learning conditions and encouragement from teachers and parents, the ability to achieve academically is a trait that almost all students can acquire or develop. In fact, Bloom (1976) argues that 90 to 95 percent of the student population have enough innate intelligence to thoroughly master the academic school curriculum. It is also Bloom's belief that "the basic differences among human beings are really very small. . . . In every nation and in every endeavor, some excel over others because they put more of themselves into it. The point is that under favorable learning conditions most people reach a high level of excellence" (1985a, 33–34).

In his five-year study of the top 150 athletes, artists, musicians, mathematicians, and neurologists in the United States, for example, Bloom discovered that these apparently "gifted" individuals studied and practiced their discipline an average of from four to eight hours per day for over sixteen years before they reached top national prominence (Bloom, 1985b, 1986). Furthermore, very few of these individuals were identified as child prodigies by teachers, parents, or experts. As Bloom indicates:

> *Only rarely were individuals in our study given the initial instruction in the talent field because the parents or teachers saw in the child unusual gifts to be developed more fully. They were given the initial instruction and encouragement to learn because their parents placed very high value on one of the talent areas—music and the arts, sports, or intellectual activities. (1985b, pp. 543–44)*

Many gifted-and-talented programs being implemented in schools appear to be based on a labelling process that reinforces a fixed entity perception of academic ability. The services offered by these programs provide challenging and enriching learning activities to overcome the boredom and frustration experienced by many high achievers in regular classrooms. Clearly, many students can benefit from these challenging and enriching learning activities. This labelling process, however, appears to be a double-edged sword; while it makes it possible for some students to obtain valuable and important services, it can also fix behavioral and achievement expectations in the minds of many teachers, parents, and students. For this reason, it is important that educators be especially careful of the labels they choose, since their connotations can have serious and far-reaching implications.

While many differences exist among individuals, to decree that a certain percentage of a school's enrollment should be *labelled* "gifted" denotes that these students are high achievers because they have been endowed with a special genetic attribute from their parents. This denotation can create anxiety and confusion for those who receive the label, since it implies that their achievements are the result of endowment rather than effort. It can also lead others to believe that they lack the "gift" to achieve at the same high levels. Although many specialists in the field do not intend to insinuate that students labelled "gifted" have genetically acquired talents different from their peers, the word *gift*, according to Webster, "often implies special favor by God or nature."

The effect of this labelling is to create a division among students based on an ambiguous fixed-entity view of student achievement and potential. Although many parents of students identified as "gifted" take considerable pride in the label, some students feel like imposters when they discover that learning does not always come easily for them. The more effort they must expend toward mastery, the less "gifted" they are likely to feel. Research by Guskin and colleagues (1986), for example, found that most of the 295 gifted and talented students they studied did not believe that being gifted was a genetic trait, and over one-third did not agree that they were gifted. In fact, they believed that giftedness can be attained by studying hard and by practice, and that gifted and talented persons only differ from other students in the effort they are willing to expend to develop their skills.

It is incumbent on educators to assist students with exceptional educational needs. Those who achieve at levels far beyond their peers should not be subjected to the boredom and frustration that come from mindless admonitions like "Just follow along with the others" or "When you finish your worksheet, help Jimmy with his." Flexible programming that provides extensions and enrichments is necessary and can benefit many students. Nevertheless, labelling a predetermined number of students "gifted" or "talented" (which may indeed describe the child prodigy), and thereby indirectly labelling most others as "nongifted" or "nontalented" may create more problems than it solves, since it is likely to perpetuate a fixed and limited view of academic ability and directly or indirectly undermine many students' persistent efforts toward academic mastery. If labels are needed, let them avoid denoting unproven genetic differences in learning potential. According to Bloom:

> *When educators try to develop talent, they often go about it by looking for the one in a hundred or the one in a thousand rather than expecting that virtually all can learn a particular talent field satisfactorily, and that the best will go even further. I think schools are wrong if they are highly selective in providing special learning experiences. (1985a, p. 34)*

Carroll's Model of Ability and Learning

In 1963, John Carroll proposed a model for school learning that challenged the traditionally held fixed entity view of student aptitude. He argued that academic aptitude might more accurately be viewed as a measure of a student's learning rate, rather than as an indicator of the depth or limit to which a student could learn a given subject, skill or concept. Rather than viewing students as either bright or dull, Carroll proposed that it was more accurate to see students as either fast learners or slow learners. He proposed the equation indicated in Figure 3-2 to express the relationship between the degree or depth of a student's learning and the student's rate of learning.

The equation indicates that the ratio between the time that a given student needs to thoroughly master a concept and the time that the child actually spends learning will determine the degree to which that concept or skill was learned or mastered. If the student actually spends as much time as he or she needs to spend, the equation would equal 1, indicating that the concept has been thoroughly mastered.

Carroll went on to define "time spent" as a function of the student's *perseverance,* or willingness to maintain active engagement in the learning process, and the student's *opportunity to learn,* which could be viewed as the amount of class time or teacher's help devoted to the concept. The "time needed," according to Carroll, was determined by the child's unique and possibly genetically determined *learning rate* for that concept, the *quality of the instruction* provided to the child by the teacher, and the child's *understanding of the instruction.* The equations in Figure 3-3 demonstrate these relationships.

FIGURE 3-2 Carroll's Equation of Academic Aptitude

$$\text{degree of learning} = f \left(\frac{\text{time spent}}{\text{time needed}} \right)$$

FIGURE 3-3   Carroll's Model for School Learning

$$\frac{\text{time spent at}}{\text{learning}} = \text{perseverance} \times \text{opportunity to learn}$$

$$\text{time needed} = \frac{\text{learning rate} \times \text{quality of instruction}}{\times \text{understanding of instruction}}$$

Carroll believed that a child's learning rate was a measure of the time needed under ideal instructional conditions. If the teacher developed a highly organized, structured, and clearly stated lesson, for example, the child would be more likely to understand the instruction, thus reducing the time needed. Experimental research by Bloom (1976) offers support for Carroll's belief that students differ in learning rates. His conclusions suggest that faster students initially learn from five to seven times quicker than slower students, but that these differences decrease somewhat when the quality and organization of instruction is improved for all students.

Carroll's model for school learning offers an alternative to the fixed entity view of academic ability. For Carroll, "time on task," a term widely used in schools today, was not a matter of exposure or elapsed time, but rather a product of the child's learning rate and the quality of instruction. Implicit in his model is the assumption that given sufficient time to learn, quality instruction, and the willingness to persevere, almost all students have the capacity to master the school's curriculum. This view flies in the face of the fixed entity view of academic ability, which implicitly at least holds that those with high ability can deal with analysis, synthesis, and problem solving, while those with low ability can only be expected to memorize rudimentary elements rather than master higher-level thinking skills.

Nevertheless, we must be honest with ourselves and with students when we conceptualize academic ability. According to Nicholls:

> Yet it would not be useful to attempt to retard the development of more differentiated conceptions [of ability] or to teach the view that one's abilities have no limits. . . . To advocate retardation of the development of the concept of ability would be to advocate ignorance. Likewise, it does not appear constructive to suggest that schools ought to prevent students from thinking they are below average. . . . Instead, students as well as educators and parents might do well to accept and find fair ways of living with the fact that everyone can't be above average. To this end we might construct interpretive frameworks that give our differences in competence a more communal function. Competence need not dominate; it can also serve. It is not likely that the injustice of competitive, ego-involving schools and societies will be alleviated by the expectation that everyone can make it to the White House or to the top of the class. (1989, p. 94)

Indeed, everyone cannot be above average, and students quickly learn how they rank among their peers on almost any skill or trait; it serves no purpose to hide this. Remaining sections of this chapter assert that finding "fair ways of living with this fact" requires that schools, (1) avoid implying that students' academic rank and self-worth are related, and (2) change instructional methods and evaluation practices that base mastery of academic goals on relative performance.

Norm-Referenced Evaluation: For Every Winner, a Loser

Parents have high hopes for their children when they send them off to kindergarten. They know that succeeding in school is crucial to surviving and flourishing in this complex world that grows more technological each year. In turn, these young learners arrive at the classroom door with equally high hopes of achievement and success. Some have practiced playing "school" long before arriving, and many have had the benefit of several years of "Sesame Street" and playing with "educational" toys. Almost all are excited and enthusiastic about the prospect of learning, and they are willing to work hard to satisfy their parents', their teachers', and their own expectations for success.

Success in school, however, has many definitions. For some it means acquiring academic skills and knowledge, earning high grades,and being included on the honor roll. For others it may mean developing self-confidence, athletic prowess, or social recognition. Regardless of definition, few parents will feel pride nor will their children feel successful if the child's academic performance is labelled "below average." Even the label "average" is a disappointment for many. After all, in many states, if college students achieve at an average or C level, they are judged unworthy to receive a teaching license.

For many parents, teachers, and students, academic success has become synonymous with the label "above average." The label implies that one's performance is "better than" or "higher than" the performance of at least half of the other students in a class or group. Since this definition of success is based on relative performance, it is necessarily exclusionary; only a limited number of students can be above average. The testing and evaluation procedures followed in most classrooms and schools are based either directly or indirectly on the practice of comparing one student's performance with that of another. Consequently, large numbers of students in any given class find it impossible to experience academic success, regardless of how hard they try.

The procedure of comparing one student's performance with that of another is called *norm-referencing,* and the results of national achievement tests, subject or unit examinations, placement tests, report card grades, honor rolls, and even daily worksheets and quizzes are usually based on this procedure. In its simplest form, norm-referenced evaluation requires the determination of the group median or mean performance on any given exercise. This referent then makes it possible to determine whether an individual's performance is above or below the norm or average. The normative terms of "above average," "average," and "below average" are so ingrained in our educational lexicon that their continued use goes unquestioned and their negative effects are seldom considered.

That for every student who is labelled above average an equal number must be labelled below average is a fact so obvious that it hardly merits mention. But one wonders how many adults truly appreciate the implication of such categorization. A biology teacher reported that the father of one of her students expressed his lack of comprehension during a parent-teacher conference: "I knew my son wasn't in the top half of your biology class, but I certainly didn't think he was in the bottom half!" And how many people in your community might become upset with your school system if the local newspaper ran the headline, "Half of Elementary Students Reading Below State Average"? One state superintendent of schools has been quoted as saying, "Without question our public school students are doing well when compared to the national average. However, we should not overlook the fact that although Wisconsin averages are high, there are a number of students who fall below the national average" (Bednarek, 1983). I'm sure that the superintendent is not alone in wishing his state was as fortunate as Garrison Keillor's Lake Wobegon, the mythical little town in Minnesota where *all* the kids are above average.

Clearly, many politicians, parents, and students have come to believe that the label "below average" on any measure of academic achievement indicates that one is incompetent, lazy, or unambitious. In fact, *A Nation at Risk* (1983), the report of former President Ronald Reagan's National Commission on Education, concluded that one reason the schools were doing so poorly was that too many of the nation's teachers came from the bottom half of their college graduating classes. The implication, of course, is that less-than-average ranking implies professional incompetence.

The national lobby group, Friends for Education, which is concerned with the lack of "truth" in the reporting of local, state, and national testing results, found that in 1988 every state in the union reported that their statewide achievement test scores were *above* the national "norm," which most parents, politicians, and news reporters equate to being above the national average (Cannell, 1989). Referring to this "Lake Wobegon effect," Cannell states, "After obtaining results from more than 3500 school districts, we concluded that 70 percent of American school children, 90 percent of American school districts, and all 50 states were testing above the publishers 'national norm' on commercial norm-referenced achievement tests" (1989, p. ix).

Several factors contribute to these confusing results. Cannell reports that they are caused by lax test security, nonstandard testing practices deceptive statistics, and misleading impressions, not improved achievement. Most upsetting, his "report concludes that outright cheating by American educators on 'Lake Wobegon' tests of school achievement is common" (Cannell, 1989, p. 5).

Pressures on students to be ranked above average are evidently shared by their teachers, parents, and state politicians. Many states, according to Cannell, have "high stakes" testing programs in which test scores can affect how far a teacher will advance up the career ladder. In California, real estate prices are influenced by the school-by-school test scores that are widely reported in the media, and, for a time, Texas even based teachers' merit pay on the standardized achievement scores of their students.

Cannell believes that the most common form of "cheating" is teaching to the test—drilling students in material likely to appear on the examinations. He quotes a Harvard-graduated inner-city teacher as saying,

> *The principal would come on the intercom each morning to discuss one or two vocabulary items from the Iowa Tests of Basic Skills vocabulary subtest: "Good morning, boys and girls, this morning we are going to have a little chat. Do you know what a 'chat' is? That's right, it's a little talk." Chat, of course, was one of the items on the ITBS vocabulary subtest. (Cannell, 1989, p. 18)*

The following is an example of one of the many letters Cannell says he has received from teachers who have written to express their frustrations with achievement tests:

> *Dear Dr. Cannell,*
> *I am a kindergarten teacher and I have watched other kindergarten teachers' IOWA scores show most of their students scoring in the ninetieth percentile. I naively thought it would not take the administration long to figure out that they were teaching the test.*
> *At one point I questioned our principal about the high scores. I was told, "confidentially," that not only did he know that some teachers were teaching the test, he also knew that some teachers walked around during the test, pointing out to their students which questions needed to be "rechecked."*
> *Although I knew my scores were making me look bad, I held out for four years. Finally, during my fifth year of teaching kindergarten, I, too, stooped to teaching the tests. I hardly spent more than one week teaching the test during the 1985–86 school year. My scores jumped to the 90th percentile, too. The administration said nothing. The 1986–87 school year I went back to not teaching the test. The scores, once again, fell tremendously.*
> *I have read your report concerning nationally normed elementary*

achievement testing with great interest. For years I have watched what was going on in our public schools. My questions and concerns have usually met with no interest. My lower IOWA test scores have led some parents to question my teaching skills. In the end, I have concluded, that there is really nothing I can do about this fraud. I would appreciate your comments on the matter. (Cannell, 1989, pp. 13–14)*

While Cannell has spent a great deal of effort researching this alleged fraud within the achievement testing system, his solutions appear to treat the symptoms rather than the core of the problem. First, Cannell suggests that students who do rank below the national average should be made painfully aware of their academic standing. "I am convinced," he writes, "that the current American epidemic of teenage pregnancy, depression, drug use, delinquency, and teenage suicide is partially related to the low standards and the low expectations so evident in America's public schools" (Cannell, 1989, p. ix). Increasing academic standards and expectations would help raise the self-esteem of many students, he argues. It is difficult to see how forcing 50 percent of our students, schools, and states into acknowledging their "below average" status would increase their self-esteem. Rather than addressing the fundamental flaws that characterize norm-referenced evaluation, Cannell offers eighteen ways to increase test security and to stop cheating. Furthermore, he advocates that the U.S. Department of Education become involved in administering national norm-referenced achievement tests, presumably because it could control test security and eliminate cheating, thereby providing a definitive answer as to exactly which students, districts, and states are to carry the "below average" label.

It seems clear that many students, parents, and politicians will go to extremes to avoid the embarrassment and degradation associated with the label "below average." I recall asking a group of teachers how they would react if they had a son who brought home a report card stating that he was achieving below the class average. Without hesitating, one mother replied, "Well, I'd grab the broomstick and take care of that problem right away!" Her assumption, of course, was that the child's rank was his own fault, and that more effort on his part, encouraged by the broomstick, would soon get him back in the top half of the class where he belonged. The odds, however, are not in his favor. While increased effort can improve achievement, moving to the upper half of the class would require that her son displace someone who was already there. Assuming that others do not increase their effort proportionately, there is a chance that he can make the displacement. Unfortunately, however, since those in the above-average

---

*From J. J. Cannell, *How Public Educators Cheat on Standardized Achievement Tests,* copyright 1985 by Friends For Education, reproduced by permission of the publisher.

group are reluctant to concede their positions, the chance is slight. Most students discover early in their educational careers that once below average, always below average.

Some teachers believe that by not "curving" their students' test scores and by using the percentage of items correct or total points earned to determine grades they can avoid the pitfalls of norm-referenced evaluation. While this approach is commendable in its departure from the standard procedure of comparing one student's performance with that of another, most experienced teachers know that no test is absolute, that they can construct a test on which almost no student earns above 70 percent, or one on which almost every student can achieve 100 percent. Regardless of scoring procedure, if it is the teacher's purpose to select test items that separate students according to their relative knowledge of the content, then indirectly, at least, the results will continue to be based on a norm-referenced philosophy. If, however, students are clearly informed of the specific content objectives beforehand, and if the test items are selected to measure individual mastery of these specific content objectives, then the evaluation procedure may be considered content- or criterion-referenced, rather than norm-referenced. In this case, slower students may be afforded opportunities for relearning and retaking, without penalty, a parallel test measuring the same objectives.

Chapter 7 provides a more detailed discussion of how standards of excellence can be identified and measured. By evaluating students against these standards rather than against others' performances, it becomes possible for all students to succeed. Bloom's research supports this optimism; his central theme is the potential equality of most human beings for school learning:

> In general, the average student taught under mastery-learning procedures achieves at a level above 85% of students taught under conventional instructional conditions. An even more extreme result has been obtained when tutoring was used as the primary method of instruction. Under tutoring, the average student performs better than 98% of students taught by conventional group instruction, even though both groups of students performed at similar levels in terms of relevant aptitude and achievement before the instruction began. (1985b, pp. 4–5)

The Threat to Self-Worth: Forced Competition

Most students believe that in school their personal worth depends largely on their academic accomplishments (Covington & Beery, 1976). This is evident in the very language used to identify or categorize their achievements: "good" students get high grades; "poor" students get low grades. Furthermore, comparative evaluation makes it quite clear that being a "good" or successful student is directly related to peer rank; success requires that one ranks above the average. There are, of course, exceptions to this assertion. Many students experience feelings of success when they earn an average grade in an exceptionally difficult course. A steady diet of *C*'s and *D*'s, however, forces one to accept an academic self-image of being less than successful.

Many environmental and personal considerations determine a student's inclusion in the above-average group; the two most important personal factors are innate learning ability, which Carroll suggests may have a greater influence on rate of learning than on capacity, and willingness to expend concentrated effort toward acquiring skills and knowledge. Only the latter is directly under the student's control.

Whether innate learning ability is a genetically determined capacity to acquire and use knowledge or whether it is a function of how quickly and efficiently one processes information, it is traditionally viewed as a norm-referenced trait that emerges naturally in the familiar bell-shaped curve. Effort, on the other hand, need not be norm-referenced; each individual is free to choose how much effort to expend on any given task. This choice is influenced by a variety of factors, but the decision to expend effort toward learning is neither genetically determined nor exclusionary. All students are capable of exhibiting intense effort—or no effort at all.

Entering school armed with their willingness to expend varying levels of effort and their norm-referenced ability, students discover that they are forced to compete with one another for the significant, but limited, official rewards for achievement. After all, not everyone can be labelled "above average," earn *A*'s, or be included on the honor rolls. The value of these extrinsic indicators of academic success is much more important to students than they admit. With few exceptions, it is only by receiving these awards that one can develop a true sense of academic self-worth.

During this competition, most students conclude that winning depends more on one's genetically determined ability than on one's willingness to expend effort. In short, their academic achievement seems all but predetermined. The grading systems used in most classrooms are based on the assumption that if all work hard, those with the greater innate ability receive the *A*'s and *B*'s, while those with less ability receive the *C*'s and *D*'s. The grade of *F* is usually reserved for those who do not attend or do not try. According to psychologist Carole Ames:

> *Normative comparisons in the classroom are explicit in grading practices and in teacher behavior as well as implicit in teachers' communications (e.g., "I like the way Allan is working."). Anecdotally, I have found on many occasions that teachers will indicate that they purposely try to de-emphasize competition in their classroom, but they readily acknowledge that they frequently wait to formulate their*

grading criteria until after they see the distributions of test scores. The point here is that competition has many faces and underscores the student's life in many, if not most, classrooms. (1984, p. 190)

Younger children do not distinguish between ability and effort as separate factors in determining achievement. According to Covington (1984), students in the primary grades see effort as an indicator of ability; those who try hard are smart. This conception changes as students move through the grades. When they reach the upper elementary years they begin to recognize effort and ability as distinct factors in determining academic outcomes, although they still believe that effort is the more important of the two. When they begin to experience the increased competitive pressures of middle and high school, however, students realize that ability, demonstrated by how quickly or easily one learns and retains academic content, becomes more important than high levels of effort for earning the official rewards of school.

We tell students that there are other important reasons and rewards for working hard in school besides being labelled "above average," receiving high grades, or being named to the honor roll. Just knowing that one is doing one's best, without regard for outcome, is a prized ethic that parents and teachers try to instill in their students. Many have said, "Regardless of the grade you receive, working hard and doing your best in school are really what's important."

I recently attended a high school swim meet and saw on the wall behind the starting blocks a rather impressive twenty-foot banner with the words "Value your effort more than your results." A smaller sign with the words "You have failed only when you fail to try" was placed on a side wall. Signs that extol the virtues of hard work and effort are inspirational to many students and certainly have their place in a classroom or an athletic contest. They are particularly effective if they remind students that increased effort can lead to improved performance–especially when improvement is measured with a stop watch.

Yet, down deep, as much as we would like to believe this sage advice, most of us know that our culture considers it a cliche–and an untrue one at that. Effort alone is not significantly rewarded, nor, as will be demonstrated later in this chapter, do most adults value effort distinct from achievement in their own lives.

Teachers do reward a student's hard work with praise and encouragement, regardless of the student's achievement. Diligent students also find that their failures are met with fewer penalties than do those students who do not try (Covington & Beery, 1976). But praise and encouragement are not significant enough rewards to sustain repeated high levels of effort without accompanying improvements in achievement. This is illustrated in the cases of Carol and Jimmy, students in Ms. Corbie's fifth-grade class. When leaving school the day before Ms. Corbie's weekly spelling test, Carol makes sure that she doesn't forget her list of forty words. She starts reviewing the list the moment she gets on the bus for the thirty-minute ride home. She also spends about twenty minutes writing out some of the more difficult words before dinner. After the dishes are washed, she talks her father into helping her review for the test. He reads the words to her as she spells them back to him. She struggles over several, but with hints from her father, she succeeds in spelling each of the words. The next morning, Carol studies her list before breakfast and looks at it again on the bus ride to school. All through the morning, she nervously waits for spelling time to arrive so she can begin the test.

As Jimmy walks out of school on the afternoon before the test, he realizes that he has left his spelling list back in his locker. Although he knows he could still go back for it, he doesn't want to be late for the soft-ball game he and his friends have planned for after school. He decides to worry about the spelling test tomorrow. After all, he looked at the list earlier in the week and already knew how to spell many of the words. After the softball game, Jimmy rides his bicycle home, arriving just in time for dinner. He helps with the dishes and then settles down for a couple of hours of prime-time television before bed. When he arrives at school the next morning, he goes to his locker for the spelling list. After reviewing it for a few minutes before the first bell, he tucks it into his reading book so he can sneak a few peeks at it during the morning silent reading time. He'll have to be careful, however, since Ms. Corbie knows he has a habit of doing this before spelling tests.

Assume that you are Ms. Corbie. You administer your spelling test of forty words. Carol spells thirty-two words correctly and earns a score of 80 percent. Jimmy spells thirty-six words correctly and earns a score of 90 percent. Jimmy's score was typical of his past spelling tests. Carol's score was ten percentage points higher than any of her previous tests. What grade would you give each student? Which student worked harder?

Although teachers vary in the method and philosophy they use to assign grades, most would typically give Jimmy an *A* or *B+*, and Carol a *B* or *C+*. We know that Carol spent considerably more time studying for this spelling test than Jimmy did. Although all teachers would praise and encourage Carol's effort, high achievement, not effort, is the primary determinant of the official rewards of school.

We tell students that working hard, regardless of the results, is what's really important in school. Will Carol feel successful from her effort regardless of the grade? Will she work as hard on next week's spelling test? The following example may help provide an answer to these questions.

Assume you are a graduate student in Professor Corry's Introduction to Educational Research course. You are a full-time teacher and this is the first course you have taken since graduating from your state university a few years ago. Since you are considering working toward a Master's degree, you want to perform well in the class. In addition, you led an active social life as an undergraduate and are not very proud of your academic record. To make amends, you decide to spend a great deal of energy in preparing for Professor Corry's class. About thirty other graduate students are enrolled in the course, and he has indicated that half of the course grade will be determined by the score on the mid-term exam. It will consist of 100 multiple-choice questions drawn from material in the rather lengthy and complicated textbook and from his class lectures.

Although you have never done well in math, you decide to study harder and prepare more for this test than you have for any other. From the onset of the course, you spend many hours each week taking copious notes from both the text and Professor Corry's lectures, and you type them into the new computer you decided was necessary if you were to become a serious graduate student. Three weeks before the exam, you work out a detailed study plan allowing yourself two-and-one-half hours per day during your busy teaching schedule to read and study for your research course. During the weekend before the exam you decide to rent a small, quiet motel room and have your food catered so that you will be free to devote all of your efforts to uninterrupted preparation for the test. You read and reread your text and copy and recopy your notes. On the night of the exam you feel confident and well prepared.

The second scenario is a bit different. Assume that you also want to do well in Professor Corry's class, but the semester has been difficult for you. You are experiencing many behavioral problems from the students in your classes, your principal is constantly complaining about your work, and, out of spite, he has appointed you chairperson of the district School Improvement Committee. Unfortunately, you discover that the rest of the committee members are too busy to attend meetings and instead want you to write the complete implementation plan and present it to the superintendent and school board. As you begin to think about writing the report, your 16-year-old daughter, who has been dating the leader of the local motorcycle gang, tells you she wants to quit high school and spend a couple of years "riding the road." When you muster the courage to share this news with your spouse, you are informed that your mate has become romantically involved with a co-worker.

Confronted with this reality, you decide that it is time for a change in your life. After cashing some old savings bonds, you phone your principal to tell her to hire a substitute for your classes, and you book a three-week cruise to the Caribbean. The pina coladas and sun help you forget your job, family, and Professor Corry's mid-term exam. You have a wonderful time meeting new and interesting people, and the three weeks pass quickly. You return home relaxed, refreshed, and with renewed energy to deal with the problems you left behind. The day before the exam you quickly skim several chapters from the text and arrive at the exam knowing you put little effort into preparing for it.

The following week, Professor Corry returns the tests and writes the scores and grade distribution on the chalkboard. Assume in both scenarios you receive the third lowest score in the class. In which of the two situations would you feel the most disappointed: when you studied a great deal for the test, or when you quickly skimmed the chapters?

If you truly believe that studying hard regardless of performance is really what is important in school, then effort is its own reward and you would be satisfied with your score in either case; the effort you expended was a valuable experience *or* you made a conscious, independent decision *not* to study, thereby choosing to limit the test's value. Most teachers, however, believe the opposite is true; they would feel more disappointed in the first scenario, in which they worked hard and did not experience success. Beyond the rhetoric regarding the virtues of effort regardless of ability, most know the personal humiliation and shame that would result from expending great amounts of effort studying for an exam, only to receive a low grade.

Forcing students to compete for the important rewards of school on the basis of learning ability rather than on their self-determined effort causes many students to retreat from the competition. It may be argued that competition is the foundation on which our society is based and that the school's role is to transmit these dominant cultural values. This view of schooling supports norm-referenced competitive procedures that differentiate and reward those who excel. Yet, if schools are to be instruments for social change and improvement, they must also foster and reinforce reasonable effort from all students, regardless of innate ability. These apparently conflicting goals have been identified by cultural anthropologist Kathleen Wilcox:

> [T]he school is a social institution upon which the culture places highly contradictory expectations. Receiving most obvious attention is the expectation that schools will maximize social equality by promoting equal opportunity; less obvious is the expectation that schools will maximize social differentiation by allocating persons to positions in a differentiated and stratified work force. (Wilcox, 1982, p. 272)

The school's use of norm-referenced evaluation is often more brutal than that applied in other segments of society. Few adults, for example, are subjected to the humiliation of zero sum norm-referencing. According to John Gardner, "The top corporate executive is apt to be particularly eloquent in defense of individual competition, but his ambitious subordinates will usually find that he has himself well protected against any unseemly rivalry on their part" (1961, p. 111). Even if valid criteria may be available, how many teachers or administrators support a norm-referenced merit system that ranks all teachers or administrators from most effective to least effective, forcing 50 percent to be below average? Such a forced ranking system would be catastrophic in a university setting, where it seems that 80 to 90 percent of the faculty believe themselves to rank in the top 10 percent of their peers.

Dreikurs warned parents and educators of the negative effects of interpersonal competition on the personalities of children:

> *Many objections are voiced to our suggestion that parents and teachers avoid competitive strife amongst the children. We are told that we should train our children in competitive efforts since they will have to live in a highly competitive society. This assumption is fallacious. The less competitive a person is, the better he can stand up under extreme competition. If he is merely content to do his job, then he is not disturbed by what his competitor may do or may achieve.* A competitive person can stand competition only if he succeeds. *(emphasis added)* *(1968, p. 78)*

Competition for excellence, in itself, is not debilitating. As many as half of our students thrive on the competition generated by the school's norm-referenced evaluative structure. Because they believe they have a reasonable chance of winning, the competition often produces their best efforts. Since these students typically learn quicker than the other 50 percent of the student population, experience has taught them that it is possible to succeed if they expend the necessary effort. Competition becomes debilitating, however, when it forces slower-learning students who have little hope of winning to compete with faster-learning students, who are far more likely to succeed.

Failure-Avoiding Behavior

During the first few years at school, most students are willing to work hard since they have been *led* to believe that effort results in success. As they move through the grades, however, slower-learning students discover that they must expend far greater effort to master what their quicker-learning friends acquire in a fraction of the time. Furthermore, since academic competition requires a scarcity of rewards, they are forced to compete against these faster-learning students in a zero-sum evaluation system that rewards some only by punishing others. While their increased effort does produce higher levels of individual achievement, slower-learning students continue to receive the lower grades since their faster-learning peers tend to exert whatever effort is necessary to remain in the upper half of the class. It is not difficult to see how this zero-sum competition creates a serious threat to the self-worth of slower students.

Some students are able to overcome this threat by finding success in extracurricular activities or in activities outside of school. Others are willing to accept their less-than-successful achievement. By refusing to equate academic achievement with self-worth, or by accepting their below-average status, they are able to persist with classroom assignments to the best of their ability. Large numbers of students, however, find it too painful to accept their below-average status. Rather than continuing to expend effort on classroom activities that do not lead to feelings of success, they often choose to focus their energies on finding failure-avoiding behaviors that protect their threatened self-identities—if they can't win, at least they can avoid losing by refusing to play the game.

Losing, of course, is a subjective judgment, one that is not restricted to a failing grade. For some students, *D*'s, *C*'s, or even *B*'s can be considered failure. Students who behave in ways to protect their self-worth, according to Covington and Beery (1976), are struggling to avoid a *sense* of failure, rather than a failing grade. While it may appear contradictory, apathy is frequently used as a defense against a sense of academic failure. If one concludes that effort will not lead to success, then opting out often appears preferable.

Dreikurs poignantly identified the burden that our culture places on adolescents:

> *They have been trained by adults to compete, and made to feel inferior if they do not excel. Their ambition, which their parents and teachers have tried to stimulate, now becomes the greatest obstacle to their adjustment. They all want to feel important, to be something special. Yet in our present culture the community offers little that gives them a feeling of significance. Some few are fortunate in finding eminence in school, academically, athletically or socially. The great majority rarely find avenues for experiencing importance in a useful way. Only in their defiance of order and discipline can they feel some semblance of power and superiority. Driving a car, easy money, gambling, drinking, and sex are the easiest ways for them to achieve a sensation of significance. (1968, p. 34)*

Covington and Beery (1976) have identified two broad strategies or "game plans" that many students use to avoid the humiliation of school failure. One set of strategies deals with ways that students try to *ensure* success in order to avoid the implications of failure. Students using these strategies may choose to drastically lower their goals and aspirations, resort to academic cheating, or become compulsive overstrivers. These tactics enable students to avoid the threat of failure by guaranteeing success. A second category of strategies enables students to disown or reject the painful implications that failure conveys regarding one's ability to achieve. By arranging excuses for failure other than low ability, failure can be defused of its threat to self-worth. Nonparticipation, false effort, or setting impossibly high goals are characteristics of these failure-prone strategies.

Avoiding Failure by Ensuring Success

One fifth-grade teacher described an example of a student who had drastically lowered his goals in order to avoid failure. She was upset that this boy refused to participate appropriately in her weekly spelldowns. As the class took its place against the wall, he would always announce loudly to the teacher and his classmates that he was going to spell his first word wrong. When his turn arrived, he smiled happily as he accomplished his goal. It would be difficult to find a clearer example of avoiding failure by ensuring success. Although his behavior earned him his teacher's wrath, this was clearly the less of two evils; he was able to satisfactorily protect his self-worth by ensuring that no one in the class would know anything about his true spelling ability. His tactic also guaranteed that he would be successful—he *could* spell the first word incorrectly. Frustrated by his behavior, his teacher tried to get the boy to participate in the cut-throat competition of her spelldown by giving him easy words to spell like *book* or *tree*. Even then, he persisted in misspelling the words. After all, why should he change the game when he was so clearly winning it? Chapter 8 provides an alternative to the unfair competition of forced spelldowns.

Cheating on homework and tests is a second way that students try to ensure success. Adults often don't appreciate the extent to which some children are dominated by the fear of failure. According to one elementary school student, "Kids don't cheat because they are bad. They are afraid that they aren't smart and what will happen if they don't do good. People will call them dumb or stupid." Another states, "I know someone who studies hard for tests and cheats, too. They feel really bad but it is better than being yelled at for bad grades." A third says, "People cheat because they are afraid of doing poorer than other kids and feeling miserable for being different and behind" (Covington & Beery, 1976, p. 55).

Overstriving is another tactic used by students driven by the conviction that one's self-worth is contingent upon one's accomplishments. Compulsive overstrivers have discovered that they can rely on overpreparedness and excessive attention to detail to ensure success in school. These students often get the highest grades in school and appear to be doing well. However, rather than generating feelings of pride and confidence, their success merely feeds the constant anxiety of knowing that they cannot avoid failure indefinitely. "Like all failure-avoiding students," according to Covington and Berry, "the overstriver has fallen victim to a misunderstanding of the proper role of failure in the learning process (1976, p. 57)."

Avoiding Failure by Withholding Effort

Many students believe that apathy is a useful way to avoid feelings of failure. While self-defeating in the long run, withholding effort on school assignments can help students temporarily ward off the humiliation and shame that accompany less-than-successful performance. When Jimmy, for example, does not do his homework assignment but says to his teacher that the reason he can't hand it in is because his dog ate it, he is still likely to receive an *F* or a zero in the teacher's grade book. While not a pleasant experience, Jimmy experiences less threat to his self-worth than he would had he expended effort to complete the assignment only to result in a similar low grade. Choosing not to participate at least places control in the hands of the student—who feels doomed to failure in any case.

Teachers and parents assure students that they fail only when they don't try. Failure-avoiding students have learned that the inverse is true; if you don't try, you can't fail. Effort, however, is a double-edged sword (Covington & Omerlich, 1979). On one edge, effort serves as a direct source of self-worth as well as a causal factor in achievement (see Figure 2-1). On the other hand, effort inheres the risk of humiliation and shame that results from lack of success. Even "cool dude" Bart Simpson, the care-free, jagged-haired elementary school iconoclast, experienced the pain of this edge when he discovered that he was about to fail fourth grade and would be required to repeat the year. Mustering all of his courage and energy, he expended a tremendous amount of effort preparing for the final exam. Receiving a score of 59 percent, he was told he flunked the exam and would be required to repeat the grade. For a rare moment in the series, Bart experienced genuine remorse and humiliation as he laid his head down on his desk and cried. He knew that he had tried his hardest, so he was forced to conclude that he will always be stupid and inept. Fortunately, in his litany of self-pity, he compares his predicament to an esoteric incident in the life of George Washington. Since he readily knew the exact month, day, and year of the anecdote his teacher gave him 1 additional point on the exam for his "incidental knowledge" and he passed the year with a *D*−. Since Bart is infamous for his efforts to do the bare minimum, he was overjoyed with his new grade: it was exactly what he wanted.

Students know that withholding effort is not without risk. Most teachers will not tolerate students who do not exert at least some effort. Blatant noninvolvement usually results in phone calls home, detentions after school, or parent-teacher conferences. To avoid these unpleasant consequences, failure avoiders must feign the appearance of effort. This false effort allows them to walk the fine line between expending enough effort to avoid the negative consequences of blatant noninvolvement, without risking a threat to their self-worth.

The following are descriptions of failure-avoiding behaviors provided by Sharon Sohner, a tenth-grade English teacher who attended a graduate course taught by the author:

Seven boys in my sixth-hour English Skills class, Jimmy, Paul, Eric, David, Jack, Lloyd, and Chuck, were motivated to avoid a sense of failure, only I didn't realize it then. I now understand the factors that contributed to their motivational stance, and I have a better idea of how I could have worked with them instead of against them. At the time, I, too, was trying to avoid a sense of failure—as a teacher.

Jimmy, when he showed up for school, presented himself to the class as apathetic and noninvolved. He would slouch, sleep or be otherwise occupied. He didn't participate; he finally dropped out. Paul would put on a good show. He'd answer questions that had already been answered or opt for the easiest assignment and become very vocal when he succeeded. He'd do half of his spelling and then say, "Well, at least I did half!" Eric and David would always say they were going to do all of the work and all of the extra credit. Then, they did nothing, although both said that they wanted to go to medical school. Jack constantly wanted to know how little he could do to get a D. Frequently Lloyd would entertain the class with his "this class sucks—the school sucks—you bitch" under his breath. Chuck would spend incredible amounts of time neatly rewriting the first two sentences of a composition, squandering his efforts in meaningless ways; he never got his assignments completed.

All seven boys cheated whenever they had a chance. There were no overstrivers. They were apathetic, uninvolved, fakers, impossible or lowest possible goal setters, and critics. They were all failing, and they were masters at avoiding a sense of failure.

I didn't understand at the time that they were avoiding failure by embracing it. If someone had told me that, I would have thought he or she was nuts. After our class discussions and my reading, I can now understand some of the factors that may have caused these students to act as they did. Jimmy felt poorly about himself. If he didn't participate, then no one would see how terribly he spelled. Only I saw this in the few things he handed in. Eventually he decided not to let me see. Paul's false effort might have been to avoid the implications that he had no ability. Eric and David wouldn't really have to worry about getting into medical school; only the bright were allowed in. They wouldn't be blamed for failure to reach such a lofty goal. And weren't they wonderful for aspiring to the American dream. Jack avoided failure by working only for a D. The rest of the group thought he was one of them because he didn't get higher grades. He would never have to really worry about not receiving a B. Lloyd became unique; a nonconformist. He got a lot of mileage from his outspoken criticisms. Chuck constantly felt that he could do nothing right. And so, he would do nothing rather than face the fact that he had not learned to write very well. Each of these boys had his own set of defenses. Ten years of low achievement clearly communicated the message of "no value" to each boy. None of them were willing to risk effort at learning again.

Researchers at the Institute for Research on Teaching at the University of Michigan analyzed how teachers, who were judged by their principals to be outstanding at dealing with students who had developed a sense of helplessness and defeatism from repeated failure, dealt with failure-avoiding behavior in their classrooms (Brophy, 1982). Although these students had rejected school and had stopped working, these highly competent teachers refused to cave in to these students by reducing expectations and treating them as if they were really unable to succeed:

Instead, they approach such students with a mixture of sympathy, encouragement, and demands. These teachers reassure the students that they do have ability and that work given will not be too difficult for them. Then, the teachers help them to get started when they are discouraged or need some support, reinforce their progress, and perhaps offer contracts providing rewards for accomplishments and allowing opportunities for students to set goals. In general, the emphasis is on encouragement and help rather than prodding through threat of punishment. Failure-syndrome students are not merely told that they can succeed, but shown convincingly that they can, and helped to do so. (Brophy, 1982, p. 23)

While this chapter has discussed several causes of academic apathy, many students have discovered that apathy is a useful, albeit self-defeating, defense to protect a threatened sense of self-worth. Students who withhold effort to avoid a sense of failure approach each new learning experience with apprehension and fear, emotions they mask with aloofness and indifference. Academic challenges are met with the conviction that "nothing ventured, nothing failed." These students are often labeled "unmotivated." In fact, they are highly motivated to protect their threatened sense of self-worth. They have discovered that if they hold the belief that school is a meaningless, boring waste of time, then the school's evaluation system will be equally irrelevant and cannot infringe on their sense of self-worth. These students have learned that it is less painful to reject school than it is to reject their own sense of competence and potential.

The following example may help demonstrate this process. Assume that a national commission is established to develop a valid and reliable instrument for measuring teacher effectiveness. The commission is composed largely of experienced teachers and is given ten years and an unlimited budget to complete its mission. Assume that the commission develops an instrument that yields exceptionally reliable content and predictive validity. Using observations, interviews, closed-circuit video monitoring, role playing, problem-solving simulations, and paper-and-pencil exercises, the instrument utilizes highly complex statistical weighing processes of twenty-three separately measured skills to yield a final score on general teacher effectiveness.

Since the test is heralded as a major breakthrough for improving the quality of teaching in American schools, your school district decides that each of its teachers must undergo the twelve-hour assessment process. Each teacher's score is then forwarded to the school board. The scores are placed into a frequency distribution, and the mean, median, and percentile scores are calculated. Of course, half of the teachers in your district will rank below average, and 25 percent will rank in the bottom quartile.

Assume that your score places you in the upper 10 percent of the teachers in your school district. Would you mind if the names of those in the upper quartile were placed in the local newspaper? Would you be strongly opposed to a proposal by your board to tie salary increases to the assessment results?

Assume, on the other hand, that your score places you in the bottom half of the district's teachers (one out of every two teachers in your district will be in this group). Further suppose that your score actually places you at the 10th percentile (90 percent of the teachers scored higher than you did). What opinions might you have about the value of this instrument? Do you think what it measures is important? Would you vote for a referendum to spend more money on teacher assessment?

In reality, 50 percent of the teachers in your district have the choice of saying to themselves and to their friends that, in regard to teacher effectiveness, they are average or below. An alternative is to reject the assessment, deciding that it is neither valid nor important. If you scored at the 10th percentile, which would you choose?

As long as schools relate academic success to the norm-referenced variance in student learning rates, large numbers of students, possibly half, will experience school as a significant threat to their self-worth—not because they are incapable of achieving, but because their achievement and, by substitution, their personal worth, is judged relative to their peers. Overcoming the destructive implications of equating self-worth to relative ability will require the courage to reexamine the assumptions on which our schools and our classroom practices are based. Richard Beery warns us that the task will not be easy:

> *The work of the educator, as I see it, is difficult. It is based on what some see as an almost heretical notion; that the personal worth of each individual is not contingent on ability, or, for that matter, on performance. Rather, each of us is valuable in our own right—and equally so. Our worth is a given, to be taken for granted, as it must be. There must be no hierarchies in personal worth. This message and the value it implies fly in the face of a very strong opposition tht often comes from within individuals, from their parents, from the academic system in which they function, and from the society as a whole. Not surprisingly, therefore, the task of the educator is not easy. (1975, p. 203)*

4

Fostering and Undermining Intrinsic Motivation

THERE WAS ONCE AN OLD and wise educational psychology professor who retired from university teaching to spend his remaining days savoring the tranquil music of the classical composers. His comfortable, modest home bordered a quiet park, and he enjoyed whiling away his days listening to his new compact disc collection and watching the seasons change outside his windows. One warm spring day, as the sounds of Bach and Mozart flooded his home, a group of teenagers appeared in the park nearby. They spent the morning laughing and horsing around while the oversized speakers of their tapeplayer blasted the piercing shrills of a rock singer. Although the professor turned up the volume of his music and closed all of his doors and windows, he couldn't prevent the clamor from overwhelming the delicate strains of Mozart.

After the pandemonium had persisted for several days, the psychologist decided it was time to modify the behavior of the noisy teenagers. He had several options: (1) He could simply ask the teenagers to move to another part of the park; (2) he could purchase larger speakers, move them nearer the windows, and try to blast out his adversaries with Beethoven; (3) he could reprimand the group for being so noisy and threaten to call the police; or (4) he could offer to pay each of the teenagers a dollar if they would leave and never return. (Which option would you choose?)

Wise and experienced, the psychologist knew that all four options were fraught with problems. Although he relished the idea of pitting Beethoven against heavy metal, he recognized that the approach could lead to his own citation for disturbing the peace. He also knew that requests are often perceived as orders and therefore easily denied; that threats usually escalate power struggles; and that paying teenagers to stop a behavior only increases the chances of it starting again—often by others looking for the same reward. Hence, he decided on a fifth option.

The next morning, a Monday, the group continued the ruckus. But when they were ready to leave the park, the old man came out of his house and told them that he loved hearing their music and laughter (years of psychological research had taught him that deception was sometimes necessary for the sake of science). If they would come back again tomorrow, he said, he would give each of them a dollar. Intrigued with the prospect of easy money, the group readily consented. Tuesday morning, they carried on as agreed and happily took his dollar in payment. The psychologist asked them to return on Wednesday, but this time he offered to give each of them only 50 cents. The adolescents agreed and returned the next day, whereupon the psychologist promptly reduced Thursday's payment to a quarter. Reluctantly, the teenagers agreed. Finally, on Thursday, the psychologist gave each boy his quarter and said that he could no longer afford to pay them. Huffily, the teenagers said that they weren't going to make their noise and play their music for nothing—and the wise old psychologist never saw the group again.

This scenario, and its many variations, provides the focus for the first section of this chapter. First, hearkening to days when the teenagers were laughing and enjoying their music, we will examine the characteristics of intrinsically motivating behavior. Second, as suggested by the wise psychologist's use of money, we will examine how external rewards can actually serve to decrease students' intrinsic motivation for certain behaviors. Yet, as most teachers know from experience, there are circumstances when external rewards can *increase* students' intrinsic motivation; this analysis will attempt to differentiate between these situations. Finally, we will examine the implications of the theory and research on intrinsic motivation for fostering student interest in school and for increasing their motivation to undertake activities that are not, in themselves, intrinsically motivating. As our apocryphal psychologist understood so well, the intrinsic motivation of some individuals can be easily undermined by the behavior of others.

Characteristics of Intrinsically Motivating Behavior

Simply stated, an intrinsically motivating activity is one in which there is no apparent or compelling reason for doing the activity, beyond the satisfaction derived from the activity itself. One of the clearest examples of an intrinsically motivating activity is putting together a challenging jigsaw puzzle. Since most puzzles are pictured on the cover of the box, there is little doubt about what the final product will look like; the motivation for completing the puzzle is the satisfaction derived from the activity itself. After having worked many hours on a particularly difficult puzzle, some individuals actually slow down as they reach the last pieces; it is as if they want to prolong the process rather than complete it.

Yet, completing picture puzzles is not always an intrinsically motivating activity. Some people work on them for the pleasure they derive from spending time with someone else who enjoys the activity. These people are not working on the puzzle because it is intrinsically satisfying, but because the activity fulfills a need for companionship. It is also possible to be both intrinsically motivated to work on puzzles *and* to desire companionship; in this situation the individual may prefer to work on puzzles in the company of others but can also find satisfaction in working alone.

Edward Deci and his colleagues at the University of Rochester have spent many years studying the characteristics of intrinsic motivation. It is their belief that intrinsic motivation is innate to the human organism and is part of an ongoing pattern in which people are driven to seek out and to master challenges that match their capabilities (Deci, 1975; Deci & Porac, 1978; Deci & Ryan, 1985b). This behavior is particularly evident in young children when they are unencumbered by the restraints or expectations of others. When encountering a challenge such as getting out of a crib, opening a door, or tying a shoelace, they will often spend hours in attempting to conquer the challenge. The task, of course, must be within their capability. If it is too difficult, they will either cry in frustration and ask for help, or they drop it until they have developed the expertise necessary to master it. If the task is too easy, they will abandon it in favor of more difficult challenges. Rarely does one hear parents complain that their preschooler is "unmotivated."

This desire to seek and to conquer challenges is at the core of all intrinsically motivating activities. It is also fueled by the intrinsic need of all human beings to feel *competent* and *autonomous*. According to Deci and Ryan:

> *The intrinsic needs for competence and self-determination motivate an ongoing process of seeking and attempting to conquer optimal challenges. When people are free from the intrusion of drives and emotions, they seek situations that interest them and require the use of their creativity and resourcefulness. They seek challenges that are suited to their competencies, that are neither too easy nor too difficult. . . . In short, the needs for competence and self-determination keep people involved in ongoing cycles of seeking and conquering optimal challenges. (1985, pp. 32–33)**

**From: E. Deci and R. Ryan, Intrinsic Motivation and Self Determination in Human Behavior,* copyright 1985 by Phenum Press, New York. This and other quotes from this source are produced by permission of the publisher and authors.

The needs for self-determination and competence were discussed in Chapter 2. To reiterate, the need for self-determination, or a sense of autonomy, is satisfied when individuals are free to behave of their own volition, rather than being forced or coerced to behave according to the desires of another. Within the context of such self-determined behavior, people also have a need to feel proficient and capable in performing the tasks they undertake.

Rather than viewing the needs for competence and self-determination as vague theoretical constructs, educators should appreciate the critical role that these two requisites play in guiding and directing student motivation in and out of the classroom. One need only observe a 12-year-old manipulating a Mario brother through a computer-generated Nintendo maze to appreciate the power and energy that a sense of competence and challenge can provide. The complex programs in these computer games provide an almost limitless progression of challenge for players at all skill levels; novices as well as experts can spend hours and days totally absorbed in these challenges as their proficiency improves.

Although parents are often forced to restrict the amount of time spent in this form of play, rarely do they insist that children must participate in it. When given the freedom to play, children typically have control over what games to choose and how long to continue them. However, as the wise old psychologist clearly knew, one's sense of self-determination within this process can be influenced and manipulated by others.

Psychologist Mihaly Csikszentmihalyi from the University of Chicago has been studying intrinsic motivation for several years. He believes the subjective feelings of pleasure and enjoyment are the intrinsic rewards that cause people to perform certain activities. He uses the term *flow* to describe the phenomenon in which individuals become so completely absorbed with a task that they are unaware of the passage of time and of their physical surroundings. When a person experiences flow, according to Csikszentmihalyi, "he or she will experience a contraction of the perceptual field, a heightened concentration on the task at hand, a feeling of control leading to elation and finally to a loss of self-awareness that sometimes results in a feeling of transcendence, or a merging with the activity and environment" (1978, p. 213). Some students experience this feeling when they solve a challenging math problem, write a computer program, or read an interesting book; others never experience it. According to Csikszentmihalyi:

> *In reality, however, most people experience flow rarely. In a sample of average U.S. working men and women we interviewed, 13% claimed never to have experienced anything resembling it, while of the remaining 87% the majority reported it as a rare event; fewer than 10% reported it as occurring daily. The flow experience is relatively rare because it requires an unusual match between the person and the environment. Specifically, a person experiences flow when personal*

capacities to act fit the opportunities for action in the environment. (1989, p. 55)

Given that adults experience the process of flow so rarely, it seems unrealistic to expect teachers to continuously orchestrate flow experiences for their students. Not only is it difficult for them to achieve the necessary match between student capacities and academic opportunities, but few educational decision makers identify these intrinsically motivating experiences as valued goals. If, however, there is a glimmer of truth in Carl Rogers's assertion two decades ago that the only truly meaningful learning is that which is self-discovered or self-appropriated, then it seems incumbent on educators to view motivation as a valuable *trait* as well as a situation-specific *state* (Brophy, 1987). When defined as a trait, motivation becomes an intrinsic disposition to strive for knowledge and mastery; it is within this context that flow becomes possible. More commonly, motivation is perceived as a situation-specific state in which individuals engage in activities that are means to ends, rather than ends in themselves. Society's emphasis on this view of motivation may explain why almost nine out of ten people rarely experience flow in their daily lives.

Suggestions for Fostering Intrinsic Motivation in the Classroom

While the intensity of flow experiences may vary, Csikszentmihalyi proposed that almost any activity can become intrinsically rewarding if it takes place in a context that: (1) is structured so that each person can adjust the level of challenge to match his or her skills; (2) makes it easy to isolate the activity in question from other stimuli that might interfere with involvement in it; and (3) has clear criteria for providing concrete feedback about one's performance. In addition, the activity itself must be structured to provide a broad range of challenges so that individuals can obtain increasingly complex information and feedback about their skills (Csikszentmihalyi, 1978). To demonstrate how these criteria can be used, Csikszentmihalyi applied them to the usually boring activity of mowing the lawn:

> *First, one needs to learn the information potential inherent in the activity: Can the speed at which I mow the yard or a part of it provide feedback to my actions? Can I tell how neatly I do this job in comparison to other times? Is it possible to develop rules about how to proceed—for instance by following a circular path, or a zigzag pattern? Or do I rather want to develop rules for my physical movements as I walk behind the machine? Or do I want to feel the freshness of the breeze or follow a*

certain chain of thought or fantasy? All of these are potentials for action that provide more or less clearly structured opportunities or challenges. In a real-life situation, one presumably will choose more than one of these "action frames." The next step consists of paying attention to the stimuli that appear in the frame and avoiding the rest. Once the relevant stimuli are isolated, it becomes easy to concentrate on them. One can then begin to "read" the feedback. Supposing I decide that I want to cut parallel swaths in the grass, making a U-turn at the end of each run without overlapping any of the runs, getting as close to the trees as possible without nicking the bark. As soon as I set up these tacit rules, they define what stimuli will be relevant for me to watch for. They also define what will be negative and positive feedback under the rules. When this is done, I am ready to go; and mowing grass becomes a moderately enjoyable activity with its own set of intrinsic rewards. (1978, p. 214)

Teachers can use Csikszentmihalyi's criteria to help students transform activities and lessons that they usually find boring into challenges that can provide some degree of enjoyment and intrinsic reward. Students can be encouraged to turn the task of memorizing multiplication tables or periodic element charts into small personal challenges by focusing on some isolated aspect of the activity that can provide both a challenge and feedback on performance. For example, a student might count how many breaths or repetitions it takes to complete the task, and then set the challenge of reducing this number, one breath or repetition at a time. When practicing musical instruments, students might set a challenge of working on one section of the musical score until they can play it a certain number of times without an error. The following example demonstrates how a student might apply Csikszentmihalyi's principles while learning a spelling or vocabulary list:

"Can I figure out which terms or words that I know well, those that I occasionally get right, and those that I don't know? Are there certain words that work with rules? Are there words that are exceptions to the rules? Are there words that don't relate to rules? Can I develop a specific study procedure to alternate between each category, or to complete each category separately?"

All or part of this information can then be used to structure an appropriate level of challenge. Each piece of information provides an "action frame." The next step is to isolate the action frame or frames being considered and then ignore the rest:

"I'll write the list of words or terms on 3 × 5 cards and separate them into piles of those I know well, those I occasionally get wrong, and those

I usually get wrong. I will then randomly select 5 cards from each pile and put the remaining cards aside. I will now review the cards in each of the three piles, selecting one card that I have mastered with each pass and place it in an easier adjacent pile. When I take a mastered card from the easiest pile, I will tear it into eight pieces which I will throw into the wastepaper basket. Under these rules, cards will progress from the difficult to the moderate to the easiest pile before being torn into pieces and discarded."

Once the rules are specified, the student is ready to start working on the spelling or vocabulary list. Under these individually determined procedures, the task can be made moderately enjoyable with its own clearly defined intrinsic challenges and rewards.

Sources of Intrinsic Motivation

Lepper and Hodell (1989) propose another conceptual framework for enhancing student intrinsic motivation. Like Csikszentmihalyi, they are concerned with finding ways that typical classroom activities might be structured and designed so as to be more intrinsically motivating to students. Their model for "motivational embellishment" is derived from the Malone and Lepper (1987) taxonomy of sources of intrinsic motivation, and they believe that a teacher's understanding of the four primary sources of intrinsic motivation—challenge, curiosity, control, and fantasy—will be useful in making routine classroom lessons more intrinsically interesting.

Challenge

The level of intrinsic motivation provided by an activity is dependent upon its ability to challenge the various skill levels of students. Structuring classroom learning activities to provide an optimal challenge for all students, of course, is no easy task; activities that may be difficult for one student may be too easy for another. Research reviewed by Lepper and Hodell suggests that, when free of external constraints, students prefer activities that represent an intermediate or moderate level of difficulty. The following chapter will examine this preference in more detail. For now, the teacher's challenge is to find ways to structure activities that reflect the initial skill levels of students and that readily adjust to changes in skill level that may occur as they continue to work with the activity. Selecting challenging activities, of course, requires that students be willing to risk failure, an integral aspect of the learning process. Yet, when rewards or high grades are used as the primary motivator in a classroom, students will forego challenging activities in order to ensure success by selecting activities they know they can accomplish easily (Pittman, Emery & Boggiano, 1982).

Lepper and Hodell also assert that students will recognize challenge in activities only to the extent that the goals of the activity have meaning to them or engage their sense of self-esteem. They contend that even the most boring of activities can be made more challenging by structuring the directions to control students' engagement in the activity. A homework assignment of thirty math problems, for example, can be made more meaningful by devising a rough difficulty index for each problem (e.g., ten problems each at difficulty levels of 1, 2, and 3) and then allowing students to complete any combination of problems as long as their number of "difficulty points" equals, say, 24. Likewise, a teacher can structure lessons on the causes of the Civil War at several levels of challenge for students. Students who lag several grades behind in reading, for example, may find it challenging to read the text while listening to a recording of the material with earphones. Faster-learning students who are more familiar with the causes of the war may find a challenge in comparing these causes to current civil unrest in other countries.

Curiosity

A second source of intrinsic motivation is found in an activity's appeal to the student's sense of curiosity. Students possess a natural inquisitiveness about activities and situations that are novel or inconsistent with their experiences or expectations. Such events provoke curiosity and incite students' interests in resolving inconsistencies.

As with challenge, curiosity is effective as a source of motivation only to the extent that the novelty or discrepancy inherent in the activity meshes with the individual student's level of experience. If the difference is too disparate, the activity is likely to be discounted; if it is too similar, it may be neglected. It is the teacher's challenge to identify aspects of a given activity that may present discrepant or incongruous information appropriate to the experiences of particular classrooms. Again, structuring tasks that merit this criteria is not easy. It requires that teachers become knowledgeable about some of the lesser-known or tangential aspects of their curriculum and that they present the material in such a way that it provokes the curiosity of their students. Discovering, for example, the characteristics of the social life of a typical middle-class teenager in the year 1860 may prompt curiosity in most students. Similarly, "proving" that 2 is equal to 1, as shown to me by a colleague and demonstrated in Figure 4-1, can trigger curiosity in many algebra students.

Chapter 10 provides structural suggestions and specific strategies that can be used to foster student interest and curiosity.

FIGURE 4-1 "Proving" That 2 = 1

1. $A = B$ Identity

2. $A^2 = AB$ Multiply both sides by A

3. $A^2 - B^2 = AB - B^2$ Subtract B^2 from both sides

4. $(A - B)(A + B) = B(A - B)$ Factor

5. $\dfrac{\cancel{(A - B)}(A + B)}{\cancel{(A - B)}} = \dfrac{B\cancel{(A - B)}}{\cancel{(A - B)}}$ Divide by $(A - B)$

       $A + B = B$

6. $B + B = B$ Since $A = B$, substitute
                                                                    B for A

7. $2 = 1$ Divide by B

       (Since $A - B = 0$, step 5 divides by 0 and the result $= 0$)

Control

Lepper and Hodell (1989) believe that students' sense of control over their behavior or environments is a third potential source of intrinsic motivation. Activities and environments that foster students' feelings of self-determination and autonomy are likely to stimulate their intrinsic interest. On the other hand, activities and environments that undermine students' sense of control have a detrimental effect on their subsequent motivation for and interest in those activities.

Chapter 7 is devoted to exploring structural changes and motivational strategies that teachers can use to help students gain a greater sense of autonomy or control over their environment. As previously discussed, however, providing students with realistic and optimal levels of choice is a powerful and easily implemented strategy for enhancing feelings of control.

Fantasy

The fourth method of engendering intrinsic motivation is the establishment of activities and environments that encourage students to draw upon and expand their imaginations and fantasies. These somewhat unorthodox activities can contribute to students' intrinsic motivation by allowing them to experience vicariously rewards and satisfactions not available to them in real life. They also foster motivation by allowing students to draw on their personal experiences to establish images of their familiar cultural settings to which they can relate relevant aspects of the curriculum.

Asking class members to close their eyes, relax in their seats, and let their minds focus on a specific memory, object, location, or image allows them to develop a personal perspective on the content being studied. Wlodkowski (1989) uses this technique to encourage a high school history class to imagine what it was like to live as a colonist under British occupation at the start of the American Revolution. The mind's eye provides a powerful view into the content we teach.

The Effects of External Rewards on Intrinsic Motivation

For many years behavioral researchers have demonstrated the positive effects of rewards on task performance and subsequent behavior. Thorndike's famous "Law of Effect," which maintains that behavior is likely to reoccur when it has been followed by a positive experience, has probably had more influence on teaching than any other empirically validated assertion. "Reward good behavior and it will be repeated" is a premise that drives virtually every teacher who has ever been in a classroom. While teachers may vary in their implementation of this principle, it remains the unchallenged foundation of most classroom learning theory.

The principle was unchallenged, that is, until Lepper and Greene (1978) reviewed a growing body of experimental research in their now-classic book, *The Hidden Costs of Reward,* that challenged the often indiscriminate and unquestioned use of rewards to control behavior. Their review clearly demonstrated that the imposition of external rewards for the performance of an intrinsically satisfying activity can, in certain situations, have a detrimental effect on a student's continued intrinsic motivation for the activity. In one of the early research studies that illustrated this phenomenon, Lepper, Greene and Nisbett (1973) introduced an enjoyable drawing activity to preschoolers during their "free-play" periods. Students could also choose from a wide variety of alternative activities, while researchers recorded their choices from behind a one-way window. Those showing the highest interest in the drawing activity were selected for the second part of the study.

The selected children were randomly divided into three individually administered experimental conditions. In the "Expected Award" condition, each child was shown an attractive "Good Player" certificate and asked if he or she wanted to engage in the drawing activity in order to earn the award. In the "Unexpected Award" condition, each child was asked to participate in the drawing activity without mention of a reward, but after finishing the activity, the children unexpectedly received the same certificate and feedback as the first group. In the "No Award" condition, children were asked to engage in the activity under the same conditions as the other two groups without expecting or receiving the "Good Player" certificate. Two weeks after these manipulations, the drawing materials were again made available during the children's free-play periods, and the researchers again recorded the amount of time that each child engaged in the drawing activity.

Contrary to the "reward good behavior and it will be repeated" principle, children in the "Expected Award" condition who had agreed to participate in the activity in order to obtain a "Good Player" certificate spent significantly *less* time playing with the drawing materials in the subsequent free-play periods than did students in the other two experimental conditions. They also showed a significant decrease in interest in the activity from the pre-experimental to the post-experimental free-play sessions, whereas children in the other two conditions maintained their same high levels of intrinsic interest in the activity.

About the same time that Lepper, Greene, and their colleagues were studying the motivational effects of rewards with preschoolers in California, Deci and his colleagues were examining the same phenomenon with college students in the East. Using a slightly different design than Lepper and Greene, the first investigations (Deci, 1971, 1972) asked students to solve interesting block-construction puzzles called Soma (distributed by Parker Brothers) by presenting them with configurations drawn on paper and requesting that they construct the configurations from the blocks provided. In the more frequently used design, students were randomly divided into an experimental and control groups and were asked to solve four puzzles, which usually took about ten minutes each to complete. Those assigned to the experimental condition were told that they would receive a payment of $1.00 for each puzzle they solved within a ten-minute time limit. Students in the control condition were asked to solve the puzzles with no mention of a payment. After each student solved the four puzzles, the experimenter said that he needed to leave the room in order to feed some information into a computer that was located in another part of the building. Additional puzzles and several magazines were available in the room and students were encouraged to do as they pleased during the experimenter's absence. The experimenter left the setting for eight minutes and, instead of going to a computer terminal, observed the student through a one-way window. By tabulating the amount of time each student spent manipulating the puzzle pieces during the experimenter's absence, it was possible to determine a measure of the activity's intrinsic motivation for each student.

Again, contrary to the Law of Effect, the students who were paid $1.00 to solve the puzzles exhibited significantly less intrinsic motivation, defined as the amount of time spent playing with the puzzles during the eight-minute free-choice period, than did students who were not paid.

When I demonstrate an abbreviated version of this research design with graduate students, almost all agree that the students who receive the money have the best arrangement. "After all, not only did they get to do something that was enjoyable—they also got paid for it!" is the typical reaction. Few predict that the rewards would have a negative effect on motivation. In fact, research by Boggiano et al. (1987) indicates that parents, adults, and college students believe that rewards, such as adding a 50-percent increase to a child's allowance, are preferable to either *reason* or *noninterference* as a way to maintain or increase a child's interest in reading. This preference was maintained regardless if they were told that the child "really enjoys reading and particularly likes to read books" or if the child "does not enjoy reading and chooses the easiest books to read." Their study also found that adults believe large rewards were more effective than small rewards in increasing student interest in reading.

The results of the archetypic studies of Deci and of Lepper and Greene have been replicated, with variations, in more than a hundred experimental studies by other researchers. (See reviews by Morgan [1984] and Deci and Ryan [1985b]. Clearly, when individuals are rewarded for performing an intrinsically satisfying activity, they can experience a significant reduction in their intrinsic interest and persistence in that activity when the rewards are no longer present. Before examining the educational implications of this conclusion, it is necessary to discuss the factors that may contribute to it.

Many people hold an intuitive belief that when rewards follow a certain behavior, they increase the likelihood that behavior will persist even after the reward has been terminated. Behavioral psychologists hypothesize that the reward strengthens the bond or association between stimulus and response, and the results of animal studies have repeatedly supported this theory. According to Deci and Porac (1978), however, a different interpretation seems more plausible. Since humans use their brains to evaluate and analyze their environments, rewards simply serve to establish the expectation that certain behaviors will lead to certain rewards. Once these rewards are terminated, humans will continue the behavior only if they believe there is a chance of obtaining the reward again. "In other words, we are asserting that rewards affect behavior not through the mechanism of strengthening associative bonds but rather through the establishment or changing of expectations about attaining desired rewards" (Deci & Porac, 1978, p. 155).

How Rewards Affect Motivation

Deci (1975) proposed what he called *cognitive evaluation theory* to explain the process by which rewards can *decrease* intrinsic motivation. Refined by Deci and Ryan (1985) and by Ryan, Connell, and Deci (1985), the theory also describes the conditions under which these same rewards can actually *increase* intrinsic motivation. While somewhat technical in presentation, the three propositions of the theory are supported by a considerable amount of research and have important practical implications for classroom teachers.

The first proposition of Deci and Ryan's theory deals with an individual's need to be autonomous and self-determining. It also assumes that individuals are intrinsically motivated when they perform an activity for no apparent reason other than the activity itself. However, when one performs an interesting activity in order to obtain a reward, then the reward becomes the cause of the behavior and shifts the reason for doing the activity from internal to external. This shift has the effect of undermining an individual's intrinsic motivation for the activity. This is, of course, precisely what happened when the professor paid the teenagers to play their loud music. Initially, the teens were hanging out in the park because they wanted to; the locus of causality was internal. But payment for their activity shifted causality from internal to external, thereby precipitating a decrease in their satisfaction for the activity in that setting. The teenagers were left with little reason to continue staying in the park once payment had stopped.

The second proposition of cognitive evaluation theory asserts that an intrinsically motivating activity supports an individual's need to be competent and to master challenges. Events and consequences that reinforce feelings of competence can actually enhance an individual's intrinsic motivation for an activity, if these events and consequences are experienced within a context of self-determination. In other words, even if individuals are experiencing competence and mastery from an activity, they will not be intrinsically motivated for that activity *unless* they are free to choose the activity of their own volition. Paul, for example, may be quite competent at adding lists of two-digit numbers, but if he is required to do so rather than choosing the activity of his own volition, his sense of competence alone will not make the activity intrinsically motivating to him.

Proposition two also asserts that activities that do not provide a sense of competence or mastery will undermine intrinsic motivation for that activity, even if they are freely chosen. Carol, for example, may freely choose to join the golf team because she enjoys walking outdoors. But when she realizes that, after several months of practice, her score is increasing rather than decreasing, she is likely to lose her intrinsic interest in golf. It makes little difference if the feedback about competence comes directly from the activity, as was the case with Carol, or from the appraisals and evaluation of others, as is often the case in the classroom.

The level of challenge that an activity presents is directly related to the sense of competence that the activity provides. If one experiences continuous success, for example, the activity may be too easy and will likely cause boredom. Conversely, if an activity is too difficult, the individual will feel incompetent, intrinsic motivation will decline, and he or she will likely choose not to participate.

The last proposition of cognitive evaluation theory proposes that the effect of rewards on intrinsic motivation is highly dependent on the context in which the rewards are given. For example, rewards like a sticker, candy bar, or an additional ten minutes of recess have both a *controlling aspect* that undermines self-determination and an *informational aspect* that conveys information about students' competence. The controlling aspect is emphasized when the teacher says, "Jimmy, if you will complete your math assignment correctly, I will give you a new scratch-and-sniff sticker." On the other hand, the informational aspect is likely to be salient when the teacher says, "Jimmy, you have completed your math assignment correctly, and I'm so pleased with your efforts I want to give you a new scratch-and-sniff sticker."

Proposition three also states that events can also have *amotivational aspects* when they convey a sense of helplessness to control one's environment or an inability to effect mastery of particular activity. These experiences carry the message that one is powerless to influence positive outcomes. A zero-sum evaluation system that forces slower-learning students into the bottom quarter of their class, regardless of their efforts, is a clear example of the amotivational aspects of a learning environment.

Implications of Using Rewards in the Classroom

Cognitive evaluation theory does *not* condemn the use of external rewards in the classroom—even when they are used with activities students find intrinsically motivating. Rewards in themselves neither undermine nor support intrinsic motivation; it is *how the rewards are used that matters.* If activities like playing a computer game, conducting an interesting science experiment, or reading a book provide feelings of autonomy and competence, they will be undertaken for their own intrinsic satisfaction. When rewards are used to enhance these feelings, they will strengthen the student's intrinsic motivation for the activity; when rewards undermine feelings of autonomy and competence, they will weaken the student's intrinsic motivation for that activity.

If teachers use rewards like extra free time, points toward grades, happygrams, stickers, food, field trips, tokens, or privileges *primarily to control* or *manipulate* students into performing activities that they may have chosen to perform on their own, then the rewards are viewed by students as the *cause* for performing the activity. When used this way, rewards undermine students' sense of autonomy and self-determination in regard to the activity and *decrease* their intrinsic motivation for it.

On the other hand, if these same external rewards are used by teachers *primarily to convey information* to students about their mastery of an activity, then the rewards can enhance students' sense of competence in the activity and *increase* their intrinsic motivation to partake in it.

Students are quite perceptive in ascertaining if their teacher's motives for using a reward are primarily to control behavior or to convey information. If, for example, the reward is dangled in front of the student as a bribe or an incentive to elicit certain behavior, the student will be quite clear about the teacher's motive. However, if the reward comes as a surprise, an obviously different intent is conveyed.

Students know if the teacher's grades and evaluative comments are used primarily to control their behavior or if they are used primarily to convey information about competence. When used informationally, grades can provide useful feedback to students regarding their study methods and their understanding of course objectives. After all, if they are to learn from their mistakes, students must be informed of what they have mastered and what needs to be corrected. Yet, too often grades and evaluations are used as rewards for students who get correct answers or as punishments for those who fail to understand the material. Furthermore, when grades are used to indicate relative performance rather than the degree of mastery of clearly stated objectives, they systematically limit the number of students who can feel competent. The personal beliefs and philosophy of the teacher will determine whether grades and evaluative comments are used to convey information and feedback or whether they are used as rewards or punishments to control behavior.

Allowing students to experience *choice* within classroom activities is one of the most powerful ways to enhance their intrinsic motivation (Ryan, Connell & Deci, 1985). According to Maria Montessori, choice leads to commitment, and commitment leads to responsibility. From cognitive evaluation theory, it is evident that choice also leads to self-determination, an important prerequisite for intrinsic motivation. Research by Zuckerman et al. (1978) demonstrated that when individuals were allowed to choose three activities from among six options during a certain time period, they showed significantly more intrinsic motivation for those three activities during a subsequent free-choice period than did individuals who were asked to work on the same activities without being given a choice. Ryan, Connell, and Deci (1985) point out, however, that:

> *Allowing choice or self-determination is not equivalent to what is commonly labeled "permissiveness."* Permissiveness *means removing all constraints and structure—for example, letting children do whatever they want. This is not autonomy, but rather neglect. The result is usually chaos for adults and excess anxiety for children. If children could take complete responsibility for themselves, they would not need teachers or parents—in short they would not be children.* Providing structure *means providing information and guidance to help develop and channel a child's growing capacities and abundant energies. But, like other exchanges between teacher (or parent) and child, guidance can be either informational—that is, autonomy supportive—or controlling. (pp. 22–23)*

Similarly, work by Lepper (1983) supports the conclusion that when rewards are made contingent on the quality of a student's performance and are used primarily to provide information about competence, they do not necessarily undermine subsequent interest in the activity. However, when these same rewards are experienced as controlling, they do undermine subsequent interest. Summarizing the research of Lepper (1983) and Pittman, Boggiano, and Ruble (1983), deCharms (1983) offers five maxims regarding the use of rewards to maintain intrinsic motivation in the classroom.

Maxim I. Do not use rewards when they are experienced by the student as controlling or constraining.

The first maxim is consistent with the first proposition of cognitive evaluation theory. All curricular areas, from art and music to math, science, and the humanities, have the potential of becoming intrinsically satisfying to large numbers of students. Yet, a substantial body of research, discussed earlier in this chapter, indicates that if teachers rely on rewards to control students' participation, they will undermine intrinsic satisfaction and interest in these activities. Using a reward to control or bribe students to complete a reading or math assignment, for example, indicates to students that these activities have little inherent value and are not worth doing in their own right. Yet, as seen in proposition three of congitive evaluation theory, if rewards are used primarily to convey information about one's competence, they will not necessarily undermine subsequent interest in the activity.

On the other hand, it is unrealistic for teachers to expect to make every aspect of a subject intrinsically satisfying. Many assignments, by necessity, are tedious, time consuming, and provide little challenge or pleasure. If Jimmy, for example, is left to pursue his own intrinsic interests, it is unlikely that he will choose practicing his spelling list over playing basketball or watching television. Jimmy's teacher will feel compelled to rely on rewards to control and reinforce Jimmy's involvement in spelling and in other activities that provide him little inherent satisfaction. In situations like these, teachers will be forced to use rewards in direct contradiction to this maxim. This contradiction will be examined in detail in the next section of this chapter. For now, it is important to emphasize that this maxim is concerned with the negative effects of rewards on *intrinsic* motivation.

Maxim II. Do not use rewards if you want children to try difficult tasks.

The second maxim addresses situations in which students are free to choose the tasks they will undertake. If the goal is to attain a reward, they will choose the easiest tasks to ensure success; when rewards are not a consideration, they will more often choose the challenging and difficult tasks. Research by Harter (1978), for example, suggests that when students are free of constraints or external pressures, they choose tasks and activities that are neither too easy nor too difficult. They seem to select tasks that provide a moderate level of difficulty relative to their personal skills or abilities; it is these activities that provide students the most intrinsic satisfaction.

However, when students have an opportunity to work for rewards rather than for the intrinsic satisfaction they gain from the activity, Shapira (1976) found they choose the easiest tasks possible to earn the reward. According to Ryan, Connell, and Deci, "Rewards and controls seem to orient people to want to succeed, but not to try out challenges or risk failure" (1985, p. 24).

The more teachers can downgrade the importance of working for rewards, the greater their chance of encouraging students to risk working at activities that provide reasonable challenges. If Jimmy, for example, is primarily concerned with how many stars or extra credit points he can earn from submitting reports on current events articles from his newspaper, it is quite likely that he will select the easiest and shortest articles that his social studies teacher will accept. On the other hand, if the social studies teacher encourages students to submit one report per week on the most interesting article they can find, Jimmy may be more likely to search for more difficult and challenging reading.

Maxim III. Do not use rewards when transfer to later nonrewarding situations is the goal.

The third maxim is supported by research that indicates that rewards will undermine a transfer of motivation for an activity if students do not expect to receive a reward in the future (Lepper, 1983). This result is particularly interesting since several studies reviewed by Lepper seemed to contradict this finding. In these studies, children were allowed to play with several activities during play time, and then, during the next phase of the study, the children were rewarded for playing with one of the activities, but not the others. Following this treatment phase, children were told that the rewards were no longer available. During the final phase of the study the children were again allowed to play with the same activities as in the first situation, without any mention of rewards. Under these circumstances it was discovered that the children were more likely to play with the previously rewarded activity—a finding contrary to Maxim III. Further analysis by subsequent researchers, however, revealed that the children appeared to play with the previously rewarded activity in order to please the experimenters (Lepper, 1983). When children were not aware that they were being observed during the final phase of intrinsic play, they showed significantly less intrinsic interest in the previously rewarded activity than did the control group who received no rewards during treatment.

Clearly, students are aware of the reward contingencies in the classroom, and, since their teachers establish these contingencies, they know what activities their teachers value. Therefore, they will often work on these activities in order to attain rewards or in order to please the teacher. However, when students are free of external constraints, they are less likely to engage in activities for which they were previously rewarded. If teachers want students to maintain intrinsic interest in activities in different contexts that are not rewarded, they may be better advised to avoid using rewards to initiate student involvement with the activity. For example, if teachers want students to develop an intrinsic interest in reading the editorial page of a newspaper, then they should avoid undermining student autonomy in this decision by the use of external rewards for doing so.

Maxim IV. Do not use rewards when they are superfluous.

The fourth maxim suggests that there are many activities in which rewards simply get in the way of children's interest in an activity and don't enhance performance even when the reward is present. Lepper (1983) reviewed research that identifies the adverse effects of rewards on immediate task performance in several contexts. When students were free to select the difficulty level of activity, for example, rewards encouraged them to select the easiest activities in order to maximize their rewards. Likewise, rewards have been shown to impair performance on activities that require creative thought or open-ended problem-solving strategies (Lepper, 1983).

Giving students rewards or extra points toward their grade for participating in an interesting discussion, reading an interesting book, or running a film projector is superfluous for many students; they would perform these activities without being controlled with external rewards. While not an easy task when dealing with a class of thirty students with different interests, teachers can encourage intrinsic motivation for activities by using rewards only when they are necessary to maintaining task involvement.

Maxim V. Do reward habitual algorithmic and memorization tasks; do not reward problem solving or creativity.

The purpose of this maxim is to help teachers determine when rewards are superfluous. As previously indicated, when students are participating in problem-solving activities that require creative and divergent thinking skills, rewards can actually interfere with and undermine the quality of students' thinking (Deci & Ryan, 1985). On the other hand, rewards have been shown to enhance students' performance when they must solve the more mechanical and repetitive algorithmic tasks like completing a page of multiplication problems.

Research supporting the second proposition of cognitive evaluation theory (Deci & Ryan, 1985) would justify an additional maxim to the deCharms list:

Maxim VI. When students choose activities, use rewards to convey positive information and feedback about their competence.

If informational feedback is used to enhance students' feelings of competence for performing an activity, it can serve to enhance intrinsic motivation for the activity. It is important, however, that this feedback be provided within a context of autonomy. As Ryan, Connell, and Deci have warned, "Telling people that they are doing well at a task will not enhance their intrinsic motivation if they do not feel self-determined in their activity. Thus positive feedback and autonomy appear to be required if intrinsic motivation is to be maintained" (1985, p. 23).

When Learning Is *Not* Intrinsically Motivating

The discussion thus far has focused on the effects of external rewards on activities that are in themselves intrinsically motivating. Activities like reading an interesting book, playing basketball, making a bookshelf, participating in the school musical, preparing a project for the science fair, or trying to solve a math equation are usually undertaken by many students for the enjoyment and satisfaction inherent in the activity itself. Yet even these apparently high-interest activities are not intrinsically motivating for all students; activities that are absorbing to some students may be drudgery for others. Aside from these personal preferences, however, many of the tasks and behaviors that are expected of students in school are not, in themselves, intrinsically appealing. After all, speaking in low voices, walking quietly in hallways, and completing pages of unimaginative math homework problems are not the vocalization, locomotion, and activities of choice for *most* students. Yet such behaviors are usually considered necessary to maintaining the social order of schools and to ensure that students master the increasingly more standardized school curricula. In short, "schools often serve the function of teaching not only *what interests the child* but also that which is felt to be *in the child's interests*" (Ryan, Connell & Grolnick, in press).

Teachers often find that they must rely on the use of external controls to encourage students to participate in activities that they do not find inherently motivating. These extrinsically motivated behaviors are driven by students' desires to attain some external reward or recognition or to avoid punishments or negative consequences. After all, if it weren't for the possibility of earning a desired grade on a report card, or the pain of an after-school detention, many students wouldn't complete their arithmetic homework problems, read the next chapter in their history text, or follow the rules and regulations of the class. According to Slavin (1991a):

> *I don't know many students who would put away their Nintendo games to do complex problems, to write reports on the economy of Brazil, to write essays comparing Shakespeare and Moliere, or to learn to use the subjective case in French. . . . There is . . . a need for teachers to try to make everything they teach as intrinsically interesting as possible. But students are unlikely to exert the sustained, systematic effort needed to truly master a subject without some kind of reward, such as praise, grades, or recognition. (p. 90)*

As discussed in Chapter 9, Slavin's cooperative learning models rely heavily on group rewards to sustain student involvement and achievement. Some educators, however, believe that such heavy emphasis on rewards may produce academic performance at the cost of intrinsic interest and motivation. In opposition to Slavin's reliance on external rewards, Kohn (1991) argued, "Slavin may be correct that few non-reward-based classrooms now exist in the U.S., but this hardly demonstrates that the best alternative to bribing individuals is to bribe groups" (p. 94).

It seems that behavioral psychology has tempted teachers to simplify and dichotomize classroom motivational approaches into either designing a curriculum to include only high-interest activities or relying on bribery to coerce students to partake in the boring ones. Although most teachers would prefer *not* to coerce students to complete assignments or follow reasonable rules of deportment, they find few alternatives to bribery or the threat of negative consequences to elicit these behaviors. Before exploring these alternatives, it is necessary to understand how students control their own behaviors.

While many students demand external rewards in payment for doing math homework or reading their history text, others who are equally uninspired or uninterested in these tasks are nonetheless motivated to do so for reasons other than bribes or threats of punishment. These students seem primarily motivated to do schoolwork in order to comply with internalized values or beliefs rather than a desire to obtain an external reward. Although these students may *prefer* to play videogames, they read their history, complete their math, or follow school rules because they value learning or social order in its own right or because they believe that these behaviors are central to their personal development.

In addition to their work on intrinsic motivation, Deci, Ryan, and their colleagues at the University of Rochester have been examining the process whereby students accept responsibility to become actively engaged in behaviors that are not in themselves intrinsically satisfying (Deci & Ryan, 1985; Ryan, Connell & Deci, 1985; Ryan, Connell & Grolnick, in press). From the point of view of an active third-grader, for example, walking quietly in the hallways is not intrinsically satisfying; running full tilt, seeing how close one can get to lockers, doors, and second-graders, is usually considered far more enjoyable. The demands of socialization, however, require that children learn to regulate their impulses to run wildly, and many teachers believe it necessary to use rewards and punishments to ensure that this learning takes place.

Yet if we are interested in helping students assume responsibility to control or regulate their own behaviors—and the development of student self-control or self-discipline is a standard element of every school's goals—then it is necessary to examine the instructional factors that support the internalization of this control. Deci and Ryan (1985) have proposed a model of internalization to help explain the process by which students move from nonregulation—doing whatever feels good—to being externally controlled by the use of rewards and punishments, to eventually becoming internally regulated through the process of identification.

Internalization, according to Ryan, Connell, and Grolnick (in press), "refers to the process by which an individual initially acquires beliefs, attitudes or behavioral regulations from external sources and progressively transforms these external regulations into personal attributes, values or regulatory styles."

Figure 4-2 presents the internalization continuum of self-regulation. At one end of the continuum are the *nonregulated* behaviors in which individuals behave in ways that feel good, without consideration of consequences. Infants and toddlers provide many poignant examples of nonregulated behaviors. If left to their own devices, these young kamikazes would quickly self-destruct as they pursue their curiosities and interests from backyards to busy streets. To control such behaviors, adults find that

FIGURE 4-2 The Development of Self-Regulation

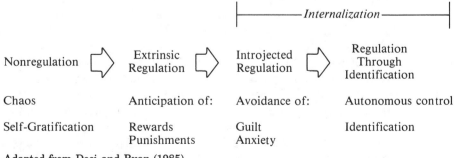

Adapted from Deci and Ryan (1985).

they must impose environmental consequences that provide a basic form of external motivation—control through the process of *extrinsic regulation.* At this level, individuals are motivated to undertake a certain activity or to control a certain behavior primarily for the purpose of gaining a specific reward or avoiding a specific punishment or negative consequence. Behavioral psychologists have been especially successful in helping teachers develop and refine the skills of controlling student behavior with external rewards. Through the process of shaping, substitution, variable schedules of reinforcement, token economies, and many other behavioral strategies, teachers have become exceptionally skillful at systematically regulating student behavior with the use of rewards. Unfortunately, the systematic use of punishments to control behavior in school seems equally well developed and pervasive, with the nature of the penalties limited only by the imagination of the teachers who impose them. Requiring students to copy innocuous sentences hundreds of times; listing names on chalkboards followed with checks; assigning detentions; revoking privileges; calling parents; and meting out failing grades, three-day suspensions, time-outs, solitary confinement (in-school suspension), and memberships in Saturday morning breakfast clubs are among the many punitive methods used, with varying degrees of success, to control and regulate students' social and academic behaviors.

Some students, however, learn to regulate their behavior independently of these tools of control in order to gain self-approval or the approval and acceptance of parents or teachers. This *introjected regulation* seems to be driven by the desire to avoid the anxiety or guilt that accompanies the failure to live up to personal standards or the expectations of others. With introjected regulation, learning or behavior control is not intrinsically motivated or valued for its own sake, but neither is it motivated by external rewards or the avoidance of external punishment. Instead, "in introjected regulation the child rewards and/or punishes himself or herself through intrapsychic, self-esteem-based contingencies" (Ryan, Connell & Deci, 1985, p. 35). When students regulate their behaviors through introjection, they are at the initial stage of internalizing control over their own behaviors. However, in this early stage of internalization, considerable anxiety and guilt are generated by an individual's struggle to avoid negative self-evaluation or disapproval from others; the student's sense of self-worth becomes linked to being a "good" boy or girl and doing the "right" thing.

For our purposes, the final level of internalization that merits attention is *regulation by identification.* (The Deci and Ryan model includes an additional level of internalization dealing with the integration of separate identifications into a hierarchy of responsible and self-determined behaviors. This integration is typically beyond the maturity of school-age individuals and will not be considered here.) With regulation by identification, students begin to rely on their own internalized values or goals to control their behaviors. The cause of their behaviors becomes internal, and actions regulated by identification are experienced as self-determined. In other words, the student takes on or internalizes the same logical reasoning for performing an activity or controlling a behavior as that held by his or her teacher or parents. In this case, students' primary motivation for reading their history chapter, for example, is not to earn a good grade or to avoid the teacher's reprimands, nor is it to avoid the guilt of not being a "good" student. Rather they choose to read their history for the same reason that their teachers have assigned it to them—to become knowledgeable in history so that they can better understand the world in which they live.

Behavior that is motivated through identification is different from behavior that is intrinsically motivated. Although in both cases students have internalized the cause of the behaviors, intrinsically motivated behaviors are undertaken because they have qualities that are inherently interesting and enjoyable in their own right. Behaviors motivated by identification need not be inherently enjoyable. Reading a history chapter, for example, may be more tiresome than pleasurable, but students who have identified with this behavior will choose to read their history because they value mastery of the material.

The developmental movement from nonregulation to the internalized regulation of behaviors is exemplified in the activities of toddlers. Almost all 18-month-old children, for example, are fascinated by the colors, lights, and smells of a fully decorated Christmas tree. If left to their own devices, most would grab for the first branch or decoration they can reach and shake it with all their might. To avoid the predictable results, parents regulate this behavior by restraining the child in their arms, by providing an attractive diversion, or by placing the child in the ignominious playpen. Nevertheless, in spite of the parents' vigilance, most children eventually find a way to reach the tree and start grabbing. At this point, parents often attempt to control the child's behavior through external regulation. Usually a sharp "No!" conveys the parental disapproval. Some parents include a mild slap to the child's hand as an added measure of external control. To avoid these negative consequences, the child will begin to regulate his grabbing behavior, although he will usually grab the tree several more times, often looking directly into the eyes of the parent, to determine whether the relationship between his behavior and the disapproval or pain on his hand is consistent and inevitable. Reward contingencies can also be devised to help the child control his behavior. In either case, rewards or punishments, the tree is saved—at least as long as the parent is in the room to administer the positive or negative consequences.

External regulation demands that parents remain in a position to control each child's behaviors. If, for example, a parent leaves the room and little Jimmy breaks a few decorations, consequences can be administered. With more than one child, however, it is often difficult to identify the culprit; "not me" has done more damage to Christmas trees than any child alive. Fortunately, introjected regulation provides the first stages of self-control and frees parents from having to continually monitor the child's presence near the Christmas tree. As Jimmy is about to grab the tree, he begins to experience an inner inhibition that helps control his impulse. A judgment, often implanted and reinforced by the parent, such as "Good boys don't grab Christmas trees" comes to mind. It is this internal, self-administered version of the parents' value judgment that helps Jimmy begin to monitor and sanction his own behavior. Shame, guilt, and anxiety become the driving forces of introjected internalization as Jimmy's perceived self-esteem becomes linked to his struggle to live up to his parents' approval.

As Jimmy moves toward identifying with the regulation, he begins to integrate appropriate behaviors into his own value system. At this stage the shame or anxiety is largely dissipated as Jimmy begins to predict and accept the logical and social consequences of his behavior. His reasoning for not grabbing the tree now becomes something like, "I like looking at the Christmas tree, and if I grab it, it is likely to fall and break some of the decorations."

A child's development and progression from nonregulation to identified regulation is largely dependent upon the environmental conditions and supports experienced at each stage of the progression:

> *Integrated self-regulation is the natural outcome of internalization that is not impeded or thwarted by environmental influences. It represents the true meaning of socialization; one does not simply do what one thinks the social values dictate, one behaves, feels and thinks in a way that is congruent with the social values because one has accepted them as one's own. (Deci & Ryan, 1985, p. 138)*

Through classroom discussions of the regulation process, teachers often can identify their students' developmental stages of self-regulation. If fourth-graders, for example, are asked if they would enjoy running in the school hallways, they will often enthusiastically describe their desire to do so. Asked why they control this impulse to run wildly, the students give answers that often demonstrate the thinking of several stages of the internalization process. If students control their impulses to run primarily because of fear of being scolded by the hallway monitors or of being kept after school, they are describing reasoning indicative of external regulation. When some say that they don't run in the hallways because "you're not supposed to" or because "the principal doesn't like it when students run," they are describing the thinking characteristic of introjected regulation. Finally, when students say that they don't run because "you may fall and hurt yourself" or "it makes other students have to look out for you," they are describing identified regulation.

A similar developmental reasoning process can be observed when students are asked why they do their homework. Some students simply do *not* do their homework, regardless of consequences. While these students may reject school in order to protect their self-images, such behaviors *appear* nonregulated. Other students are externally regulated and do their homework because they want to earn high grades, obtain "good student" certificates, get a few dollars from their parents, or avoid their teachers' threats. Others are motivated to do homework because they are supposed to or because they feel guilty or anxious if they do not. These students are regulated by introjection, and while they also enjoy receiving rewards for completing assignments, such rewards or external controls are not necessary to maintain their motivation; the guilt usually suffices. Some students do homework because it helps them learn skills and acquire knowledge that they value. While they may not enjoy it, they do homework primarily because they have identified with its positive purposes. Finally, there are some students who do their homework because it is fun, enjoyable, and challenging. Although these intrinsically motivated students may not exist in large numbers, they seem to be spawned by teachers who also see learning as fun, enjoyable, and challenging.

The following section will examine ways that educators can help students identify with the logical realities for doing their nonintrinsically motivated schoolwork or for controlling their socially disruptive impulses.

Fostering Self-Control and Internal Motivation in the Classroom

Teachers can foster students' self-control and internal motivation by setting limits, illuminating choices and logical consequences, and acknowledging conflicting feelings.

Informational Limit Setting

Helping students control their disruptive but self-gratifying impulses and fostering an appreciation for the value of working hard to master academic content are formidable tasks. They require understanding, patience, and a knowledge of student needs and perceptions. Punishments, threats, bribes, and verbal hammering have all been used by teachers to control student behavior. While these techniques may provide teachers a temporary respite from classroom chaos, they do little to help students develop, identify, and internalize the reasoning necessary for self-control and internal motivation. Controlling students' impulses for immediate self-gratification and pleasure always requires that teachers *set limits* on the behavior of students in the classroom. But how teachers set these limits and how students perceive the nature and context of the limit setting will determine whether students learn to assume responsibility for their own behavior or whether they will simply learn to obey.

Limit setting requires that teachers provide a classroom structure that defines behavioral expectations and restrict behavior that is not conducive to learning. Deci and Ryan (1985) propose that teachers can establish limits in either an *informational* or a *controlling* manner. Informational limit setting is based on the teacher's responsibility to support the social order and logical reality of the classroom. In this environment, students understand the purpose for and necessity of restricting behavior that interferes with the social and personal process of learning. A controlling approach to setting limits is characterized by an emphasis on the use of rewards and punishments to manipulate student behavior. The teacher establishes and maintains student obedience by relying on fear of consequences for noncompliance or by creating expectations for external gratifications if compliance is achieved.

An important experiment by Koestner and colleagues (1984) clearly demonstrates the effects of informational and controlling limit setting. In designing the informational limit-setting phase of their study, they relied on the following four-step approach to positive limit setting recommended by psychologist Haim Ginott (1972; Orgel, 1983): (1) Acknowledge students' feelings or wishes; (2) state the limit clearly; (3) where possible, identify alternative ways that students can express feelings; (4) help students express feelings of resentment they may experience when constraints are imposed (Koestner et al., 1984).

The experimenters asked forty-four first- and second-graders to paint pictures in three randomly selected limit-setting situations. In the *controlling-limits* group, the experimenter gave the students the following directions:

> *"Before you begin, I want to tell you some things that you will have to do. There are rules that we have about painting. You have to keep the paints clean. You can paint only on the small sheet of paper, so don't spill any paint on the big sheet. And you must wash out your brush and wipe it with a paper towel before you switch to a new color of paint, so that you don't get the colors all mixed up. In general, I want you to be a good boy (girl) and don't make a mess with the paints."* (p. 239)

Students assigned to the *informational-limits* group received the following similar instructions:

> *"Before you begin, I want to tell you some things about the way painting is done here. I know that sometimes it's really fun to just slop the paint around, but here the materials and room need to be kept nice for the other children who will use them. The smaller sheet is for you*

to paint on, the larger sheet is a border to be kept clean. Also, the paints need to be kept clean, so the brush is to be washed and wiped in the paper towel before switching colors. I know that some kids don't like to be neat all the time, but now is a time for being neat." (p. 239)

The *no-limits* group was allowed to paint without receiving limit-setting instructions. Clearly, the informational-limits group was given directions that acknowledged the potential conflict between being messy and being neat and that were designed to be free of surplus control. Directions for the controlling-limits group did not acknowledge the inherent conflict of interest and seemed to make the externally controlled nature of the task salient.

All students were given ten minutes to paint whatever they wanted. At the end of this time, the experimenter collected the paintings and said that he would have to take them to another room and would return in a few minutes. Two additional sheets of paper were placed on the desk and students were told that they could paint some more if they liked, or they could play with some puzzles on another table. When the experimenter left the room, an assistant unobtrusively observed the students for eight minutes. The number of seconds of free-choice time spent in painting was used as a behavioral measure of intrinsic motivation. At the completion of the free-choice time, students were asked to indicate on a "happy-face" scale how much they enjoyed the painting activity. In addition, the original student paintings were evaluated by outside raters to obtain a measure of creativity.

Results indicated that students in the controlling-limits group demonstrated significantly less intrinsic motivation for the activity, as measured by the number of seconds they spent painting during free-choice time, than did the informational-limits or no-limits groups. Results on the self-report of enjoyment scale revealed that the controlling group also expressed somewhat less enjoyment for the painting activity than did the informational group. In addition, outside raters judged paintings from the informational-limits group as being significantly more creative than the paintings from the control-limits group.

It appears from the Koestner et al. study that even though it may be necessary to place limits on student behavior, these limits can be imposed in ways that students perceive as either informational or controlling. When the limits are controlling, they undermine intrinsic motivation; when they are informational, they can offset the detrimental effects of control inherent in the limits themselves.

The internalization of self-control is both an intrinsically satisfying process and one that is best fostered in informational environments that do not place undue pressure or control on students. These environments allow students the opportunity to experience some degree of autonomy as they experiment with the regulation of their own behavior. Successes and failures are a natural and necessary part of this experimentation if the student is to attain an internalized sense of self-control. Such experimentation, however, makes the teacher's job especially difficult. Pandemonium is common in classrooms in which twenty or thirty bubbling bodies are experimenting with the process of gaining control over their own social and academic behaviors. Explaining the reasons for limits is important to creating informational environments.

When limits are needed to control student behavior, it is important that teachers explain the reasoning behind them. If deadlines for assignments have been established to help the teacher balance his or her workload or to help students better organize their time, then it is helpful to students' internalization processes if the reasons for these deadlines are explained. Likewise, if students are to be in their assigned desks when the bell rings in order to ensure a productive start to the class or to avoid wasting the limited instructional time, then it is helpful to students to tell them that. As Deci makes clear, such explanations "are legitimate reasons. On the other hand, 'Because I said so' is not a legitimate reason. It's a power maneuver and only invites defiance" (1986, p. 44).

Choice

When teachers foster and support choices in the classroom, students experience a sense of self-determination about the tasks that they choose (Deci & Ryan, 1985). In establishing a classroom's structure and limits, teachers must consider the age and maturity of the students. While it is important to explain to students the reasons for the necessary limits, it is also important to provide students as much choice as possible within these limits. For example, if students are required to complete several assignments before recess, it will build their sense of autonomy if they can choose the order in which they will complete the work (Deci, 1986). Similarly, choice within assignments serves the same purpose. Rather than assigning the odd or even problems, for example, it will be more autonomy engendering if students can choose to do the odd *or* the even. Correspondingly, if you want students to complete the first five or ten problems in an assignment, it may be more productive to allow them to choose *any* five or ten problems from the group. While this may create a bit more work for the teacher, it allows students a feeling of self-determination over their work. In addition, some students will complete twice the number required just to make sure they have found the five or ten problems that they know are correct.

According to deCharms:

> To enhance motivation is neither to force children nor is it to let them do anything they want. The most basic principle is that choice, even a small choice, gives a person some feelings of personal influence and

security. Learning to make choices leads to commitment and to respon-sibility for the results of choice. This chain (choice, commitment, respon-sibility) is the core of responsible Origin behavior, and all the links of it have to be learned. Small but real choices must be given in the beginning, and small but real changes in motivation will result. Too many choices or choices that are too difficult to make are just as bad as too few. A person who is overwhelmed with choices is just as much a Pawn as one who has no choices. (1977, p. 446)

Research by deCharms (1976) found that the major characteristic of teachers who were able to motivate students toward academic achievement was their skill at carefully nurturing students' ability to make choices within the classroom. Furthermore, these teachers expanded their students' opportunities for choice as they learned to manage this increased responsibility.

If teachers hope to increase their students' opportunities for choice, they must ensure that the choices are *real.* Letting students decide how to run the class or if they want to play or do school work are not real choices—they are examples of irresponsibility and abdication. Furthermore, teachers are well advised to avoid offering choices if they can't live with the results. If they want students to complete specific assignments, teachers are on much safer ground if they simply inform students where they have no choice, rather than hoping that they choose "right" (deCharms, 1977).

Logical Consequences

The use of logical consequences, including temporary exclusion, may be necessary for teachers to create and maintain a sense of social order and productivity within the classroom. Logical consequences, however, are not punishments (Raffini, 1980; Dreikurs, Grunwald & Pepper, 1982); the following factors may be helpful in distinguishing between the two:

1. When using logical consequences, the teacher's tone of voice is usually unemotional. A simple, matter-of-fact statement is made in a calm, friendly manner. With punishment, the authority usually shows anger or resentment—either open or concealed—toward the student.
2. The consequence imposed is dependent on and logically related to the unacceptable behavior. The relationship is direct and easily discernible. Punishment rarely is directly or logically related to the unacceptable behavior.
3. Judgments of individual goodness or badness are absent when using logical consequences. The focus is on the unacceptable behavior and its relationship to the consequence. Punishment has moralistic over-tones and equates unacceptable behavior with badness.

4. Logical consequences are designed to enable students to assume responsibility for changing their behaviors. With punishment, responsibility for changing student behavior rests with the authority.

5. Logical consequences express the reality of the situation. Punishment expresses the personal power of the authority.

Acknowledge Conflicting Feelings

As Ginott (1972) noted several years ago, adult acknowledgments of a student's feelings enables the student to know that his or her thoughts and emotions are being understood. This is especially important when the student's behavior is being restricted for the good of the student or for the good of the class. If Leslie, for example, must come in after school to make up work she missed during a recent absence, the teacher might say, "I know that you are disappointed that you will be late for basketball practice because I've asked you to come in after school, but this is the only opportunity we will have to go over the material before Christmas vacation." By acknowledging these conflicting feelings, the teacher shows acceptance of Leslie's perceptions. If Eric is becoming frustrated in his efforts to factor equations, the teacher might comment, "I can see that this material is frustrating for you, Eric. Many students have difficulty with it at this stage. If you can give me a few minutes during lunch time, I think I can help you sort out some of the obstacles." Not only do these overtures acknowledge Eric's feelings; they express faith in Eric's ability to solve the problems, thereby empowering him to do so. As Deci clearly states: "Children aren't wrong for feeling what they feel, though they may be wrong for doing what they do. They can't—and shouldn't—be forced to change their feeling. But if that feeling is acknowledged and accepted, they'll find they're able to behave in ways they don't really want to" (1986, p. 44).

Minimally Sufficient Control

While teachers' use of external control in classrooms appears to be well established, the question often overlooked is the amount of control necessary to create an orderly and productive environment without stifling student autonomy and the internalization process. As noted, research by Boggiano and her associates at the University of Colorado has clearly demonstrated that both college students and parents believe that if they want students to develop a long-term interest in academic tasks, regardless of their initial enjoyment, they should use the *largest* reward possible (Boggiano et al., 1987). This belief conflicts directly with the goal of building student autonomy and self-regulation and contradicts research reviewed by Boggiano et al., which indicates that larger rewards undermine intrinsic motivation more than smaller rewards do. Apparently, adults do not recognize each student's varying levels of interest in an activity. They seem to view all school tasks as "work" and therefore infer that rewards are needed for all types of school activities; in this context, adults believe that the larger the reward, the better.

It seems evident that many parents and educators fail to realize that, while external control may be necessary for the initial development of the prosocial and academic behaviors of students, the intrinsic motivation of these students and their development of self-control is best supported when the use of rewards and punishments is guided by the *minimal-sufficiency principle* identified by Lepper (1981). This principle proposes that when it becomes necessary for parents or teachers to use extrinsic controls to regulate a student's social and academic behaviors, they should endeavor to use the *smallest* reward or punishment possible to meet their objective, since research shows that less powerful social control techniques are more effective with helping students internalize a willingness to comply with requests than are stronger ones. According to Lepper, "Parents' use of overt power-assertive techniques, involving the heavy-handed use of physical punishment, withdrawal of tangible rewards, and so on, correlates negatively with subsequent moral behavior in situations outside the home, whereas the use of induction and reasoning . . . shows consistent positive correlations with subsequent internalization of moral standards and behavior" (1981, pp. 203–204).

The minimal-sufficiency principle enables adults to control student behavior initially, when compliance would not otherwise be obtained, while increasing the likelihood that students will eventually internalize the regulation as their own. This principle, of course, is violated every time a teacher or parent promises a child a reward to engage in an activity that he or she would voluntarily undertake.

The use of the minimal-sufficiency principle seems especially appropriate in elementary schools, where prosocial behavior and schoolwork are often regulated with the use of gold stars, stickers, smiley faces, time on the computer, "good student" certificates, and a host of other apparently innocuous rewards. Do we really *need* or *want* a pizza restaurant chain to use free pizzas to bribe elementary students to read? Making pizza contingent on reading is likely to create an obvious shift in locus of causality that blatantly conveys to young readers that a primary purpose for reading books is to obtain free pizza. If the restaurant chain really wanted to foster a love of reading in young children, its goal might be better served if it was to reverse its program and make reading contingent on pizza—for every two pizzas that students eat, for example, they earn a certificate good for one free book at their local bookstore. A reading teacher objected that her poorer students who couldn't afford the pizza would be deprived of the books. Besides, she said, her students really liked the current program because they enjoyed the reading *and* the free pizza. While both students and educators may be enticed by these short-term benefits, the long-term effects may be far more costly than the price of a few pizzas. Psychologist John Nicholls believes that the long-term consequence of the current program is likely to be "a lot of fat kids who don't like to read" (Kohn, 1991, p. 84). It seems apparent that in their quest to obtain free pizzas, many young readers are being needlessly tempted to forego the pleasures and challenges of a variety of reading materials in order to maximize their payoff, by seeking out the shortest and simplest books available.

In summary, the minimal sufficiency principle suggests that if teachers intend to help students develop a sense of self-control in regard to their interpersonal behaviors and to help them develop a love of learning, then they must carefully monitor the use of external controls to ensure that (1) they are really needed, (2) they are no more extensive than necessary, and (3) students are weaned from them as soon as they are no longer required.

While it *may* be necessary for teachers to use rewards as a form of bribery to get students to put away their Nintendo games and work on their math problems (some will argue that it is not), it is incumbent on all teachers, kindergarten to graduate school, to be cognizant of the minimal-sufficiency principle, the importance of self-determination and competence for building intrinsic motivation, and the developmental process of self-regulation.

Chapters 7 and 8 identify structural suggestions and specific motivational strategies that teachers can use to help all students increase their intrinsic motivation toward learning by developing their sense of self-determination and competence. In addition, Chapter 9 presents suggestions for using group rewards in cooperative learning situations.

5

Developing a Motivating Classroom Personality

MOST EXPERIENCED TEACHERS can tell when it happens. Sometimes they must wait until after Easter vacation; other times it's evident before Thanksgiving. Sadly, some classes never achieve that stage of development at which students begin to acquire a sense of unity and trust and begin working together for their common benefit. As this feeling grows, individual self-consciousness is reduced, and most participants become willing to risk expressing their thoughts and opinions. In short, the class members begin to work as a cohesive group, meeting mutual needs in a spirit of cooperation and acceptance. While there are too few rewards in school teaching, one of the most satisfying is the pride of accomplishment that comes from teaching in a classroom that has developed this level of cohesiveness.

This chapter is based on the assumption that the group of students within a classroom, like the individuals in it, develops a unique personality during the course of the group's existence. The disposition of this personality is produced by the behaviors of the students who make up the group and by the beliefs, goals, and strategies of the teacher who leads it. While both the teacher and the students influence and are influenced by this classroom temperament, it is the teacher who has the authority and responsibility to set its tone and pace.

This chapter analyzes three components of classroom personality that can significantly influence student motivation to learn: (1) *teachers' beliefs* about learners, learning, and teaching; (2) the *organizational patterns* developed by teachers; and (3) the primary *goal orientations* that the classroom fosters within students. The character of each of these components is primarily determined by teachers, although it is strongly tempered by students, parents, colleagues, and administrators.

Teachers' Beliefs about Learners, Learning, and Teaching

The teachers' beliefs component of classroom personality is probably the most influential and the most illusive of the three to be considered. It is based on teachers' personal opinions and philosophical assumptions regarding which students can learn, what and how they learn, and the teacher's role and responsibility in this process. These beliefs determine how teachers structure teacher/student communication, establish norms for the classroom, and select a style of leadership. Combined, they have a significant impact on the development of each classroom's unique personality.

These beliefs can also strongly influence the classroom's goal orientation; some beliefs support the development of content mastery for all, while others tend to support the sorting and ranking of students so as to reward those who excel. The application of these beliefs is also represented by the structure and organization of the specific learning activities selected by the teacher. In summary, a teacher's beliefs regarding learners, learning, and teaching creates the overriding disposition of a classroom's personality. The character and temperament of this personality are shaped by the teacher's leadership style and by the goal orientation he or she fosters in students.

Which Students Can Learn

Chapter 3 proposed that students' perceptions of their academic ability are important in determining whether they view learning activities as challenges or threats. This chapter asserts that these student perceptions are heavily influenced by teachers' beliefs regarding each student's potential for achievement. The following examples demonstrate differences in these teacher beliefs:

> Mr. Genes: *Tom Genes has been a middle school math teacher for twelve years. He was instrumental in establishing the math tracking program and requiring all students in the state to take a standardized math aptitude test at the beginning of sixth grade. He strongly believes that students who have little aptitude for grasping important mathematical concepts should not slow or penalize brighter students from being challenged by a high-level mathematical curriculum. He takes pride that his math program was the first in the school district to offer Algebra 1 to sixth graders, and he enjoys teaching the fifteen students selected for this special class.*
>
> *Mr. Genes also teaches two sections of remedial sixth-grade math. Although he often becomes frustrated by the poor attitude and lack of diligence of these students, he is quite willing to spend extra time reexplaining math concepts and procedures to any student willing to*

come in before or after school. He also provides extra credit projects for students who do poorly on tests to raise their grade to a C (Mr. Genes believes that students in remedial classes should not earn A's or B's). Few take advantage of either offer, which further reinforces Mr. Genes's belief that most kids today have a poor attitude toward school and don't care how they perform on the newly devised ninth-grade statewide math performance test.

Mr. Hart: *Hugh Hart, a recent graduate of State University's teacher training program, is in his third year of teaching middle school math. Math students at his school are not ability-grouped, nor are they required to take sixth-grade math aptitude tests. Mr. Hart finds that students in his class demonstrate a wide range of math skills. When he introduces a new concept, some students seem to grasp its meaning almost immediately, while others are perplexed and confused. These students often require additional instruction, more concrete explanations, further practice examples, and repeated review opportunities before they comprehend its meaning.*

During Mr. Hart's first year of teaching he noticed that his faster-learning students became bored and listless when they were required to sit through additional explanations, examples, and review problems dealing with concepts they had clearly mastered. He struggled to find a teaching pace that would allow slower students the time they needed to assimilate important math concepts without boring the faster-learning students.

During Mr. Hart's second year he realized that it was impossible to find a teaching pace suitable to all students. He therefore decided to change his approach by teaching a major concept or unit to all students, determining who had mastered it, and then establishing fortification activities for these students that would help enrich their depth of understanding and enjoyment of math while he provided additional explanations and examples for those who did not grasp the material during the first instruction. Mr. Hart soon found that this approach to teaching math required more preparation on his part, although he also found that the librarian and the newly appointed fast-learner supervisor were quite willing to help him in designing meaningful fortification and enrichment activities. A few of these faster-learning students also volunteered to help Mr. Hart find alternative ways to explain the unit concepts to students who had difficulty understanding them the first time.

Mr. Hart was especially surprised that many students were willing to come in outside of classtime for additional help. They seemed encouraged by Mr. Hart's policy that allowed them to retake another version of the original test once they had mastered the concept. As a result, almost all of his students ended the year with a grade of B or A, and

*all but one scored above the state "standard" in a newly devised
statewide math performance test.*

Clearly, Mr. Genes and Mr. Hart differ in their philosophical beliefs
regarding which students can learn. Furthermore, the expectations
generated by these beliefs govern their judgments about how they teach
math. Mr. Genes appears to believe that a certain number of students can
be expected to become proficient in understanding the intricacies of middle
school mathematics, a smaller number can be expected to excel, and a certain number will lack either the ability or volition to undertake the task
seriously. Mr. Hart, on the other hand, ascribes to the belief that a major
difference among students is the amount of time required to learn certain
math skills. Given a sufficient amount of time and varied instructional
procedures, he believes that almost all students can be expected to become
proficient at middle school math. Faster-learning students who acquire this
proficiency quickly can be challenged to pursue collateral interests.

The beliefs of Mr. Hart, of course, have been influenced by the theory
of student differences identified by John Carroll and discussed in Chapter
3. The reader will recall that Carroll (1963) proposed that rather than view
students as either bright or dull, it would be more precise to see them as
either fast or slow learners, and that major differences among students
could more accurately be viewed as an indicator of a student's learning
rate, rather than the depth to which a student is capable of understanding a given subject.

Effort = Expectancy × Value

Understanding why students in Mr. Hart's class are willing to seek help
with their math before and after school might best be achieved by examining the Atkinson *expectancy × value* theory of student motivation
(Atkinson, 1957; Feather, 1982; Brophy, 1987). This theory provides a
useful model for discerning why some students choose to become actively
involved in learning, while others withdraw from active participation and
choose academic apathy as an alternative.

In its broadest terms, the expectancy-value theory of motivation is
based on the following equation:

$$\text{effort} = \underset{for\ success}{expectation} \times \underset{success}{value\ of}$$

The equation implies that students' willingness to expend effort to to
become actively involved in learning tasks is a product of: (1) the degree
to which students *expect* to be successful at accomplishing the task, assuming they apply a reasonable amount of energy; and (2) the degree to which
they *value* task participation, defined as the intrinsic or extrinsic reward

or benefit derived from successful task completion. Like all mathematical equations, the theory assumes that no effort or energy will be expended to accomplish a task if either of the factors is zero, regardless of the strength or magnitude of the remaining factor. In other words, students will not exert effort on a task, even if they are certain of success, if they do not value the outcome. Likewise, students will not expend effort, even though they may value the outcome, if they are convinced that they cannot succeed.

Paul, for example, may strongly value having his name listed on the school honor roll, yet if he believes that there is little chance of that happening, regardless of how hard he studies, he is unlikely to expend effort working toward this outcome. On the other hand, Mitzie, who is sure that if she studies diligently she will be quite capable of earning a C instead of a D in math, will expend little effort toward this outcome if she does not value C's.

Teachers' beliefs about each factor in the expectancy × value equation significantly influence their decisions regarding the organization and structure of their classrooms. These decisions, in turn, influence the classroom atmosphere and goal orientation that result.

Expectancy of Success

The expectation of success factor in the equation is based on students' beliefs that if they expend reasonable effort on learning tasks, they can expect to experience feelings of success. Each student, of course, defines success and failure differently—for some a grade of C implies success; for others a grade of B means failure. Teachers often tell students that with a resonable amount of effort, they can expect to earn a C in a particular subject or class. Many students, however, do not experience success from a grade of C. If these students can't expect success—often defined by an A or B—from a reasonable amount of effort, then this factor in the equation approaches zero and little effort will be expended. As discussed in Chapter 3, many students try to protect their sense of self-worth by withholding effort on tasks that they do not believe will provide them with a reasonable chance for success.

Psychologist Jery Brophy offers teachers several research-supported suggestions for enhancing student motivation to learn (Brophy, 1987). He emphasizes, however, that an essential precondition for the effectiveness of these suggestions is that learning tasks must be structured in a way that allows students "to achieve high levels of success when they apply reasonable effort" (p. 42). Educational psychologist Raymond Wlodkowski (1989) concurs that a prerequisite to student motivation is the student's belief that effort can lead to success.

I recently discussed this assumption with a group of teachers representing a broad spectrum of teaching levels. Since colleges usually do not accept C students, and since many states will not allow students with

C averages in college to become teachers, I proposed the assertion that the only grades that convey true academic success are *A*'s or *B*'s. After some discussion of this assertion, I played the role of a student who wanted to know if he could expect to earn a semester grade of *A* or *B* if he expended a reasonable amount of effort in the teachers' classes. As might be expected, confusion quickly surrounded the words "reasonable amount of effort." Continuing the simulation, I encouraged the teachers to define specifically the amount of effort toward learning they considered reasonable at their grade or in their subject. In my conversation with a ninth-grade math teacher, for example, I agreed to devote my complete concentration to math for one hour per day, seven days a week, outside of class. There would be no television or music playing in the room where I studied, and I convinced the teacher that I would diligently give my total and undivided attention to math for the full sixty minutes.

The math teacher, with agreement from most of the others, was unwilling to assure me that I could expect to receive an *A* or *B* in her class; my grade, she explained, would depend upon my performance on the unit tests. (Typically, only about half of her students earned *A*'s or *B*'s). I persisted, increasing my commitment to ninety minutes per day of assiduous devotion to math. While few in the room doubted my sincerity, most were reluctant to assure me that I could expect to receive an *A* or *B*; again, we would have to wait for the test results.

Many teachers conceded that, if I were sincere in my efforts, I would receive at least a *C* in the class. Others tried to comfort me by saying that there was nothing wrong with the grade of *C*, and that I should be happy with it. Still others said that the report card included a section to evaluate a student's level of effort and that a high mark in this area would reward my commitment to math. The kindergarten teachers were the only ones willing to encourage me to expect an *A* or *B* from my high level of effort, although most did not use letter grades in their classrooms.

While an occasional *C* probably will not have a detrimental effect on a student's expectations of success, few students take pride or experience feelings of success from a steady diet of *C*'s. As a student's expectations for meaningful success decrease in school, so does his or her willingness to devote meaningful effort toward mastering school-related tasks.

Contrary to the suggestions of Brophy and Wlodkowski, it is difficult to expect teachers to assure students that reasonable effort will automatically lead to success in their classrooms. Even if it were possible to measure effort accurately, grades have been primarily used to indicate a student's level of performance, and it would be unrealistic and confusing to try to change this. What is important, however, is that teachers do everything possible to establish instructional and evaluation procedures that support effort-outcome dependency. Students must believe that if they are committed to expending reasonable effort, then it is highly likely that this effort will lead to outcomes that demonstrate mastery of the course content.

This means, *first,* that the outcomes to be measured must be based on clearly defined objectives that have been made available to students prior to instruction and that define the focus and emphasis of all instructional activities. The specific knowledge and skills required of students should not come as a surprise to them on an exam question; if effort is to lead to mastery, students need to know exactly what it is they are expected to master.

Second, performance must be evaluated against absolute standards rather than against the relative performance of one's peers. This means that the grades of *A* or *B* indicate a predetermined level or percentage of content mastery (often 90 percent and above for an *A*, and 80 to 89 percent for a *B*) rather than one's relative ranking within the class; percentages—not percentiles—are a prerequisite to assuring students that effort can lead to success. This requires that teachers avoid artificially restricting the number of *A*'s or *B*'s that will be distributed. While some may worry that this practice may lead to "grade inflation," educators will be unable to attain "achievement inflation" without increasing the chances for all students to experience success.

Third, the method and pace of instruction must accommodate both faster- and slower-learning students. There is no single pace of instruction that is appropriate for all students. Slower-learning students become frustrated when they are not given adequate time to master the content, and faster-learning students become bored if the pace is too slow. Chapter 8 will examine how outcome-based education and mastery learning can accommodate both faster- and slower-learning students. It will also offer ten specific recommendations for helping teachers assure students that reasonable effort will lead to success. For now, however, it is important to emphasize that learning can no longer be viewed as a race between fast and slow learners. If we hope to maintain our democracy and standard of living in the next century, we must be committed to structuring classrooms so that they motivate all students to achieve at high levels, rather than reward those who can do it first.

Value of School Success

While the value of success in school seems obvious, we often fail to teach this value to students or relate this value to the specific content being taught. "Because I said so" is simply not reason enough for students to commit their efforts to schoolwork. As indicated in Chapter 3, imparting to students the value of school success is further complicated by the finding that school grades and test scores of non–college-bound students had a negligible impact on the wages they earn immediately after high school (Bishop, 1989). On the other hand, students interested in attending selective colleges and universities understand that high school grades are important to the selection process, and, consequently, they tend to be quite grade-conscious.

Psychologist John Atkinson (1957) proposed that the degree to which one prizes or values an accomplishment in achievement situations is directly related to the task's difficulty. Furthermore, when students are free to select the difficulty level of a task, their basic motivational disposition significantly influences this decision (Raffini & Rosemier, 1972). Atkinson's original theory of achievement motivation was based on the assumption that the incentive value for accomplishing a certain task relates to the probability of achieving that task. Table 5-1 shows this relationship as it applies to Atkinson's classic ring toss experiment (Atkinson & Litwin, 1960). Participants threw ten rings at a peg to see how many ringers they could make. The throwing area had fifteen marks on the floor at a distance from one to fifteen feet away from the peg (Table 5-1 establishes the maximum distance at nine feet to simplify the calculations). Participants were told to see how well they could do and that they were free to throw from any distance they preferred. (What distance would you choose?)

Atkinson and Litwin hypothesized that when human beings were placed in an achievement-oriented situation, their behavior was influenced by a basic motivational disposition composed of both a motive to achieve success and a motive to avoid failure. Their results indicated that when individuals were more oriented toward achieving success than avoiding failure, they had a tendency to throw their rings from a distance where the probability of making a ringer multiplied by the incentive value of the ringer would be the highest.

For example, assume one was throwing the rings in a room with other students and an applause meter with a 9-point scale was available in the front of the room. Assuming that the probability of making a ringer from a distance of one foot would be very high, say .9 (you should make about nine ringers with every ten throws), the incentive value of the ringer (using our applause meter to measure the group's reaction) would probably be quite low, likely only a 1 on our scale. As indicated in Table 5-1, the

TABLE 5-1 The Relationship Between Probability and Incentive

Distance from Peg	Probability of a Ringer	Incentive (Applause Meter)	Product of Probability Times Incentive
1'	.9	1	.9
2'	.8	2	1.6
3'	7	3	2.1
4'	.6	4	2.4
5'	.5	5	2.5
6'	.4	6	2.4
7'	.4	6	2.1
8'	.2	8	1.6
9'	.1	9	.9

Adapted from Atkinson and Litwin (1960).

product of the probability multipled by the incentive would be .9. If you were to select a distance of moderate difficulty, say five feet away, where your probability of a ringer is about .5 (you have about a 50-50 chance of making a ringer with each throw), the applause you might receive with each ringer would also be moderate, say 5 on our 9-point scale, and the product would be 2.5. On the other hand, if you were to stand nine feet from the peg, where the probability of making a ringer would be quite low, say .1 (you should make about one ringer with every ten throws), making a ringer from this distance would have a very high incentive value, probably warranting a standing ovation that would register a 9 on the applause meter. However, the product of the two would still be only .9.

Atkinson's research indicated that success-oriented individuals selected a distance where they believed that they had a 50-50 chance to make ringers. However, individuals who were more concerned with avoiding failure rather than attaining success had a tendency to select a distance where the product of probability and incentive was the smallest; they either stood very close where they could be quite certain that they would not fail, or they stood very far away where no one expected them to succeed. (For a revised and more detailed mathematical model of this theory, see Atkinson [1982].)

Atkinson's theory of achievement motivation can help teachers better understand the motivation and behavior of many of the students in their classrooms. When Jerry, for example, who has never written anything longer than two paragraphs, says that he is going to write a thirty-page paper about the causes of the Civil War, the teacher might hypothesize that Jerry's unrealistic goal is probably motivated by his desire to avoid feelings of failure. Jerry will not experience a genuine sense of failure if he does not complete the paper because both he and the teacher do not expect him to do so. Jerry can only fail when he chooses a goal he has a reasonable chance of achieving.

But in order to experience authentic success, students must be willing to risk failure. Those who have had a history of success have learned that failure is an inevitable part of the learning process; this distinction is important because it robs failure of its capacity to threaten their sense of self-worth. However, for students who have experienced continued failure, each additional failure becomes unbearable; while success may be valued, it is not worth risking additional failure and further jeopardizing their self-worth.

Given the way that our increasingly technological society has exalted the personal and monetary values of a good education, it is difficult to imagine a student who would choose academic ignorance over academic competence, all things being equal. Yet, as discussed in Chapter 3, when students begin to believe that academic success is beyond their reach, they are forced to reject the value of education in order to protect their sense of self-worth. If we want these students to expend genuine effort toward learning, we are compelled to change the learning environment so that all students can expect that genuine effort is likely to result in feelings of success.

Attribution Theory

Assume that you are a middle school teacher and your administrator has decided to send you to a three-day out-of-state conference. After returning to your classroom you find that the bookshelves have been cleaned, new bulletin boards have been posted, and a beautifully wrapped box of chocolates is sitting on your desk. Imagine how you would feel. While some teachers would feel delighted and appreciated, others would feel suspicious and skeptical. In either case, the nature of a teacher's feelings will result from the assumptions he or she makes regarding the cause for the changed environment. Did you receive these presents because the students missed you? Or are they a bribe to appease your anger because your students did not complete their assignments on time? Your answers to these questions will influence your response to the presents.

Attribution theorists such as psychologist Bernard Weiner (1979; 1980; 1986) propose that an individual's feelings and reactions to events are closely related to his or her judgments about why events occur. Weiner has been primarily concerned with the effects of these perceived causal attributions as they relate to success or failure outcomes in achievement situations. In the context of the classroom, for example, students who receive an *A* or an *F* on a test or homework assignment make assumptions about why these outcomes have occurred. According to Weiner, the most common attributions given for success or failure in achievement situations are the presence or absence of personal *ability* or natural aptitude, *effort* toward success, *task difficulty,* and *luck* (Weiner, 1980). Although each student makes his or her own interpretation about the causes of an event, there are three dimensions that characterize these causal elements, as identified in Table 5.2. According to Weiner (1979), the first dimension, *locus of causality,* is concerned with whether the cause of an event is inherent within the person or whether it results from external events. The attributes of ability and effort are internal because they originate within the individual; task difficulty and luck are external because they are caused by factors outside an individual's control.

The second dimension of attributes, *stability,* addresses the question of whether one can depend on the attribute to provide consistent success or failure in future encounters with the task. Ability and task difficulty are considered stable, since a student who is a capable speller today, for example, can count on having that spelling ability again tomorrow. Likewise, if solving simultaneous equations is a difficult task today, it will likely be a difficult task next week. On the other hand, effort is considered

TABLE 5-2 Attributions for Success and Failure, Classified According to Locus, Stability, and Controllability

Dimension	Ability	Effort	Task Difficulty	Luck
Locus of Causality	Internal	Internal	External	External
Stability	Stable	Unstable	Stable	Unstable
Controllability	Uncontrollable	Controllable	Uncontrollable	Uncontrollable

Adapted from Weiner (1979).

unstable, since although individuals have expended great effort today, they cannot be sure they will be able to repeat the effort tomorrow. Luck, like effort, cannot be relied on over time and is also considered unstable.

The third dimension of attributions, according to Weiner, is *controllability*. Although individuals can personally control how much effort they choose to expend on a given task, they have little control over their innate ability to perform the task, the difficulty of the task, or of the luck they believe they have when performing it.

These three dimensions identified by Weiner are important in understanding the feelings that one may experience when success or failure is ascribed to a particular attribute. When students attribute their successes to their ability, they experience pride and confidence. The pride results from the internal locus of causality that is characteristic of ability attributes; the cause of the success is within the person. Since ability is also stable, it can be relied upon in the future, which, in turn, results in feelings of confidence.

When students attribute their successes to effort, they experience feelings of pride since effort is both internal and individually controllable. However, the unstable nature of effort often produces feelings of relief rather than confidence since one cannot rely on having the energy or willingness to expend similar levels of effort to produce success in the future. Like winning a lottery, success attributed to luck produces feelings of surprise and pleasure even though luck is an external attribute. Yet luck is unstable and therefore unreliable. And although the level of a task's difficulty is stable, attributing success to the fact that tasks are easy produces feelings of indifference since the locus of causality is external. For example, if one earns an *A* on a test that was considered to be exceptionally easy, one feels little pride in this accomplishment.

When failure experiences are attributed to one's lack of ability, they generate feelings of shame and hopelessness. Since ability is internal, no one else can be blamed; since it is stable and uncontrollable, future attempts are likely to produce similar results. Failure attributed to lack of effort also produces feelings of shame or embarrassment, but because effort is both unstable and controllable, it is possible to expect that increased efforts could lead to greater success.

Teachers' beliefs regarding student abilities help determine the attributes students select to explain their successes and failures. These attributions, in turn, contribute to the development of classroom personalities that either support or undermine student motivation to learn. Using the earlier example, students in Mr. Genes's classroom are more likely to attribute their failure in math to lack of ability or to task difficulty than are students in Mr. Hart's class. Mr. Hart has organized his instructional procedures to help students experience a direct relationship between effort and outcomes; when they fail, they are more likely to attribute their failure to lack of effort.

Stipek (1988) identifies three antecedents that affect students' perceptions about the cause of their achievement outcomes. First, *consensus information* based on the performance of others can influence students' judgments about the reasons for their successes and failures. If everyone in the class, for example, is unable to solve a particular math problem, students are likely to attribute their own failure to solve the problem to the external and uncontrollable factor of task difficulty. Second, a student's personal *history of performance* can also influence his or her causal attributions. If Jimmy, who has always performed poorly in math, again receives a low grade, he is likely to attribute his lack of success to stable causes such as lack of ability or task difficulty. On the other hand, outcomes that are inconsistent with one's past history of performance are likely to be attributed to unstable causes. If Jimmy received an *A* on his math test, he would likely attribute his success to unstable attributes like luck or an unusually high level of effort.

Finally, according to Stipek, students' *beliefs about competence* influence their judgments about the causes of their achievement outcomes. If Jimmy believes that he is competent in science, he is likely to attribute his success on a test to his ability; if he fails on the test, he will seek attributions that are consistent with his perception of competence, such as an unfair test or a lack of preparation. Conversely, if students believe that they are incompetent, they will attribute failure to their lack of ability and success to external factors such as luck or task ease. According to Stipek:

*Weiner admits that relatively stable individual differences in percep-
tions of the cause of achievement outcomes may exist, but he claims
that individuals make attributional judgments primarily on the basis
of information in the current achievement situation. Past experience
in similar achievement contexts is relevant, but it is only one of many
factors that the student considers. Weiner's view is optimistic because
it suggests that we should be able to change students' causal
attributions—whatever their previous experiences in achievement
contexts—by manipulating variables in the current classroom environment. (1988, p. 84)*

Stipek's point is well taken; changing student attributes for success
or failure is much more difficult than it appears. Nevertheless, attribution theory has several immediate implications for creating classroom personalities that support student motivation to learn. First, when students
expend high levels of effort on a required task at which they are unable
to succeed, they are forced to conclude that they lack ability. Teachers can
help students avoid this sense of hopelessness by trying to match their
assignments to the achievement levels of their students. This is difficult
to accomplish in a classroom with thirty or more students. It requires that
teachers task-analyze their assignments so that they can divide complicated
procedures into more easily managed subprocedures for those students who
need them. Only then will it be possible for all students to discover that
effort leads to success. As Maria Montessori discovered long ago, students
should never be allowed to fail at tasks until they have a reasonable chance
to succeed. If they do, they have no choice but to attribute their failure
to lack of ability and will therefore stop trying. On the other hand, when
they believe that higher levels of effort offer a possibility for success,
students will persist in spite of the inevitable failures that accompany
learning.

Teachers often try to encourage effort from students by telling them
that the task they are being asked to complete is really quite easy. Attribution theory, however, suggests that this approach be avoided. Since
task difficulty is an external factor, attributing success to task ease results
in feelings of indifference and makes it impossible for students to experience the pride that comes from success through effort. Furthermore,
students are destined to feelings of shame and embarrassment should they
fail at a task labelled "easy." Teachers can help students avoid this shame
and embarrassment by telling them that the tasks they are being asked
to perform are *difficult,* but with reasonable effort they can expect success. Since effort is internal and controllable, students can experience genuine pride from their accomplishment, and they may eventually develop
feelings of confidence from their increased perceptions of competence.

Many teachers also try to encourage their students by wishing them "good luck" as they are about to undertake a task. Since luck is also external and uncontrollable, this practice actually reinforces an external attribution. If success does result, students are likely to feel surprised rather than competent; if failure results, they are likely to feel indifferent. Wishing students "good effort" may be more awkward, but it also may help them experience more pride and confidence from their successes.

Attribution Retraining

Attribution retraining is a process by which apathetic and failure-avoiding students are encouraged to change their perceptions of the causes of their failing behaviors from the uncontrollable attributes of luck, task difficulty, and low ability to the only controllable attribute—effort. As Stipek has suggested, the process of attribution retraining is not easy; since failure-avoiding students tend to ascribe their occasional successes to external factors, they feel little ownership or responsibility for their occasional successes. By helping these students reassess their causal perceptions for success and failure and by helping them attribute their successes to internal rather than external factors, it may be possible to rekindle their active involvement with learning.

Teachers' verbal comments contribute to a motivating classroom personality, and they are essential in influencing the success and failure attributions of students. In reviewing attribution retraining studies, Licht (1983) found that when teachers helped students attribute their failures to insufficient effort, students began to increase their persistence and improve their performance on tasks. The use of informational feedback, discussed in the previous chapter, can help students attribute failure to effort rather than to lack of ability. Comments like "I can see that you're really working hard on your math, Jimmy—all of that work sure is improving your skill with multiplying and dividing fractions" can help students realize that increased effort can lead to success.

Failure identities are difficult to change; moving students from hopelessness to hope requires more than a single high grade or a few informational comments. In fact, students who believe that they cannot succeed in school will need many effort-outcome feedback experiences before they begin to experience pride and confidence. Yet the teacher's beliefs and philosophical assumptions are crucial to the development of students' causal attributions and to the process of attribution retraining. In the final analysis, teachers' faith and confidence in their students *precede* students' faith and confidence in themselves.

Control Versus Automony

Some teachers believe that their primary responsibility in the classroom is to maintain order and control over the behavior and learning of students.

Other teachers believe that their primary obligation is to develop in students a sense of autonomy and self-determination. In both cases, the personality of each teacher's classroom will reflect these beliefs.

Deci and Ryan (1985, 1987) believe that all human beings perceive their environment from an autonomy-control orientation that influences their beliefs about the causes of behavior. Individuals who have a strong *autonomy orientation* tend to seek out situations that allow them choice and the opportunity to determine their own direction. They usually prefer activities characterized by flexibility and options that provide occasions in which they can pursue their own goals and interests. In short, autonomy-oriented individuals choose to be captains and navigators of their own ships, rather than below-deck passengers following the dictates of others.

Individuals with a strong *control orientation* perceive that their behavior is driven by external factors or internal compulsions. They tend to undertake activities or perform behaviors because they "must" or "should" or because these activities or behaviors will lead to extrinsic compensation. A control orientation leads individuals to comply with real or imagined regulations and expectations; one's behavior, like that of a puppet, is controlled by others.

As discussed in Chapter 4, proposition three of cognitive evaluation theory proposes that external rewards have both a controlling aspect and an informational aspect. When the controlling aspect is salient, the purpose is to elicit a particular behavior from the recipient. When the informational aspect is salient, the purpose is to provide the recipient with performance feedback. Chapter 4 also discusses research that indicates that rewards decrease intrinsic motivation only when the controlling aspect is salient for the recipient.

Deci and colleagues (1981) hypothesized that the philosophical beliefs of teachers are among the factors that determine whether the controlling or informational aspect of an event or reward will be salient. If teachers, for example, use rewards to manipulate the behavior of their students, then clearly the controlling aspect of the reward will be salient. Similarly, if the teachers' primary purpose in granting the reward is to provide feedback to students regarding their competent performance, then the informational aspect of the reward will be salient.

Viewing an individual's philosophical beliefs or orientations toward control and autonomy as a continuum, Deci et al. (1981) developed an instrument to measure teachers' orientations toward control versus autonomy when dealing with students in classroom problem situations. They believed that the instrument would allow them to determine whether a person's orientation toward control versus autonomy would influence the emphasis he or she placed on the controlling or the informational aspects of rewards and communications.

Their instrument, called the *Adults' Orientations Toward Control Versus Autonomy with Children Scale,* was designed to measure whether teachers would select more controlling or more autonomous options when dealing with student problems in the classroom. "Highly controlling" (HC) options are those in which the teacher decides on the solution and then uses sanctions to ensure that the solution is implemented. "Moderately controlling (MC) options are those in which the teacher determines the solution but tries to get the student to implement it by the use of guilt or by emphasizing that it is in the student's best interest. In "moderately autonomous (MA) options the teacher encourages the student to compare his or her behavior to that of other students. Finally, in "highly autonomous" (HA) options, the teacher encourages students to consider the various elements of the situation in attempting to arrive at their own solution to the problem. Deci et al. asked teachers to rate each option for dealing with the problem situation on a 7-point scale ranging from "very inappropriate" to "very appropriate." The following is an example of one of the eight vignettes used in the scale:

> *Jim is an average student who has been working at grade level. During the past two weeks, he has appeared listless and has not been participating during reading group. The work he does is accurate but he has not been completing assignments. A phone conversation with his mother revealed no useful information. The most appropriate thing for the teacher to do is:*
>
> > *(MC) 1. She should impress upon him the importance of finishing his assignments since he needs to learn this material for his own good.*
> >
> > *(HA) 2. Let him know that he doesn't have to finish all of his work now and see if she can help him work out the cause of the listlessness.*
> >
> > *(HC) 3. Make him stay after school until the day's assignments are done.*
> >
> > *(MA) 4. Let him see how he compares with the other children in terms of his assignments and encourage him to catch up with the others. (Deci et al., 1981, p. 644)*

Research using the Orientations Scale has found that students in the classrooms of teachers who score higher on autonomy orientation are more intrinsically motivated, perceive themselves as more competent, have higher self-esteem, and believe that their teachers are more supportive than do students of teachers who score higher on control orientation (Deci et al. 1981). Furthermore, research by Deci, Nezlek, and Sheinman (1981) found that control-oriented teachers tend to use rewards controllingly, while autonomy-oriented teachers tend to use rewards more informationally. Their data also indicated that students perceive autonomy-oriented teachers as facilitating personal responsibility and internal control more than control-oriented teachers.

Clearly, when teachers believe that one of their primary responsibilities is to support the advancement of autonomy and self-determination in their students, they behave in ways that contribute to a motivating classroom personality. When they believe that students should learn to assume responsibility for their own behavior, they convey faith and trust in the ability of students to act in constructive ways. Most students rise to meet this level of expectation, and the classroom atmosphere becomes friendly, supportive, and productive.

Organizational Patterns

When a teacher and twenty-five or thirty students meet daily for several months, they create a unique culture; stable interaction patterns develop between the teacher and the students, both teacher and student behaviors become predictable, and a clearly recognizable ambiance permeates the classroom. In short, this collection of individuals, under the leadership of the teacher, acquires its own personality. Once the personality is formed, outsiders who enter the room can feel the currents of discontent or the bonds of unity that characterize the class and either support or undermine student motivation to learn. Richard Larson at the University of Wisconsin-Milwaukee has proposed a model for understanding how organizational patterns influence the formation of a classroom's personality (Larson, 1992). Table 5-3 identifies seven major organizational patterns typically found in classrooms, and Figure 5-1 provides Larson's characterization of these patterns. An eighth organizational structure, the adhocracy, seems consistent with Larson's model and has been included in Table 5-3 and Figure 5-1.

As the leadership style of the teacher begins to influence and be influenced by the classroom's organizational pattern, predictable communication pathways become established, a sense of isolation or belonging develops, and the unspoken norms of behavior become defined. The interrelationships among these variables produce a unique classroom personality that either supports a productive, mastery-oriented learning environment or generates conflict, resentment, and maladaptive behavior. The characteristics of each organizational pattern will be discussed individually.

Individualist (Programmed Isolation)

An individualized organizational pattern fosters a closed classroom environment in which each student becomes an independent and self-contained

TABLE 5-3 Organizational Patterns and Classroom Personality

	Individualist	Separatist	Anarchy	Dictatorship	Benevolent Dictatorship	Cooperation	Quasi-Democracy	Adhocracy
Communications	Closed	Status determined	Random	One-direction	One-direction	Between and within	Open	Collaborative and reciprocal
Belonging	Low	Selective	Conspiritorial	Unified resentment	Low	High within groups	High within class	Moderate and temporary
Norms of behavior	Personal and isolated	Defined by cliques	Chaotic	Teacher-defined, enforced, and fragile	Teacher defined and enforced	Shared and pluralistic	Shared and mutually defined	Situational specific
Leadership Style	Technical	Political	Crisis management	Power through fear	Power through bribery	Facilitating groups	Facilitating class	Shared decision making
Descriptor	Programmed isolation	Insiders and outsiders	Everyone for themselves	The Steel fist	Steel fist with velvet glove	Sink or swim together	One for all, all for one	A solution for every problem

Adapted from Larson (1992).

112

FIGURE 5-1 Organizational Patterns

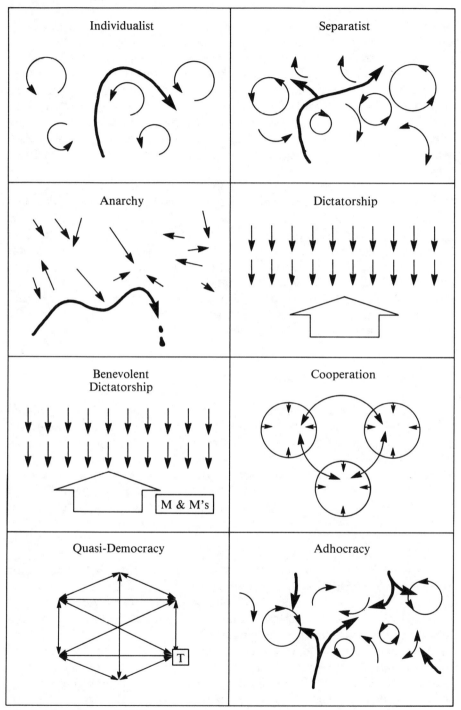

Adapted from Larson (1992).

learning system. The teacher's mission is to move about the room encouraging and helping each student to master specifically programmed learning activities. Although this organizational model may be useful for meeting clearly identified and hierarchial learning objectives, the resulting classroom personality is muted since the closed communication patterns stifle the sharing of mutual ideas and concerns. Most communication among students is unnecessary and therefore discouraged. Instead, students communicate with the teacher as required, although the highly sequential instructional material reduces the need for even this perfunctory form of communication.

Individualized classrooms do not engender a sense of belonging among their members, nor does this style of organization contribute to the development of common norms or of a unified set of beliefs regarding behavior. Each student operates in isolation with little reason or opportunity to build a sense of group identity; personal needs rather than consensual expectations determine behavioral norms. The leadership style is classified as technical or clinical since the teacher relies heavily on assessment instrumentation to monitor, graph, and evaluate student progress. The highly specific instructional material is clearly organized and individually matched to each student's skill level.

Separatist (Insiders and Outsiders)

Some classrooms become organized around tightly closed cliques of students with little communication between groups. These extremely selective cliques are composed of students with homogeneous backgrounds and interests; members are typically selected on the basis of family income, race, athletic ability, gender and/or social attractiveness. Not all students, however, are accepted into a group since the cliques pride themselves on their exclusivity. Those rejected are forced to survive in isolation within the classroom. While a sense of belonging may be evident within the cliques, members of other cliques, isolates, and the teacher are either regarded as intruders or summarily rejected.

Teachers do not consciously set about organizing their classrooms around a separatist personality. This dysfunctional structure develops as a result of several factors, but the teacher's inability to provide strong and facilitative leadership is often a major contributor. Once firmly established, separatist organizational patterns force teachers to become political in their leadership style. (Here the term "political" is meant to suggest the act of bartering for power and control between groups or individuals.) Teachers in these classrooms are compelled to bargain with each clique separately as they attempt to cajole the class to progress through the curriculum. This process is made more difficult by the unequal distribution of influence and power among the cliques. The teacher's bargaining position, unfortunately, is built on a foundation of weakness; he or she has little choice but to rely on trade-offs in the process of bartering privileges for student compliance.

The norms of a separatist classroom are split among the circles of students, with each circle defining the unspoken but clearly communicated behavioral expectations for its members. Although some of the students excluded from cliques staunchly assert their independence, many others withdraw into lonely isolation and avoid drawing attention to themselves. While they may pursue academic objectives, they are usually careful to avoid the teacher's recognition, as it is likely to cause others to notice their rejection.

Anarchy (Everyone for Themselves)

When classrooms dissolve into anarchy, their organizational pattern becomes chaotic, and their personality is characterized by normlessness and whimsical self-gratification. While the teacher barters for control and student learning in separatist classrooms, in anarchical classrooms the teacher has lost control and is powerless. Unable to establish order and maintain academic integrity, the teacher either feigns a semblance of authority or withdraws into painful isolation. This cultural anomie produces sporadic and random communication among students and between students and the teacher. A conspiratorial sense of belonging may develop among some students as they band together in opposition to the teacher's attempts to regain control.

The overt norms for classroom behavior are either chaotic or nonexistent. Students continually push the limits of acceptable deportment as they challenge the teacher's power to control the classroom. Classmates often become embedded in covert competition to see who can generate new avenues of resistance or defiance. Teachers, of course, still retain the threat and power of the school administration in reserve. But they, as well as the students, know there is a limit to the number of times any teacher can surrender control to this greater authority, thereby conceding his or her inability to maintain classroom order. Such tentative and restricted support requires that the teacher refrain from calling upon administrative intervention until student transgressions reach critical proportions. More than one teacher has entered the professions of real estate or insurance sales after having encountered crisis after crisis in anarchical classrooms with little hope of changing their resulting personality.

Dictatorship (The Steel Fist)

Fearful of anarchy, many teachers organize their classrooms as dictatorships with themselves firmly and unquestionably in control. This pattern of organization relies heavily upon unidirectional communication from the teacher to the students, and, as in the individualized organizational pattern, communication among students is discouraged and quickly extinguished. Most interactions are teacher initiated and dominated by commands, judgments, and edicts of punishment. Threats are seldom used; dictatorial teachers have discovered that severe and consistently enforced punishments are much more effective in eliciting student compliance.

A morose sense of student belonging may develop, but it is usually accidental and established in the group's mutual resentment of the teacher's severe and unilateral use of power. The external norms of the classroom are clearly defined and enforced by the teacher; the unspoken norms are mute since they make little difference to the rigid behavioral demands of the dictator. Yet the overt norms are quite fragile since any change or lapse in the teacher's vigilance will quickly produce a strong backlash in the release of student latent hostility and resentment.

The leadership style in a classroom dictatorship relies heavily on the teacher's ability to maintain unquestioned control over student behavior with the efficient and forceful use of punishment. This leadership style, however, extracts a heavy toll of psychic energy from the teacher, since it requires constant vigilance in discovering student transgressions and in immediately dispensing consequences. Its success is completely dependent on the students' realization that nothing is negotiable; each transgression must result in swift and severe repercussions.

The steel fist often hides a fearful heart. Many teachers mask their insecurities, doubts, and fears of anarchy with a leadership style that focuses on power and the need to dominate others. To dictators, conflicts are simplistic win-lose encounters, where winning means strength and power and losing implies weakness and impotence.

Benevolent Dictatorship (Steel Fist with Velvet Glove)

Similar to the dictatorship is the organizational pattern of the benevolent dictatorship. Here again the communication pattern flows from teacher to student, and scant student-to-student communication is encouraged or allowed. Most interactions are teacher initiated, but rather than dispense punishment to enforce orders and commands, the benevolent dictator relies on the use of rewards to ensure compliance. Since a mutual enemy is not present and since students are required to compete with one another for limited rewards, only a minimal sense of belonging develops in these classrooms.

The norms of classroom behavior are clearly leader-defined and enforced, but because students experience less resentment toward the teacher, their existence is much less fragile than under the dictatorship. The motives of the benevolent dictator are clearly more student-oriented than those of the dictator. After all, the teacher points to the long-term legitimate interests of students to justify the classroom's one-directional and dogmatic personality.

In regard to leadership, the benevolent dictator relies on bribery and moral suasion rather than on punishment to elicit from students appropriate academic outcomes and social behaviors. Yet this pragmatic approach to leadership clearly legitimizes the teacher's use of any means short of punishment necessary to attain these justifiable ends.

Cooperation (Sink or Swim Together)

The cooperative organizational style establishes a classroom personality based on small and cohesive learning groups that share the common goal of mastering content objectives. (Chapter 9 provides a detailed analysis of cooperative learning groups.) Communication within each learning group is reciprocal, honest, and direct; it focuses on both the academic tasks and the interpersonal relationships among the group members. Communication between groups is less developed and often focuses on the competition and rivalry among the various clusters.

In a classroom characterized by a cooperative organizational pattern, the teacher is able to establish a sense of companionship and belonging within each group. These feelings are less developed within the classroom as a whole, since little time or effort is taken to engender a larger group identity. The norms or beliefs about how students are to behave are jointly established between the teacher and the students and can be considered pluralistic since every student is valued regardless of gender, race, economic status, or ability.

The leadership style of the teacher in cooperative organizational patterns is facilitative and shared. As a facilitator, the teacher attempts to follow all students to express their ideas and concerns, and to help them understand the purposes and necessity for classroom decisions. The teacher also fosters shared leadership responsibilities within each of the learning groups.

Quasi-Democracy (One for All, All for One)

Finally, according to Larson, the quasi-democratic organizational pattern is one in which the teacher shares both the leadership and decision-making power with all class members. Although power is shared, this organizational pattern is not a true democracy since the teacher is not free to surrender to group consensus his or her authority over the curriculum or educational operations. Yet within this environment communication flows openly among and between the teacher and all class members. This reciprocal communication supports the development of a strong sense of group identity; each participant is encouraged to feel like a valued and contributing member of the class. Larson's definition of a healthy group is that each member of the group cares about every other member and that every member cares about the group.

The norms of behavior are overtly defined and shared by all participants. Furthermore, each member of the class believes that compliance with the norms supports the goals and objectives of the group as a whole. The teacher's leadership style facilitates both the personal and academic concerns of each member and is instrumental in developing a group identity in which all participants support the feelings and concerns of one another.

Adhocracy (A Soution for Every Problem)

As schools become more outcome-oriented, it may be useful to add an eighth organizational structure, the adhocracy, to those suggested by Larson. Popularized by Alvin Toffler in his book *Future Shock,* the term *adhocracy* is used by Mintzberg (1979) to describe a complex but loosely organized administrative arrangement in which specialist teams function as units to solve specific problems. In the 1960s, NASA's Apollo project was one of the first and clearest examples of an adhocracy. With the single goal of landing an American on the moon before 1970, NASA developed an administrative and organizational structure that abandoned the traditional bureaucratic line-staff decision-making structure that characterized most similar organizations. In its stead, NASA created a system designed to facilitate functional decision making through a system of constellations of staff experts working together in ever-shifting relationships.

Skrtic (1987) argues that schools could be far more effective if they were organized to function as problem-solving adhocracies in which teams of classroom teachers and specialists collaborated reciprocally to meet the needs of all students. By drawing upon the collaborative expertise of learning disabilities instructors, reading specialists, human relations workers, counselors, and school psychologists, adhocracies could help each student maximize his or her chances for academic success by providing these services in a supportive and stigma-free environment.

As indicated in Table 5-3, communications within adhocracies are collaborative and reciprocal, both among experts as they consult and plan instructional strategies to help students overcome specific problems, and between experts and students as they interact during the implementation of these strategies.

Students develop a moderate sense of belonging within adhocracies, but since there is a steady shifting of the individual experts required to deal with constantly changing problem-solving tasks, this sense of belonging is often temporary. While two or three students, for example, may develop a sense of unity as they work with a learning disabilities teacher on a specific task, their work group will eventually dissolve and be reorganized with other students as needs and learning problems change.

Since the instructional staff is constantly changing to meet the needs and problems of the group's members, the norms for expected behavior within an adhocracy are defined by each specific learning situation. If three students, for example, are working with a reading specialist, the norms for their behavior may emphasize cooperative sharing. On the other hand, if a student is working individually with the speech clinician, he is free to pursue his personal needs in ways similar to those that characterize an individualized organizational pattern.

The leadership style within adhocracies is based on shared decision making between the teacher and the support staff. The expertise of each staff member remains the primary factor influencing decision making as the instructional team works to help students solve specific learning problems.

Organizational Designs and Student Motivation

Clearly, classrooms with personalities that are characterized by unity, cooperative purpose, and mutual acceptance provide a motivating environment for all students. While several of Larson's organizational patterns are designed to stimulate student achievement, only the cooperative and the quasi-democratic patterns generate classroom personalities that support both academic outcomes and the interpersonal process of learning. In the cooperative environment, each of the separate groups endeavors to support collaboration, teamwork, shared leadership, and an *esprit de corps* as the members focus on mastering the content objectives of the course. The quasi-democratic classroom attempts to develop these same supportive processes and academic outcomes within the class as a unit. While adhocracies are primarily concerned with developing academic outcomes, they can also support the interpersonal aspects of learning as students, teachers, and experts collaborate to solve learning problems.

Unless the organizational design of the classroom deliberately and systematically assists students in satisfying their needs for esteem, autonomy, competence, and belonging, student motivation to learn will be little more than a response to bribery or coercion. Educators will find that when they organize classrooms to support both the process and product of learning, they increase the probability that students will be motivated to learn in order to satisfy their own personal and academic needs.

Organizing to Develop Unity

Much has been written about the interpersonal dynamics that support group cohesiveness, and many researchers agree that several sequential stages can be identified in its development. Tuckman (1965), in a review of more than fifty studies dealing with group development, identified four stages that appear common to most groups. The first stage is characterized by a period of uncertainty and initial confusion about the norms of the class and about how one fits in with others. Second is a "storming" phase in which conflicts arise and members begin to rebel. Third, assuming these conflicts are resolved, the group moves into a stage of cohesiveness. Finally, the fourth stage, characterized by acceptance, tolerance, and flexibility, emerges as the group achieves its shared goals.

Much of the research conducted on group development is based on "leaderless" groups in which the designated leader makes little effort to direct the group through its developmental stages. Assuming this role, it is argued, eliminates the possibility that leadership will emerge from within the group itself. Consequently, much floundering is necessary before members begin to assume this shared leadership responsibility.

In classrooms with academic as well as interpersonal objectives, few teachers are willing to tolerate the inefficiency of such floundering. Furthermore, much of the conflict and rebellion observed in Tuckman's "storming" stage appears to result from dissatisfaction with its leader for not providing direction. Because teachers must take a more active role in providing leadership, Stanford (1977) argues that teachers cannot simply wait for leadership roles to emerge; they must take responsibility for providing experiences that develop unity and cohesiveness. To help with this responsibility, he identified five stages that classroom groups experience as they become productive units that support student motivation to learn (Stanford, 1977).

Stage One: Orientation

Students generally experience some anxiety and uncertainty when they start a new school year or come into a new classroom. They have concerns about what is expected of them, what others are like, how they are going to fit in, and how they are going to be treated. If they have been together in other classes or grades, students will experience less anxiety than if they are entering a new group for the first time. New students entering an established group experience an especially high level of apprehension and need help with this transition.

Ice-breaking activities that allow each member to contribute his or her opinions and information about previous experiences in nonthreatening ways are useful during this stage. One useful exercise involves establishing pairs of unacquainted students, allowing them a few minutes to get to know each other, and then inviting each to introduce his or her partner to the rest of the class. Assigning a host or welcome partner to a new class member is a simple but important procedure for helping new students feel welcomed. Clear descriptions of course and grade requirements are especially helpful for reducing student anxiety in the upper grades.

Stage Two: Establishing Norms

Once students begin to feel comfortable within the group, they need to have the expectations of their classroom behavior clarified. The teacher can assist in the process by helping each member assume responsibility for his or her individual behavior as well as for the collective behavior of the group. If the group is to grow toward maturity, its members must develop the skills and attitudes necessary for productive group activities. It is during this stage that individuals begin to identify with the group as a whole and start to share the responsibility for setting and reaching group goals. According to David and Roger Johnson from the Cooperative Learning Center at the University of Minnesota, teachers need to help students develop a sense of *positive interdependence* that requires all participants to view the learning situation with a "we-are-all-in-this-together" orientation (Johnson & Johnson, 1987). This requires that learning tasks be structured so that no student can succeed unless all do.

Establishing norms that foster positive interdependence requires that students be given instruction and opportunities to practice the skills of interpersonal communication. Active listening and responding through the use of paraphrasing, reflection of feelings, and "I" messages (Gordon, 1974) are necessary if students are to learn to accept the thoughts and opinions of all group members. In several of the organizational patterns previously discussed, communication is teacher-centered and most verbal exchange involves the teacher and individual students. If classrooms are to develop motivating personalities based on a sense of cohesiveness and group membership, it is necessary that students learn to listen carefully to one another and to interact directly. By developing good listening skills through group discussions and role-playing activities, students can become conscious of their interaction patterns and be encouraged to support and value one another's thoughts and ideas.

Stage Three: Coping with Conflicts

Interpersonal conflicts occasionally will surface in classrooms in which students begin to communicate more openly and directly. It is important, therefore, that students also have the opportunity to learn conflict resolution skills so that conflicts can be addressed without destroying relationships or the self-esteem of those involved. Teachers, of course, are important role models in this process. How they confront and resolve their own conflicts within the classroom will set a tone and pattern that students will follow. According to Fisher and Ury (1981), successful negotiation should: (1) produce an agreement acceptable to both sides, if possible; (2) maintain and possibly improve the relationship between the participants; and (3) take a reasonable amount of time. Figure 5-2 provides a conflict negotiation strategy designed primarily to help teachers resolve conflicts with students who exhibit disruptive behavior in the classroom. It can provide a useful model for helping students negotiate conflicts among themselves.

Beliefs of Successful Negotiators

Before discussing each of the phases within the negotiation process, it may be useful to examine some of the beliefs and assumptions of teachers who are successful negotiators:

FIGURE 5-2   Conflict Negotiation: A Problem-Solving Process

INVITING

Invite students into the learning process by
building positive teacher/student relationships.

CONFRONTING

Be clear about who owns the problem,
and utilize the skills of "I" messages, descriptive
confrontation, and inquiry confrontation.

FACILITATING

Use the skills of paraphrasing and reflecting feelings
to help the students identify their goals and needs.

EVALUATING

Ask students to evaluate their behavior
relative to their needs and goals and to the needs
and goals of the teacher and others in the class.

RESOLVING	CONSEQUATING
Help students work out a plan for alternative behavior that will meet the needs of the student, the teacher, and others in the class. Discuss the students' commitment to the plan; possible difficulites in keeping it; and teacher, classroom, and/or environmental changes that will assist in making it work.	If students are unwilling to evaluate their behavior or explore alternatives, use logical consequences until alternative behaviors can be found.

ENCOURAGING

Reinforce behavioral changes through descriptive or
appreciative verbal approval.

---

1. *While stopping classroom disruptions is of major importance, teachers who have success negotiating conflicts have an equally strong desire to help students meet their needs in nondisruptive ways.* Students cannot be allowed to meet their needs at the expense of the teacher or of other students in the class. Disruptive behavior, by definition, makes it difficult for the teacher to teach or for others to learn and such behavior cannot be allowed. Yet in the process of eliminating classroom disruptions, teachers should help students find positive, acceptable alternatives to their maladaptive behaviors. Eliminating disruptive behavior is insufficient; teachers must also help students to identify behaviors that meet their needs in ways that do not disturb the learning of others.

2. *They endeavor to understand a student's point of view, though they may not agree with it.* To listen, to paraphrase, and to understand a student's concerns or feelings does not mean that the teacher must agree with them. While it is difficult to listen sincerely to a person with whom one disagrees, listening does not mean that one must approve of a student's behavior or agree with the student's perception; it simply means that one accepts the student's perception as being real for the student.

3. *While they may reject a student's behavior, they try not to reject the student.* Separating what a student does from what a student is, is never easy. Yet teachers who have success with negotiating conflicts endeavor to believe that within each student is the potential for constructive behavior. Given this, there is no reason to ever give up or to reject a student. Likewise, while teachers and students differ in experience, they are equal in their humanity. This equality makes it wrong for teachers to demand more respect than they are willing to give.

4. *They do not assume responsibility for the behavior of students. Rather, they try to help students assume responsibility for their own behavior.* Teachers cannot force students to change their behavior; they can only hold students accountable for the consequences of their behavior. They can also help students explore these consequences and encourage them to make more productive choices.

5. *They try to show faith, trust, and belief in students and focus on student improvement rather than past behavior.* The process of encouragement requires that teachers believe in students' ability to learn and to behave in productive ways. These beliefs precede students' faith and trust in themselves. Teachers who have success negotiating conflicts focus on students' assets rather than liabilities, they emphasize strengths rather than weaknesses, and they try to nourish and expand these strengths.

Conflict Negotiation Strategies

The first step of the conflict negotiation process presented in Figure 5-2 requires that teachers be *inviting* toward students. This means that teachers should be willing to build positive relationships with all students, but especially those who seem unmotivated to learn or to participate in class activities. This, of course, is more difficult than it sounds. It requires that teachers be willing to smile, to speak in pleasant tones, and to show faith and trust in students who often behave with hostility and defensiveness. According to Purkey and Novak (1984), if teachers hope to build positive relationships with students, they need to send verbal and nonverbal invitations. Furthermore, since students are free to accept or to reject these invitations, teachers need to send them in abundance.

When a student's behavior makes it difficult for the teacher to teach or for other students to learn the teacher has little choice but to *confront* the student with the problem. If Jimmy, for example, starts talking to one of his friends while his teacher, Ms. Mercy, is presenting the directions for a new math activity, then Jimmy's behavior is creating a problem for his teacher. It is important to remember, however, that it is Ms. Mercy who owns the problem—not Jimmy. After all, he's probably quite happy talking to his friend. Nevertheless, Jimmy's behavior is creating a problem for the teacher, and she needs to confront Jimmy with the problem. Gordon (1974) suggests that teachers confront students with the use of an "I" message that describes the student's behavior nonjudgmentally, conveys the teacher's feelings, and identifies the tangible effects of the behavior on the teacher. In Jimmy's case, Ms. Mercy might say, "Jimmy, when you talk to Bill while I'm trying to give directions, I'm getting frustrated because I would like to help the others get started on this activity."

An alternative to an "I" message is an inquiry confrontation, which can be defined as a nonrhetorical query regarding the student's perception. Based on the suggestions of William Glasser (1977), an inquiry confrontation asks the student to reflect on his or her behavior and its probable consequences. In the current example, the teacher might say, "Jimmy, what are you doing?" It is assumed that the teacher is willing to listen to Jimmy's response and help him evaluate the consequences of his behavior. Many teacher questions, however, are rhetorical and defy answers. When Ms. Mercy says to Billy, "What did you say!" when he shouted out "Damn!" while struggling with a math problem, she would probably be even more upset if Billy gave her an honest answer to her question.

A third type of confrontation is to simply describe the student's behavior and its effects. This descriptive confrontation is an "I" message without identifying feelings. In Jimmy's case the teacher might say, "Jimmy, when you talk to Billy while I'm giving directions, it is disrupting the class."

The following suggestions may be useful for determining which style of confrontation to use: (1) When the student's behavior appears intentional or when the student's emotions seem stronger than those of the teacher, an inquiry confrontation may be more appropriate; (2) when the teacher is experiencing strong emotions or is discussing a conflict alone with a student an "I" message may be more appropriate; and (3) when the teacher's emotions are not strong or when the behavior appears inadvertent, a descriptive confrontation may be more useful.

The third step of negotiating conflicts is to *facilitate* a discussion of the problem from the student's point of view. This requires that the teacher make a concerted effort to listen and to clarify the student's opinions of the situation. Paraphrasing students' ideas and reflecting their feelings facilitates a more open dialogue between teachers and students and encourages students to describe their needs and beliefs.

After the initial confrontation, the teacher can usually determine if the student's inappropriate behavior was the result of a minor lapse of judgment or a symptom of a more involved, underlying problem. If the incident appears to stem from the latter, the teacher will usually find it more productive to find a time and place to continue the dialogue in private. If Jimmy, for example, responds to Ms. Mercy's descriptive confrontation with, "I broke my pencil and was just asking Billy for another," she might just hand Jimmy a pencil and end the matter. On the other hand, if Jimmy appears to be using his broken pencil as an excuse to gain some attention by disrupting the class or if he responds with, "This stuff is boring; besides, I'm not talking any more than the others in here," she may want to acknowledge Jimmy's feelings and set a time or place to continue the discussion: "It sounds like you're a bit angry because you think I'm picking on you, Jimmy. I'd like to discuss this with you at the end of the period."

When the conversation resumes, the teacher will want to continue to try to understand the student's feelings, thoughts, and needs:

"Thanks for waiting, Jimmy. It sounds like you're not finding much value in what we were doing in class."

"Yeah, this stuff's for the birds. I don't like doing math."

"Math doesn't seem to be very exciting to you and you would rather talk to Billy than work on your assignment?"

"Yeah, anything to relieve the boredom."

Once the teacher begins to understand the student's perceptions, the next step is to encourage the student to *evaluate* the results of the behavior. The teacher has already decided that the behavior is unacceptable. Now it is up to the student to evaluate the consequences of the behavior for himself and for others in the class. Continuing the example with Jimmy and Ms. Mercy:

"It seems as though there are two problems here, Jimmy. You don't want to do your math because you don't find much interest or enjoyment in it, and you think I'm hassling you when you talk to your friends."

"Yeah, that sums it up pretty good."

"I can understand your boredom with math, Jimmy, and I think there are some ways I can help you find more value in it. I cannot, however, allow you to talk to your friends when you feel like it."

"What are you going to do to me?"

"I don't want to do anything to you, Jimmy, except help you find some value in math."

"Well, that's a lost cause. I just don't like math. I was never very good at it. And besides, all that stuff on dividing fractions really has me confused.

I can't understand how dividing a number by a fraction makes it bigger, and multiplying it by a fraction makes it smaller. I tried to stay with it at the beginning, but now I don't care. I guess I'd just rather walk around and talk to my friends."

"It sounds like if you could understand fractions a little better you wouldn't need to walk around the room so much."

"Yeah, but I'm so confused I'll never be able to understand it. Besides, I like talking to my friends, too."

"I think I can find a way to help you work through all that confusion with fractions, Jimmy, but I can't let you continue to interrupt the class."

"Well, I suppose I could try to not talk to the others during the class."

Since Jimmy has agreed that his behavior is not in his best interest or the best interest of the class, Ms. Mercy can now help him *work out a plan* for alternative behavior. The purpose of this step is to help students find alternative ways of meeting their needs that do not disrupt the class. The plan should include both what Jimmy is not going to do, as well as what he will do. Ms. Mercy could build Jimmy's commitment to the plan by discussing some of the difficulties he may have with keeping it and any changes that might be required in the class that may assist Jimmy in making the plan work. Plans seem to have a greater chance of success when they are suggested by students. In any event, plans must be clearly understood and acceptable to both parties. Continuing the example with Jimmy and Ms. Mercy:

"I'm glad to hear that you are going to try not to interrupt class by talking to your friends, Jimmy. Let's also set up a time when I can help you clear up some of that confusion with fractions."

"I can't come in after school because I have to catch the bus."

"Yes, I thought that would be a problem. We'll have to try to work out another time during the school day. Would you be able to come in during the second half of your lunch period? I have some prep time then."

"Well I usually like to be with my friends then. But I guess I can try it for a while."

"Good, it shouldn't take too long; I think I can get you back on track in a few days."

"Boy, I don't know. I'm so far behind that I don't think I'll ever catch up."

"You sound pretty discouraged."

"Yeah, I guess I am. My dad says I wasn't around the day the good Lord handed out brains. Maybe he's right."

"Oh yes, I remember that day very clearly. And I know you were there because you were sitting three rows ahead of me. As I recall, when the brains were handed out you got out of your seat and started to talk with Billy." [Jimmy breaks out in a big grin.]

"I'll have to tell that to my Dad the next time he says that to me. Boy, will be surprised! [Pause] Do you think you really can help me learn fractions?"

"I'm certain of it, Jimmy. But it's going to take some time and effort on your part."

"Well, I'm willing to give it a try. I'll also try not to talk to Billy and my other friends during class time. Maybe if I can understand fractions I'll be able to do some of my work then."

"That sounds fine to me, Jimmy. When do you want to start?"

"Can we start tomorrow?"

"Fine, I'll see you then."

If Jimmy had been unwilling to discuss his perceptions or explore alternative behaviors, Ms. Mercy may have had to impose a *logical consequence* until Jimmy was willing to agree to try to control his behavior. The use of logical consequence is an attempt to tie the results of unacceptable behavior as closely as possible to the behavior itself. If, for example, a student spills paints during art class, the logical consequence is that he or she cleans them up. Unlike punishment, a logical consequence is logically related as closely as possible to the unacceptable behavior. If the teacher decides to give a detention to the student who spills paints or forces him or her to write a hundred times, "I will be more careful during art class," the teacher is using a punishment rather than logical consequence. While punishment may occasionally stop unacceptable behavior, it often produces anger and resentment on the part of the students, and it has a high possibility of turning the teacher/student relationship into a struggle for power. Driekurs, Grunwald, and Pepper (1982) provide a detailed discussion of the differences between logical consequences and punishment.

Temporarily removing a student from a group or from the class until he or she is willing to follow the rules seems to be a clear and logical consequence of intentional disruptive behavior (Glasser, 1977). In Jimmy's case, the use of a logical consequence was not necessary. However, had he been unwilling to discuss the situation or work out a plan, Ms. Mercy might have had to temporarily remove Jimmy from the group until she could discuss the matter further with him.

Rather than a sequential progression, the final step to negotiating conflicts permeates the entire process. The importance of *encouragement* cannot be overestimated; it forms the foundation of all successful teaching. Encouragement is the process of extending psychological support to students and showing faith in their ability to act responsibly. Inherent in this process is the teacher's belief that students' lack of skills or inappropriate behavior in no way diminishes their value as human beings.

Teachers who have internalized these beliefs and who use the language of encouragement seem to have several characteristics in common:

- They focus on students' assets rather than on their liabilities. They emphasize strengths rather than weaknesses and try to nourish and help students expand on these strengths. Effort and improvement are recognized and appreciated.

- They try to avoid making value judgments about their students' behavior. When they like or dislike something a student does, they say so in a way that avoids judgments of goodness or badness.
- They tend to respond to students in ways that convey acceptance; their students don't have to be perfect to be valued.
- They try to exhibit their confidence and trust in students. They believe that their students can move in positive, responsible directions. This makes it possible for their students to eventually begin to believe this themselves.

Stage Four: Productivity

This is the stage in a group's development when a sense of identity emerges within the class, the members become productive in accomplishing academic tasks, and the emotional and psychological needs of the class members have been acknowledged and supported. The productivity stage is the stage that most teachers hope to reach with their classes. Each student has learned to pull his or her own weight, and "slackers" or "hitchhikers" who let others do all of the work are not tolerated. Members of the class strive for mutual benefit and are actively involved in learning. Clearly, when teachers are able to utilize organizational patterns and leadership styles that guide students to this stage of group cohesion, apathy toward learning becomes significantly reduced. According to McDaniel, "When students learn the joy of working productively together toward common goals, motivation inevitably improves (1984, p. 47).

Attainment of this stage of group development, according to Stanford, is directly related to the development of the norms and skills identified in the previous stages. Groups are unlikely to reach the stage of mutual productivity by chance; patience, skill training, and strong teacher leadership are prerequisites. Furthermore, the dynamics of human interaction require that groups periodically assess how well they are working together and meeting each other's needs so that they can continually examine ways to improve relationships among members (Johnson & Johnson, 1987).

Stage Five: Termination

Termination is the final stage in a group's life. As the semester or year ends, group members recognize that they will be going their separate ways. If the class has remained an aggregate of individuals without having developed a sense of belonging and group identity, this stage is viewed with indifference or relief. However, if the class has established cohesiveness and interdependence, then the emotional bonds that have been developed may make separation a difficult and unsettling period for many students. Teachers may find it helpful to help students discuss and express their feelings about separating so that they can resolve these concerns and move on to new experiences.

Goal Orientation

Chapter 1 proposed that schools are currently producing academic winners and losers in about equal numbers. Although this dichotomy risks oversimplification, most teachers of the upper elementary grades and above can clearly identify hard-working students who concentrate on mastering academic tasks from those who have disengaged from serious academic involvement. A major difference between these two groups of students is that the academic winners have acquired adaptive motivational patterns embedded in personally valued *learning goals*. These students expend high levels of effort toward learning new skills, persist in the face of obstacles, and express a preference for challenging rather than easy tasks. They are strongly influenced by the belief that reasonable effort will lead to success, and, in general, their behavior is directed toward understanding and integrating the knowledge and skills offered by teachers.

Academic losers, on the other hand, demonstrate maladaptive motivational patterns primarily concerned with gaining favorable judgments about their learning ability in order to protect their self-worth. As Dweck (1986) has suggested, they acquire *performance goals* characterized by academic apathy, avoidance of effort, low persistence, and other failure-avoiding strategies previously discussed.

Nicholls (1989) uses the terms *task orientation* and *ego orientation* to describe similar constructs and behavior patterns. In conjunction with his colleagues, he has developed scales to distinguish between the two orientations among high school students. Items such as "I feel most successful in school if I get a new idea about how things work" and "I feel most successful if something I learned really makes sense to me" measure task orientation. Ego orientation is measured by items like "I feel most successful if I score higher than other students" and "I feel most successful if I do better than other students" (Nicholls, 1989, p. 96). As one might expect, Nicholls's research indicated that students who scored highest on task orientation expressed more satisfaction with school learning, while those scoring highest on ego orientation acknowledged more academic alienation and a desire to avoid schoolwork (Nicholls, 1989).

In addition to task and ego goals, Maehr (1984) identified two additional goal categories to describe student achievement patterns in school: *Social solidarity goals,* which are concerned with students' desires to gain social approval from parents, teachers, or peers, and *extrinsic rewards,* which are associated with earning grades, money, or prizes. Maehr hypothesized that when students were confronted with challenging tasks, they would respond according to their goal orientation. Students with task goals would be highly motivated to undertake moderate challenges; these were the success-oriented students who were more motivated to attain success than to avoid failure. Ego-oriented students would respond similarly if they had a high sense of confidence in their ability, but they would avoid moderate challenges and seek easy or extremely difficult challenges if they had a low sense of confidence; these were the failure-avoiding students mentioned earlier in this chapter and described by Dweck in Figure 3-1. Students with social solidarity goals would be highly motivated to succeed, regardless of the difficulty level of the challenge. These students, according to Maehr, would show little preference for or opposition to challenges, since their primary purpose was to please others. Finally, extrinsically oriented students would be motivated to take the easiest path to the highest reward. They would have discovered that there is little value in confronting a challenge when one is primarily concerned with gaining an extrinsic payoff; it is the reward, not the challenge, that they seek.

Because of the similarities between task and learning goals and between ego and performance goals, Ames and Archer (1988) have integrated these goal orientations by using the terms *mastery goals* to describe the former and *performance goals* to describe the latter. When students pursue performance goals, they are primarily concerned with gaining favorable judgments about their ability relative to that of others; when pursuing mastery goals, they are more concerned with developing new skills and understanding course content.

While academic winners and losers vary in their goal orientations, the personality of a classroom can have a significant effect on the goal orientation embraced by each student. Table 5-4 provides a performance and mastery goal analysis of different classroom personalities or climate dimensions. When grade competition is emphasized or when students are subjected to repeated social comparisons in regard to achievement, some pursue the goal of gaining favorable judgments about their ability by working hard at getting the highest grade in the class, being the first finished, or achieving a higher score than the person at the next desk. Others attempt to protect unfavorable perceptions about their ability by withholding effort or by resorting to some of the other failure-avoiding strategies discussed in Chapter 3.

However, when the personality of the classroom is characterized by support for student cooperation and self-improvement, clearly defined outcomes that can be attained through reasonable effort, and an inclusive view of success, students become oriented toward mastery goals. Under these conditions, students define success in terms of improvement and competence, value success through effort, view mistakes as part of the learning process, and focus on acquiring information and learning skills.

Research by Ames and Archer (1988) indicates that when students perceive their classroom as emphasizing a mastery orientation, they have

TABLE 5-4   Classroom Achievement Personality and Student Goal Orientation

Achievement Dimensions	Classroom Personality Characteristics	Goal Orientation Reinforced
Success	A) Defined by high normative performance; grade competition	Performance
	B) Defined by improvement, progress, and competence	Mastery
Mistakes	A) Always penalized; to be avoided; elicit anxiety and failure-avoiding behavior	Performance
	B) Natural part of the learning process	Mastery
What is Valued	A) Having more ability than others; competition	Performance
	B) Success through effort; cooperation	Mastery
Evaluation Criteria	A) Performance relative to others; frequency distributions; ranking on the curve; no retests	Performance
	B) Progress toward absolute performance standards on clearly defined outcomes; retests encouraged	Mastery
Focus of Attention	A) How students are performing; performing better and faster than others	Performance
	B) How students are learning; acquiring information and skills	Mastery

Adapted from Ames (in press, b) and Ames and Archer (1988).

a more positive attitude toward the class, prefer challenging assignments within the class, and have a stronger belief that success follows from one's efforts than do students who do not perceive their classroom as emphasizing a mastery orientation. Furthermore, when students perceive their classrooms as emphasizing a performance orientation based on competition and social comparisons, they evaluate their ability more negatively, and they are more likely to attribute their failures to lack of ability.

Ames and Archer's research indicates that if teachers can decrease their emphasis on social and normative comparisons within classrooms, they are likely to reduce students' tendency to focus on their ability and to evaluate it negatively. Yet this change does not ensure that students will substitute mastery goals for performance goals. If we want students to seek challenging tasks, to develop more positive attitudes, and to expend reasonable effort toward learning, we must develop classroom personalities that are specifically designed to foster mastery goals.

Target Structures

With this in mind, Epstein (1989) proposed a framework for identifying the manipulatable structures within a classroom that can contribute to the development of mastery goals. using the acronym TARGET to label these structures, she defines task, authority, reward, grouping, evalution, and time as the six broad categories within a classroom that can be manipulated by the teacher to create a classroom personality that supports mastery goals.

Task Structure (T)

The task structure within a classroom deals with the organization, composition, and design of the learning tasks or activities that teachers require of students. According to Epstein, "It includes the content and sequence of the curriculum, the design of classwork and homework, the level of difficulty of the work, and the materials required to complete assignments" (1989, p. 93). While the specific objectives and outcomes required of a particular grade or class are usually predetermined, most teachers have considerble flexibility in determining how to design instructional activities to reach these outcomes. The difficulty level and requirements of assignments, for example, may be identical for all students or may be tailored to fit individual or small-group needs. Teachers may design tasks that emphasize a didactic, linear approach or tasks that are organized to emphasize a discovery or problem-solving structure.

To foster mastery goals in all students, it is incumbent upon teachers to structure tasks that provide challenges to both faster- and slower-learning students. By understanding the skills and prior knowledge of students, and by tailoring assignments to these individual differences, teachers can design learning activities that are neither too easy for some nor too difficult for others. While clearly stated performance standards may be required of all students, it is only by varying the structure of learning tasks that all students can experience success through reasonable effort, thereby ensuring progress toward achieving these outcomes.

Authority Structure (A)

The authority structure within the classroom, according to Epstein, concerns the nature of decision making as it occurs between teachers and students. "In some settings, authority is exercised only by the teacher; in other settings, teachers and students share responsibilities for making choices, giving directions, monitoring work, setting and enforcing rules, establishing and offering rewards, and evaluating student success and teacher quality" (1989, p. 94). While the primary authority or control within a classroom clearly rests with the teacher, how the teacher shares this control can influence students' commitment to the learning process.

However, teachers can share authority and control only if they have it. There are some classrooms, particularly in middle and high schools, where the students have assumed control, either through abdication on the part of the teacher or after a prolonged and intense power struggle. Needless to say, these classrooms have developed personalities that have allowed socializing and wasting time to replace academic learning. Furthermore, in environments in which students value physical retaliation and personal power over others, shared authority is often perceived as weakness. So-called "democratic" or "humanistic" teachers are laughed at, ridiculed, and pushed around. Foster (1974) has documented many examples of these conflicts. In addition, his *Four-Phase Rites of Passage* describes the process whereby many teachers learn to share control within the classroom.

Adapted by Raffini (1980), the first phase in this developmental process is *permissivism.* Uncertain about their relationship with students and wanting to avoid the role of "dictator," many new teachers approach the class with a warm, friendly disposition, hoping that by treating the students as "adults" they will respond in mature ways. This is often a difficult and frustrating time for new teachers. Wanting to like and be liked by students, the insecurities of beginning teachers often cause them to personalize most things students say and do. Desperately wanting to feel successful and liked, these new teachers are shocked by the realities of some classrooms. Foster's description of his first day as a teacher in an inner-city school can bring nightmares to anyone who must face such an environment for the first time:

> Next, I discovered a new word: "Teach." One of my students walked up to me and said, "Hey, Teach, we work a period, read comics a period, and then take off the last period—Ok?" To which I replied with something like, "Look, I'm a vet, and I'm the teacher now. I intend to stay and we are going to work all three periods. You guys are not going to drive me out of here the way you drove out all those other teachers."
>
> From then on everything seemed to happen at once. Someone crumpled up a piece of paper and threw it at me. A near miss. I thought of my Psychology I and II courses ("make a joke out of things" or "decontaminate through humor") and said, "If that's the best you can do, you better hang up." Whereupon all hell broke loose. The class showed me they could do better!
>
> Students ran across the table tops throwing T-squares and drawing boards. Others ran in and out of the room. The noise was deafening. T-squares and drawing board missiles flew through the air. The classroom was not only noisy but dangerous. And do you know what I did? You know that section in the teacher's desk where the teacher puts his legs when he sits down? I hid there—in the kneehole.

After what seemed like an enternity, five or six teachers stuck their heads into the room to see what was going on. I looked up sheepishly from my shelter without saying a word. Since the din continued even with their presence, they threw both doors open and my students took off. (1986, p. 12)

The second phase in the "rite of passage" for teachers is called *disillusionment*. This is the period of rejection and chaos during which many teachers question their beliefs and aspirations. Confused and isolated, the teacher may reassess his or her career goals or may simply "blame" the students and/or the system for being so primitive and unresponsive. When disillusionment sets in, teachers can choose to either grovel in self-pity, find an "easier" school, leave the profession, or move to phase three.

The third developmental phase experienced by most teachers is *control*. This is when the teacher begins to establish order out of the chaos. Firmness and resolve become essential. As Foster says, "At this phase, some sensitive teachers begin to hate themselves for what they are doing in the name of discipline. (I tell new teachers when they begin to hate themselves for this toughness, they are beginning to grow and make it as teachers . . .)" (1974, p. 243).

Many teachers reject shared authority and quasi-democratic teaching during this phase. Finding themselves saying and doing all the things they hated other teachers for saying and doing, they feel betrayed by their democratic philosophy and are no longer willing to trust students. They have equated democracy and humanism with first-phase permissivism and, after a painful period of disillusionment, have rejected both.

A small number of teachers eventually move beyond phase 3 to phase 4: *humanism*. Again, Foster's description is valuable:

The phase 4 classroom has a relaxed atmosphere where feelings are expressed. The students have run their testing games and have learned the teacher's limits. Learning takes place in this positive, structured, yet relaxed atmosphere. Students move around the room knowing that no one will pick on them, that no one will steal their clothing from the closet, and that their teacher is fair and will answer their questions. He respects them and they respect him. Their teacher is in charge and in control; and they can now relax. (1974, p. 243)

The transition from phase 3 to phase 4 is not easy; few teachers make it. Foster estimates that between 70 and 80 percent of the teachers in ghetto schools are fixated at phase 3. Distrustful of students, they are continuously on guard, maintaining control through fear and busywork.

Control and authority are necessary in the classroom—learning cannot take place in chaos. Establishing control, however, does not mean that teachers must disregard an understanding of student needs and interests.

Firmness is necessary in the classroom, but it need not be derived from totalitarianism. When it is based on holding students accountable for their behaviors and enforcing logical consequences rather than punishments, students will begin to believe that they have a place in the classroom and that they can achieve success through reasonable effort. It is only when control is established through firmness and fairness, and then shared, that a classroom's personality will encourage student motivation toward mastery goals.

Reward Structure (R)

The reward structure in a classroom, according to Epstein, concerns the procedures and practices used by teachers to reinforce student achievement. Teachers can be highly selective when distributing rewards, or they can be quite generous in determining what students, behaviors, and achievements are worthy of reinforcement. As discussed in the previous chapter, when rewards are used to undermine student autonomy, they may extinguish intrinsic motivation and undermine self-regulation.

Yet rewards do define the achievements and behaviors that teachers consider important, and when rewards are used to convey information about student comptence at these activities, they can enhance students' motivation to learn. Epstein believes that in most schools only a few students receive the official recognition and reinforcement conveyed by rewards. She suggests that if teachers try to keep in mind a student's *history* of past accomplishments and skills, *plans* or goals for which a student is striving, and *outcomes,* or actual accomplishments, it will be possible to design reward structures that more widely acknowledge the efforts and achievements of all students. Knowing students' past accomplishments and goals, for example, can help teachers keep a record of students' "personal best" accomplishments and thus reward student improvements more fairly. According to Epstein:

> *[O]f the three elements of evaluation—history, plans, and outcomes— only outcomes regulate the reward structure in most subjects in most schools. If the reward structure is ignored, teachers may find that their distributions of grades, honors, and other awards support and boost the energies of some students, while the same practices alienate and destroy the energies of others (1989, p. 95)*

Group Structure (G)

Grouping structure concerns the manner in which students are segregated and grouped for instructional activities. Few practices in education are as controversial as grouping and tracking students according to their academic ability. Those who argue in favor of ability grouping believe that teachers can do a better job of meeting student needs when the variance in student achievement is reduced through combining or tracking students of similar abilities. According to Walberg, "Educators should be realistic about individual differences. Teaching students what they already know or are as yet incapable of knowing wastes effort. We can't simultaneously teach consumer mathematics and calculus" (ASCD, 1989, p. 5). Scott makes a similar argument when he asserts that ability grouping is crucial to restoring America's stature as a world power:

> *Teachers are confronted by a wide range of student abilities. The academic achievement spread in a 10th grade class can span a dozen grade levels. Elimination of ability grouping would place an inordinate burden on teachers. In responding to varied learning needs, teachers have three primary instruction options: they can expect all students to adhere to rigorous academic standards, they can teach for the average student, or they can "dump down" the material. The first option is politically unacceptable, the second invites frustration and disengagement from less able students, and the third is likely to elicit boredom and mischief from more capable students. (ASCD, 1989, p. 5)*

The strongest support for ability grouping seems to come from those concerned with the effects of heterogeneous groups on the more able students. According to Feldhusen:

> *Grouping gifted and talented youth for a least part of the school day and offering a differentiated curriculum leads to higher achievement, engenders better attitudes and motivation, and does no harm to less able youth. Failure to do so will increase the ranks of the gifted underachievers and continue the low standing of American students in international comparisons. (ASCD, 1989, p. 4)*

Those on the other side of the controversy oppose ability grouping and tracking because it perpetuates educational inequity by locking large numbers of students into groups that are stereotyped as incapable of learning. According to Slavin:

> *Students assigned to lower groups or tracks are less likely to graduate or go on to college than are students of the same ability assigned to higher tracks. Their teachers have lower expectations for them and may teach at too slow a pace. In integrated schools, tracking usually creates racially identifiable groups, which can create inequities along racial or ethnic lines. For these reasons, grouping by ability should be avoided as much as possible, and used only when there is a clear educational justification (ASCD, 1989, p. 4)*

An even stronger indictment comes from Jeannie Oakes of the RAND Corporation, who has spent many years researching the effects of ability grouping:

> *Nearly all ability grouping schemes place limits on most students' access to high-quality learning opportunities. The highest groups usually get the best teachers; learn the most rigorous, challenging, and interesting curriculums; and are bolstered by high expectations. Top track classes spend more time on learning and less on discipline, socializing, or classroom routines. Teachers give them more homework. Top group teachers typically show more enthusiasm, make instruction clearer, and are less likely to criticize or ridicule. Learning tasks are better organized and more varied.*
>
> *Such differences point to ironic school inequities. Students who need more time to learn get less; those who have the most difficulty learning get the poorer instruction. Poor and minority children are disproportionately affected by these factors. (ASCD, 1989, p. 4)*

Stipek (1988), quoting comments made by elementary school children in an earlier study, provides a direct and personal view of ability grouping:

> *Kids in the bottom group don't care . . . I'm in the high group . . . Kids in the other other groups are retards.*
>
> *They're just not good enough.*
>
> *Makes me feel like I'm not much good. This puts you off school and soon you spend most of your time trying to avoid work.*
>
> *Being in the low group you feel like, well, you're being put there out of the way. It's sort of a punishment for being too dumb to do the work.*
>
> *You feel that if other kids can do it, why can't you . . . there has to be something wrong. (p. 126)*

Clearly, it is beyond the scope of this discussion to explore the research supporting and refuting each of the positions on ability grouping. As Oakes suggests, however, as "educators become increasingly disenchanted with tracking, they may not need to throw out the baby (possible benefits to the top students) with the bathwater (likely disadvantages to the rest)" (1988, p. 42).

By viewing ability as a malleable rather than fixed trait and by restructuring classrooms to allow for differences in learning speeds, it may be possible for teachers to help students of all abilities benefit from being taught together. Ames (1991) suggests that when classrooms provide flexible and heterogeneous grouping arrangements, and when they allow students multiple grouping opportunities, student motivation to learn can be enhanced.

Evaluation Structure (E)

The fifth classroom structure identified by the TARGET acronym that supports mastery goals is evaluation. This structure concerns the manner by which teachers establish expectations and measure and judge student performance relative to these expectations. Chapter 2 provides an extended discussion of the effects of criterion- and norm-referenced evaluation procedures on student motivation to learn. According to Epstein (1989):

> *An effective evaluation structure—with important, challenging, yet attainable standards, fair and clear procedures for monitoring progress, and explicit and frequent information about progress—should lead students to a higher level of understanding about their own effort, abilities and improvement. An ineffective structure can embarrass or confuse students and misdirect their efforts for improvement, by withholding information on what and how to improve, or by setting standards too high to attain. (p. 97)*

Since norm-referenced evaluation artificially restricts the number of students that can experience success, it seems evident that when student achievement is compared to clearly stated performance standards and when students are given adequate time to master necessary skills, most students will be motivated to learn, since they will have a reasonable opportunity to experience success from their efforts.

Time Structure (T)

The final manipulable classroom structure that can foster mastery goals is the amount of time allocated to learning tasks. As Spady (1988) has suggested, the current educational paradigm is based on keeping instructional time a constant. Biology, for example, is usually what high school students learn for forty-five minutes a day during the 180 instructional days of their freshman or sophomore year. Of course, achievement in biology varies considerably among students. Spady argues that outcome-based learning is designed around a major reversal in these variables; achievement needs to become the constant, and time the variable. If we want all students to attain the same high level of mastery or competence in biology, then we may need to allow slower-learning students forty-five, sixty, or ninety minutes a day for 180, 250, or even 300 instructional days to attain the same high level of competence. If a competent level of achievement is to be a constant, then time *must* be a variable.

Ongoing research by Carole Ames and her associates at the University of Illinois (Ames, in press a, b, 1990; Ames & Archer, 1988) focuses on helping teachers use the TARGET dimensions to develop mastery-oriented experiences for at-risk students. After searching the motivational literature to identify general and specific strategies and principles that support a mastery-oriented philosophy and goal structure, Ames grouped these strategies and principles into the six manipulable classroom categories identified by the TARGET acronym. Table 5-5 provides a summary of these mastery-oriented motivational strategies. In Ames's experimental design (Ames, 1990), elementary teachers were encouraged to use as many of these strategies as they could in their classroom instructional procedures but were instructed to use strategies from at least one TARGET area each week. Preliminary results of the Ames research indicated that when teachers attempted to systematically create mastery-oriented goals within their classrooms, they were able to arrest the downward trend in motivation that tends to characterize at-risk students. According to Ames (in press b):

> *When the environment conveys a mastery goal orientation, children are more likely to exhibit adaptive motivational processes. An approach to restructuring the environment requires identifying those principles and strategies that will make a mastery orientation salient to the individual participants. With this approach, "motivational training"*

TABLE 5-5 Motivational Strategies within TARGET Areas

TARGET Area	Strategies
Task	Design activities for variety, individual challenge, and active involvement. Help children set realistic, short-term goals.
Authority	Involve children in decision making and leadership roles. Help students develop self-management and self-monitoring skills.
Recognition	Recognize individual progress and improvement. Ensure equal opportunities for rewards. Focus on each child's self-worth.
Grouping	Use flexible and heterogeneous grouping arrangements. Provide for multiple grouping arrangements.
Evaluation	Use criteria of individual progress, improvement, and mastery. Involve children in self-evaluation. Make evaluation private and meaningful.
Time	Provide opportunities and time for improvement. Help children establish work and practice schedules.

Adapted From "Achievement Goals, Motivational Climate, and Motivational Precesses" C. Ames. In *Motivation in Sport and Exercise* (pp. 173) by G.C. Roberts (Ed.), 1992. Champaign, IL: Human Kinetics. Copyright 1992 by Human Kinetics Publishers, Inc. Adapted by permission.

involves a comprehensive restructuring which focuses on ways to envelop children's experience with mastery goal principles. It involves changing the strategies and practices of the teacher, parent, or leader.

A prerequisite to the development of mastery goals is the establishment of a psychologically safe classroom; a prerequisite to a psychologically safe classroom is the belief by students that their self-worth will be protected and that success can be experienced from reasonable effort. Table 5-4 is a useful starting point for teachers interested in creating a classroom personality that downplays performance goals and emphasizes the development of mastery goals. Once teachers are committed to helping students develop mastery goals within each of these personality dimensions, then the TARGET catagories can be manipulated to reinforce mastery learning experiences for all students. Table 5-5 provides a useful list of instructional strategies or suggestions for helping teachers create a mastery-oriented learning environment.

Although the fifty motivational strategies in the next five chapters are designed to meet specific psychological and academic needs of students in classrooms, all are compatible and useful for helping teachers develop mastery-goal orientations. To assist in this process, the TARGET areas appropriate to each strategy have been identified.

6

Enhancing Student Self-Esteem

The Pimple*

He was so proud of his handsome face;
Just the right eyes in just the right place,
His perfect nose and his perfect chin
Above and below his beautiful grin
And surrounded by his satiny skin.

He started each day in front of the mirror
Admiring his hair, his brow, and his ear or
Touching his jaw with its wonderful dimple.
He was so beautiful, life was so simple—
Until the day he discovered—a pimple!

There it was, on his perfect nose,
As big as a ski hill, as red as a rose,
Right on the tip, where he couldn't hide it,
Where his perfection could not have denied it—
It sat like an egg, and someone had fried it.

He smeared it with cream, he dabbed it with powder,
He rubbed on an ointment, a smelly thick chowder
That was intended to dry up that lump,
That scarlet and screaming and insolent hump
On his perfect nose, an imperfect bump.

He squeezed it and probed it and pushed it and pricked it;
Too bad. It would have been wish to predict it
Would only get bigger and bigger instead,
This ugly volcano so angry and red
On his perfect nose. He wished he were dead.

He went to school with his visor pulled down,
His once perfect face in a wrinkled frown,
His shoulders hunched in a slinking pose,
Hoping that no one would notice there rose
A gigantic pimple on his perfect nose.

*From R. Larson (1991), *Why is a Wild Pig Called a Boar? Poems for Kids Growing Up, and Adults Growing Down* by Richard Larson, Ph.D. Copyright 1991 by Richard Larson, reproduced by permission of the author.

As he walked with his imperfection,
There came down the hall from the other direction
The girl of his dreams, the one who inspired
The wish to look perfect that he so desired;
Perfection was what her presence required!

She came ever closer; when she was near,
He lowered his head, his heart full of fear
That she would catch sight of the hill that grew
On his nose. It was then that he knew
That he was finished, his life was through.

But he peeked up as she sauntered by.
He thought she looked different but didn't know why,
Until she turned toward him to expose
A flowering, burgundy, full blooming rose
That grew on the tip of her beautiful nose.

He lowered his shoulders, he lifted his face.
He took off his cap, and felt no disgrace
As he displayed for public inspection
His now unimportant, small imperfection.
He turned and he hurried in her direction.

RICHARD LARSON (1991)

AFTER EXTENSIVE TESTIMONY and deliberation, the California Task Force to Promote Self-Esteem and Personal Social Responsibility defined *self-esteem* as appreciating one's own worth and importance, having the character to be accountable for one's self, and acting responsibly toward others (Reasoner, 1982). This three-part definition is useful to educators who are looking for methods and strategies to increase student self-esteem and motivation to learn. Before examining each component of this definition, it may be useful to distinguish the term *self-esteem* from *self-concept*. As indicated in Chapter 2, a person's self-concept is the picture or perceptions that the individual holds of his or her strengths, weaknesses, abilities, values, and temperament. Self-esteem, like self-worth or self-value, refers to the judgment of merit or value that an individual places on the various facets of the self (Kaplan, 1990). For example, a student might have a self-concept that includes being an uncoordinated athlete, but it is the value he or she places on athletics that determines how this self-view will effect the self-esteem.

The first component of the California Task Force's definition of self-esteem concerns recognizing the significance of one's inherent worth and importance as a human being. According to Reasoner:

Being alive as a human being has an innate importance, an importance to which the Declaration of Independence refers when it declares that all people "are endowed by their Creator with certain unalienable rights . . .". This conviction concerning the dignity of every human personality has long been a part of our nation's moral and religious heritage. Every person has unique significance, simply because the precious and mysterious gift of life as a human being has been given. This is an inherent value which no adversary or adversity can take away. (1982, p. 9)

Glasser (1969) has suggested that in order to help students value their inherent worth, teachers should attempt to treat all students with kindness, courteous, and respect at all times—*regardless of how they treat the teacher.* The last phrase, of course, is what makes Glasser's suggestion so difficult to implement. It's easy to be friendly and courteous to students who respond in kind. Yet it is the failure-avoiding students who hide behind facades of anger, cynicism, or apathy who can benefit most from our encouragement and respect and who, because of their behavior, are the least likely to receive it.

As discussed in Chapter 2, Covington's self-worth motive holds that an individual's desire to enhance and to protect his or her self-worth is fundamental to all human motivation; people seek experiences that generate feelings of pride and accomplishment, and they avoid experiences that cause them to feel valueless. The preceding chapters have discussed several factors inherent in the practices of many schools that denigrate opportunities for "appreciating one's own worth and importance." It is the purpose of this chapter to focus on specific recommendations and strategies that can help students at all grade levels feel more significant and more valued.

The second component of the Task Force's definition deals with "having the character to be accountable for one's self." Character, according to Reasoner, proceeds from a healthy, positive sense of self-worth and must be nurtured, both in the home and in the school. As Reasoner suggests, "there is no fully adequate substitute for a loving family as the environment in which people learn to appreciate their own worth" (1982, p. 10). Yet the reality in current classrooms is that large numbers of students come to school without having experienced a loving family. To increase the chances of enhancing positive self-esteem in students, teachers have little choice but to build classroom personalities that nurture human integrity, character, and accountability.

The last part of the Task Force definition, "acting responsibly toward others," suggests that all individuals need to learn to respect the uniqueness of others as they learn to value their own. Valuing the differences among others requires that students have a solid base of self-worth and a willingness to listen to the thoughts and feelings of their peers. The insecurities and self-doubt of many students, however, make establishing this base a much more difficult task than it appears. It requires that teachers consciously and systematically provide activities that help students experience their uniqueness and worth, learn skills of empathetic listening, and assume responsibility for their own behavior. Teachers should find the suggestions and strategies in this chapter useful in this process.

Borba (1989), drawing on the earlier work of Reasoner, has clarified five components characteristic of individuals considered to have high self-esteem. All of the components—security, self-hood, affiliation, mission, and competence—can be influenced by teachers. While each of the five components clearly contributes to one's judgment of self-worth, some authors have considered each as a separate human need (need Chapter 2). For our purposes, the affiliation and competence components of self-esteem will be considered separately; strategies for enhancing students' sense of affiliation or belonging will be discussed in Chapter 9, and strategies to enhance students' need for competence will be considered in Chapter 8.

Security

Consistent with Maslow's hierarchy of needs, Borba and Reasoner have argued that the security component of self-esteem is a prerequisite to all other components. Students who have developed a sense of security feel safe and secure in their environment, know what is expected and required of them, and feel assured in their faith and trust of others. Building a teacher/student relationship based on trust and mutual respect can help students begin to value their worth as human beings. The seminal research of Stanley Coopersmith (1967), based on an analysis of the antecedents of students with high self-esteem, found that unconditional acceptance from parents and significant others was significantly related to a student's positive self-image. Unconditional acceptance, of course, implies that one is valued regardless of individual weaknesses or shortcomings. It does not, however, mean agreement. Acceptance means we take what a person says or does as being real for them—not for us. It implies that we can reject a student's behavior without rejecting the student.

Acceptance of students is shown through *empathy,* which simply means letting people know that we are trying to understand their feelings and concerns. It's not enough, however, to just say that one understands; many people remember parents or teachers saying they understood a feeling or situation when clearly they did not. The skills of paraphrasing and reflecting feelings, discussed in Chapter 5, represent essential feedback that shows people they are being understood. While empathetic and facilitative listening and responding are learned skills, they also require a philosophy toward teaching and students based on the following beliefs regarding acceptance:

1. Teachers have to *want* to hear about their students' concerns and have to take the time and effort to get involved. They have to genuinely want to be helpful.
2. While not always agreeing, teachers must be willing to accept students' feelings as being real for *them,* whatever those feelings may be or however different they may be from those of others.
3. Teachers need to have a deep feeling of *trust* in students' capacity to handle their feelings, to work through their problems, and to find their own solutions.
4. Teachers must be able to see students as persons separate from themselves—as distinct individuals—with their own lives and own identities.

Suggestions for organizing classrooms to develop student unity, discussed in the previous chapter, are also useful for building a sense of trust and security in the classroom, thereby enhancing student self-esteem. In addition, Reasoner (1982) offers the following four suggestions for establishing a classroom climate or personality that fosters a sense of security in students:

1. *Set realistic limits.* Students need to know what behaviors are expected of them and what behaviors are inappropriate within the classroom. It seems generally agreed that broad parameters with clearly defined limits, procedures, routines, and expectations help students feel secure.

2. *Enforce rules consistently.* Clearly defined rules are of little value when they are seldom or capriciously enforced. By using natural and logical consequences rather than punishments (see Chapter 5), teachers can help students learn to assume responsibility for their own behavior within a safe and secure climate.

3. *Encourage the development of self-respect and responsibility.* Put-downs, sarcasm, and ridicule have no place in the classroom for the simple reason that, although they may stop or change a student's behavior, they undermine the student's self-respect and dignity. Students learn responsibility by being encouraged to explore their behavioral options and being held accountable for their behavioral choices. There is no contradiction between friendliness and firmness in the classroom—neither doormats nor dictators help students develop self-respect and responsibility.

4. *Build trust.* Building trust in a classroom is a slow process and results from many small incidents in which the teacher has responded honestly and dependably. It is easy to trust "trustable" students, but it is the "untrustable" students who need systematic trust-building experiences. For example, when Mr. Hart asks Jimmy—who is notorious for his recalcitrance, poor attendance, and negative attitude—if he thinks he can take the attendance list to the office and be back within two minutes, he is providing Jimmy with an opportunity to be trustworthy. While some

students may occasionally abuse this trust, they need repeated opportunities to learn and practice this character trait.

Selfhood

The *selfhood* component of self-esteem, according to Borba, deals with the development of feelings of individuality; for Reasoner, it is a process of establishing one's sense of identity. Both authors use the term synonymously with self-concept. As previously defined, self-concept is an individual's perceptions of his or her attributes and roles. Through the use of positive feedback, teachers can help students establish an awareness of their unique characteristics while they learn to develop more accurate self-descriptions. This requires, of course, that students' strengths be recognized as teachers and students establish a trusting and accepting relationship. Assisting students to identify and express their emotions and opinions is also effective in helping them perceive their individuality (Borba, 1989).

Starting when they are young children, the self-concept of students evolves from the feedback they receive from others and from their own self-evaluation. The process of establishing a sense of identity becomes important during adolescence and revolves around one's search for an answer to the question "Who am I?" In the early 1960s, psychologist Erik Erikson proposed a psychosocial theory of human development that described a series of stages or psychosocial crises that people pass through in the process of their lfetimes that significantly shape their personality (Erikson, 1963). It is during stage five, ages 12 to 18, that students struggle to find out who they are and where they are going. The positive outcome of this search is the formation of a solid and secure sense of personal identity. This process of self-definition is not always easily resolved. Some adolescents fail to honestly confront the question of who they are, choosing instead to conform to the identity described by expectations of their parents or peers. (Edgar Friedenburg poignantly describes this process in his book *The Vanishing Adolescent.*)

Other individuals become overwhelmed by the question of self-identity and leave adolescence with a sense of emptiness and confusion. While periods of confusion are a natural part of the process of establishing a firm identity, these individuals seem to drift aimlessly through their adolescent years, as if trying to cross an ocean in a rudderless boat with no clue how to jury rig it.

It is easy for teachers to become impatient with the confusion and inconsistency that are frustrating but necessary byproducts of self-definition. Students need encouragement to explore their options, feedback on their strengths and weaknesses, and unconditional acceptance if they are to make successful landfalls in the voyage to selfhood.

Mission

Similar to self-identity, establishing a sense of mission or purpose in life is another component of self-esteem identified by Borba (1989) and Reasoner (1982). Students with high self-esteem are more likely to succeed in life because they have a clear sense of direction regarding their priorities and their goals. They are able to reflect on their plans and aspirations and then take the necessary steps to achieve success.

The interdependence of ambition and goal-direction, high self-esteem, and motivation to learn makes it difficult to ferret out cause-and-effect relationships. In this analysis, it seems reasonable to assume that students who have a purpose in life have high self-esteem and are motivated to accomplish their goals. It is, therefore, useful to teachers to help students improve their ability to make decisions, set realistic goals, and monitor progress toward accomplishing their ambitions.

The following chapter, "Enhancing Student Autonomy," provides a discussion of the steps involved in setting and achieving attainable goals. It seems more appropriate to place the discussion of individual goal-setting within the context of student autonomy because helping students set goals allows them to encounter the process of choice, a fundamental prerequisite of self-determined behavior.

Recommendations for Enhancing Student Self-Esteem

The following recommendations to improve student self-esteem were gleaned from many sources and were selected for their adaptability to all grades and subjects. Teachers who consistently and systematically implement these ideas can expect to see increased self-esteem in their students. While this objective makes these recommendations valuable in their own right, teachers can also expect that students with high self-esteem will also become more predispositioned to expend effort at mastering learning tasks.

1. *Set high expectations for all students and assist students in achieving them.* There is ample evidence that teacher expectations can generate self-fulfilling prophecies. As Haim Escalentes, the Los Angeles math teacher whose behavior inspired the film *Stand and Deliver,* has so clearly demonstrated, students will rise or fall to the level of expectation of their teachers. Self-esteem grows from the beliefs of others. When teachers believe in students, students believe in themselves. When those you respect think you can, *you* think you can.

2. *Provide all students with ample amounts of positive information feedback.* Positive information feedback is positive, descriptive feedback regarding student strengths, achievements, attitude, deportment, skills, or social behaviors. Most importantly, this feedback provides students with information rather than judgments. Saying, "Good work, Jimmy" is a vague value judgment; it provides little information. It is more enhancing to Jimmy's self-esteem if the teacher says, "I've enjoyed reading your paper, Jimmy. Your ideas about the causes of the war are clearly described." The second statement, while taking more time to write, shows appreciation for Jimmy's effort and identifies his strengths.

3. *Always try to explain the reason or purpose for rules, assignments, and learning activities.* Research reviewed by Brophy (1986) suggested that the failure of teachers to identify the purposes and values of assignments was a major reason for low student motivation. In more than 100 hours of observing elementary teachers, Brophy noted that of the 250 statements made in the process of introducing assignments or tasks, "not one of the teachers made any reference to the fact that students could derive personal satisfaction from developing their knowledge or skills" (1986, p. 8). When pressured to increase student performance, it is easy to forget to teach the value and purpose of the assignments themselves. Only by drawing attention to the value of activities students are expected to complete can teachers help students experience the personal importance and satisfaction that accompanies achievement.

4. *Learn something unique about all your students and occasionally mention it to them.* It is useful to have the students describe on a 3 × 5 card something they believe makes them unique from others in the class. This difference may be a physical trait, an accomplishment, a personal belief, or any other characteristic or experience that only they possess. The teacher can then comment or discuss this uniqueness with the student individually. If students agree, these unique characteristics and experiences can also be shared with the class (see Strategy 6.2).

5. *Value students' efforts as well as their accomplishments.* Hard work and concentrated effort, regardless of outcome, need to be appreciated and reinforced. Repeated effort without success can lead to discouragement and apathy. It is important, therefore, that teachers task-analyze assignments and match components to the skills of the student, so that concentrated effort can lead to success.

6. *Help students learn to accept their mistakes and successes by modelling self-analysis of errors and achievements.* Some students respond defensively when they make an error, while others seem to deny or negate their successes and accomplishments. Modelling self-talk that demonstrates your acceptance of mistakes or reinforces you achievements helps students appreciate their own strengths and limitations (e.g., "It looks like I have added incorrectly; being a fallible human being, I'll have to be more careful next time," or "I feel wonderful about today's lesson; I worked hard preparing it, and everyone met the objectives."

7. *Accept students as valuable, worthwhile human beings, although you may have to reject particular behaviors.* It is often difficult to distinguish

between what a student does and who a student is. When we must stop a student's behavior or when a student fails to behave as expected, we must endeavor to communicate our concern, frustration, or anger in a way that separates the behavior from the person. This requires that we avoid evaluating the student as a person and focus exclusively on the student's behavior. Students are not bad, inconsiderate, or mean for what they do—although, at times, specific behavior may be all of those things. We are all more than what we do, so there is never reason to give up on students.

8. *Celebrate the accomplishments and achievements of all students.* This can be done during the class, but it is important to avoid embarrassing students. Short notes or comments on papers can be especially valuable for recognizing the accomplishments of all students. It may be helpful to remember that "we can complain because rose bushes have thorns, or we can rejoice because thorn bushes have roses." We must see through student misbehaviors to find attributes that we can acknowledge and support.

9. *Encourage students to evaluate their behavior relative to their goals and prior level of achievement.* Help students keep a record of their achievements so that they can observe improvement and progress toward their goals. Personal journals, in which students can also be encouraged to include their feelings about themselves, are particularly useful for this purpose. Students experience genuine success when they make progress along the path that leads to clearly defined goals.

10. *Create a psychologically safe climate in which students are encouraged to express their opinions and risk being different.* A psychologically safe classroom is one that protects all students from ridicule and embarrassment. It takes courage to be different, and students need support and encouragement to express ideas that vary from those espoused by their peers. Classroom environments must protect the dignity and security of all who inhabit them; teachers must be firm and consistent as they insist that such environments prevail.

Strategies for Enhancing Self-Esteem

─────── **STRATEGY 6-1** ───────

Positive Day

Purpose
This strategy is designed to enhance feelings of self-esteem by encouraging students to make only positive statements during a specified class period or day. It also stimulates academic interest by adding novelty to the daily routine.

Continued

STRATEGY 6-1 *Continued*

TARGET Area
(T), (A)

Grade Level
This strategy is appropriate for all grade levels. It is particularly useful in instrumental music classes, physical education classes, and other skill-oriented classes.

Procedure
Select a day or class period one or two weeks in the future, write it on the chalkboard, and announce to your students that this will be a special day (or hour) in your classroom. On this day everyone in the room, including the teacher, will strive to make *only* positive comments when speaking to others. You can build anticipation and interest by discussing some of the difficulties students might foresee in meeting this challenge. When the day arrives, ask each student to keep a personal record of any negative comments they hear, but not to point them out to others. You might start the following day with a discussion of how the students felt during the Positive Day, what difficulties they had in making only positive comments, and the examples of negative comments they recorded.

Variations
Depending on the reaction of your students, you may want to use this strategy several times during the semester.

Source: Jerry Borchardt, middle school instrumental music teacher.

_____ **STRATEGY 6-2** _____

Mystery Kid

Purpose
This strategy fosters feelings of self-esteem by focusing attention on the positive achievements of each student. It also can help develop a sense of group relatedness and cohesion.

TARGET Area
(T), (R)

STRATEGY 6-2 *Continued*

Grade Level

Useful for all grade levels, but particularly suited to elementary and middle school.

Procedure

At the beginning of each year or semester the teacher asks students to make a list of all of their personal accomplishments. Some students may have difficulty with this task, so it is important that the teacher help in this process by explaining to students that they can list almost any achievement about which they feel proud, regardless of how insignificant it may appear to others.

Encourage students to select those accomplishments that are likely to be original and unique, such as being the best ping pong player in the family, having the cleanest room in the house, being able to put up the family tent without help, being capable of spitting watermelon seeds farther than an older sibling, having built his or her own radio, and the like. Encourage students to identify as many accomplishments as possible but not to mention them to others since they will be used in a special activity during the school term.

Select a small bulletin board section and decorate and label it as the "Mystery Kid of the Week" area. Choosing a different student each week, take five of his or her most obscure and unique accomplishments and, using a felt pen, write them out on a 3 × 24 slip of white poster board. Starting on a Monday, add one clue to the bulletin board each day of the week.

Encourage students to try to guess the Mystery Kid, but to keep their guess a secret. When they think they know the Mystery Kid's identity, they can write it on a slip of paper along with their name, date, and time and place it in a box set aside for this purpose. On Friday after the fifth clue has been posted and all of the students have had a chance to guess the Mystery Kid, the box can be opened and the identify of the Mystery Kid revealed.

Material

Decorated bulletin board area, personal accomplishment sheets for each student, a small box to collect guesses, and poster board to write clues.

Variations

Younger students might be encouraged to draw pictures of their accomplishments or discuss them individually with the teacher so that he or she can keep them on file. Students seem to enjoy identifying those accomplishments that others in the class do not know.

—————— **STRATEGY 6-3** ————————————————————————

Celebrity of the Week

Purpose
This strategy enhances self-esteem by providing an opportunity for each student to focus on his or her positive attributes and to be on "center stage" for a week. It fosters feelings of importance, acceptance, and belonging. It also helps each student gain an awareness of the uniqueness of each class member.

TARGET Area
(R)

Grade Level
This strategy is especially useful for preschool through elementary school, but it can be adapted to other grades.

Procedure
At the beginning of the year the teacher assigns a week during the year for each child in the classroom to be "Celebrity of the Week." This is not to be used as a reward for good behavior; each child is entitled to his or her "week in the sun," regardless of behavior. A note should be sent home explaining the activity and indicating the week that has been chosen for the child. In the week prior to the chosen week, a reminder note is sent home.

It is important that the teacher develop a list of special privileges and awards that all students receive when they are Celebrity of the Week. Some examples might be: a signed certificate suitable for framing (if you need help, your media specialist or a student experienced in computers can easily design one for you); the privilege of being first in lunch line; a Celebrity of the Week coupon good for an extra trip to the drinking fountain; a special five-minute interview in front of the class where the celebrities are encouraged to discuss their hobbies, interests, and aspirations; the privilege to run audiovisual equipment or take attendance or notes to the office; lunch with the teacher (maybe even in the faculty lounge); or acting as the reader of daily or weekly announcements.

The nature of the privileges selected would depend on the grade level of the class. It is useful to make a list of the special privileges for Celebrities of the Week and post them in the classroom.

It is sometimes useful to have a special suitcase in the class that each celebrity takes home on Monday or Tuesday to bring back something special for the class to see and discuss. Students can play twenty questions to guess what the child has in the suitcase.

STRATEGY 6-3 *Continued*

While these little privileges and awards seem insignificant and don't cost anything, they can often become very important to the students. It is important that the teacher not use this strategy unless there is enough time in the class term for *each* child to be Celebrity of the Week.

This strategy can be effectively combined with Strategy 6-2. Once identified, the Mystery Kid can spend the following week serving as Celebrity of the Week while a new Mystery Kid is selected.

Variations

The teacher might take instant pictures of each Celebrity of the Week and display them in an appropriate location. A semantic map can be constructed for each child, including things like hobbies, family facts, favorite foods, turn-offs, etcetera. Other students can write a story about the Celebrity and make a picture to put into a special keepsake book. Students might also write an autobiography during the week prior to their turn as Celebrity, so that they can read it to the class on Monday of their special week.

A librarian, counselor, or administrator might run a similar program for teachers, with the Celebrity Teacher of the Week receiving privileges such as a reserved parking spot in front of the school, an extra prep period, or early dismissal on Friday.

This activity has been called Super Kid, Star of the Week, First Grader of the Week, Student of the Week, Special Kid, and Very Important Person (VIP) of the Week by different teachers. Starting the year by letting students vote on the name for the activity can build group unity and self-determination.

When planning the celebrity schedule, you might want to start with students' birthdays and, where possible, schedule the students' celebrity week concurrent with their birthday week.

Source: Many teachers have suggested versions of this activity. Pam Kiskunas, a third grade teacher, and Kristine Carlson, a fifth grade teacher, were two of the first.

STRATEGY 6-4

PIT Calls (Positive Information Telephoning)

Purpose

This strategy is designed to get parents involved in reinforcing student self-esteem and feelings of competence.

TARGET Area

(R)

Continued

STRATEGY 6-4 *Continued*

Grade Level
PIT calls are useful for all grade levels.

Procedure
This strategy requires that the teacher set aside fifteen minutes each week to telephone the parents of one or two students to inform them of their child's positive accomplishments during the past week or two. The conversations can be kept short and should focus on a specific behavior of the student.

It is important to try to schedule a consistent time each week for making the PIT calls. While most teachers believe in the value of positive phone calls to parents, they are often overlooked or pushed aside by busy schedules.

It is also important to avoid discussing student problems or difficulties during the PIT calls. These concerns should be set aside for another conversation, since the positive effects of the PIT calls will be lost if negative information is mentioned.

While it is easy to find positive information or accomplishments for hard-working students, it is important for the teacher to look very carefully to find at least one small accomplishment for the reluctant learners. It seems that the more difficult it is to find positive information about a student to share in a PIT call, the greater the potential for that student to benefit from such calls.

Variations
It should be possible for elementary teachers to contact the parents of all of their students at least once each semester. Given the work schedules of some parents, it may take considerable persistence to achieve this goal. Specialty and secondary teachers who see many students each week will have difficulty calling the parents of all or most of their students. In such cases, the teacher may find it more effective to focus on those students who are likely to benefit the most from such phone calls. Calling thirty or forty parents each semester, however, can go a long way in fostering and reinforcing the self-esteem of many students who wouldn't otherwise develop it.

PIM (Positive Information Mailing) notes serve the same purpose as PIT calls and are a useful alternative to PIT calls for difficult-to-reach parents. They are written statements of a student's accomplishments, usually on a computer designed and decorated form, that are mailed weekly to two or three selected students. Sending notes home with students is less effective than using the postal service to deliver the positive information—the small amount of postage required is well worth the cost.

Source: Adapted from a suggestion by Chick Morman, educational consultant.

STRATEGY 6-5

Five-Year-Old Humor

Purpose
This strategy can build self-esteem and confidence by helping students realize that it is okay to make mistakes; even teachers do it.

TARGET Area
(T)

Grade Level
Preschool through early elementary.

Procedure
When young children begin working in language activities, they often learn nursery rhymes by listening and discussing the stories, by acting them out, and by illustrating them in art activities. In this activity, the teacher starts a class by asking if any of the children know the teacher's new friend, Jack, who also has a friend, Jill. The teacher continues the stimulus questions until most students have recognized the rhyme. The teacher can then recite the rhyme with a few of the obvious facts changed, such as, "Jack and Jill went up the elevator . . . ," or, "Jack fell down and broke his nose . . . ," or "Jill called 911," and so forth.

The children seem to thoroughly enjoy laughing at the humor and correcting the teacher's mistakes. After a few trials, and to the delight of the class, the teacher finally recites the complete poem correctly. He or she then thanks the children for their help.

When young children become bored or restless, the five-year-old humor strategy can often help them refocus on classroom activities.

Variations
Students can be encouraged to work with partners, and each can take a turn making up his or her own version of the rhyme while the partner tries to spot the inaccuracies.

Source: Sally Marks, early elementary special education teacher.

STRATEGY 6-6

Family Biographer

Purpose
This strategy enhances self-esteem by encouraging students to examine their family heritage and thereby discover their own unique individuality.

Continued

STRATEGY 6-6 *Continued*

TARGET Areas
(T), (R)

Grade Level
Upper elementary school, middle school, and high school.

Procedure
As a family biographer, the student investigates their nationality and family tree by interviewing one or both parents, guardians, or relatives. They can also gather information on the country that contributes the most to their nationality. Students should record their findings in notebooks, where they might include family photographs, documents, maps, or other information. Each student should be free to decide whether or not to share this information with the group.

Possible research questions for parents or relatives might include:

1. What did you like most about your parents?
2. What was the best thing that happened to you when you were my age?
3. Who in the family speaks our native language?
4. What aspect of our heritage makes you most proud?
5. What ethnic customs do you remember?
6. Have you visited or talked to relatives who have visited our ancestral home?
7. What have you learned about it?
8. What's the most difficult thing about being a parent or guardian?
9. What do you like most about being a parent or guardian?

Variations
This is a good activity for helping students get to know one another. Students with similar nationalities might meet to share their findings. These students can help organize geography lessons about their ancestral homes; information on dress, food, agriculture, religion, and politics can be incorporated into their presentations. A bulletin board of flags, maps, and pictures can present the heritage of each class member, including the teacher. Older students might want to construct an in-depth genealogy of one or both sides of the family.

Source: Adapted from Kim Johnson, elementary school teacher, and Bernadine Butt, middle school English teacher.

—————— **STRATEGY 6-7** ——————————————————————————

Identity Cube

Purpose
The purpose of this activity is to enhance self-esteem by encouraging students to identify and share their individual attributes, beliefs, and experiences.

TARGET Area
(T), (R)

Grade Level
Primarily useful in elementary or middle school, but can be adapted to other grade levels.

Procedure
Start this activity with a discussion of student differences and how these differences make people more interesting. Hand out cube patterns (Figure 6-1) and then write a series of directions, appropriate to the grade level, on the chalkboard, similar to those that follow. Encourage students to draw illustrations or symbols on each of the cube faces that express their thoughts regarding the statements that corresponds with the cube face number.

Possible questions for each cube face:

1. Illustrate something that you do exceptionally well.
2. Illustrate something that you wish you could do better.
3. If you had to move to a new city tomorrow, what words would you want people to say about you after you left?
4. Illustrate what you will be doing for most of your time, ten years from now.
5. What slogan or motto demonstrates your outlook on life?
6. Illustrate your happiest moment.
7. List three words that describe you.
8. Illustrate something that people like about you. When finished, the cubes can be stacked in a pyramid or arranged into a design or word.

Materials
You will need construction paper and pencils, crayons, or markers. It may be a bit easier if students cut out their cubes *after* they have completed their illustrations. You may want to laminate the cubes before they are assembled.

Continued

STRATEGY 6-7 *Continued*

FIGURE 6-1   Identity Cube

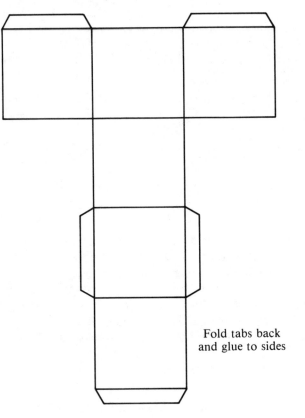

Fold tabs back
and glue to sides

Variations
Younger students can cut pictures out of magazines to illustrate statements
and questions. Students may want to glue photos of themselves to one of
the cube faces. After the cubes have been displayed for an appropriate time,
you might put them away so that you can return them at the end of the
year as a class remembrance. You may want to display the cubes in such
a way that students can change the faces they want showing, according
to their moods.

Source: Adapted from Lynn Zimmerman, elementary education student.

—————— STRATEGY 6-8 ——————————————————

Death to Put-Downs

Purpose
The purpose of this activity is to create a safe and secure environment in which students will be able to express their feelings and beliefs without fear of being ridiculed or embarrassed.

TARGET Areas
(T), (A)

Grade Level
Can be used at all grade levels.

Procedure
Start this activity with a discussion of why students use verbal put-downs with one another and how it feels to receive a put-down from another student. Then hand out paper and have students write down all of the put-downs that they have heard within the past year. Give students time to write as many as possible, stopping periodically to have students volunteer to read their lists.

When the full spectrum of put-downs has been identified, have the students place their lists into a small cardboard box that you set aside for this purpose. Tape the box closed, and, if possible, take the class outside to a far corner of the schoolgrounds where you dug a hole earlier in the day. Place the box into the hole, and then take out a eulogy that you have previously written and read it to the group. Any eulogy will work; include things like "We are saying good-by to a life-long friend, someone we have known well, and will miss dearly. This friend has been very dependable, and was always around when you needed him. He has been an important part of all of our lives, and we will think of him often."

After reading the eulogy, take a shovel and start to cover the box with dirt. Allow an opportunity for each student to throw a shovelful of dirt on the box. When the box is buried, take the group back to the classroom. Then take out a prepared tombstone, drawn on poster board, that includes the statement, "R.I.P. Put-Downs" and place it on the front bulletin board. Try not to talk anymore about the activity at this point, and redirect the class back to their normal routine.

The very next time that you hear a student use a put-down in your class, walk up to the student and quietly say, "I'm sorry, 'dirt-ball' (or whatever was said) is not with us any more." At this point, most students will realize the significance of the previous "funeral."

Materials
You will need a small cardboard box, tape, paper and pencils for writing, a shovel, a prepared eulogy, and a headstone on poster board.

Continued

STRATEGY 6-8 *Continued*

Variations

Instead of burying the box, you might want to stage a cremation at the school incinerator. You might want to make an audiotape of the class reading their put-downs and place it into the box, along with the written put-downs.

Source: Adapted from a suggestion by Chick Morman, educational consultant.

───────── **STRATEGY 6-9** ─────────────────────────

Secret Supporter

Purpose

This strategy is designed to enhance self-esteem by allowing all students to give and receive positive statements.

TARGET Area

(R)

Grade Level

Can be used at all grade levels.

Procedure

Prepare slips of paper with each student's name written on them, and place them into a container. Start this activity with a discussion of how it feels when you receive a genuine compliment from another student. Discuss the nature of these compliments, how the tone of voice conveys meaning, and why it can be difficult to say positive things to a peer. Then ask the students if they would like to participate in an activity that can help improve their skill at giving and receiving positive statements. Respect students' desires not to participate; take their names out of the container, and continue with the activity. When you are alone with the student, you may want to discuss the reasons for the student's decision not to participate in this activity.

Explain to the students that they each will become a "secret supporter" to another student whose name they select from the container. In this role, they will look for opportunities during the next week in which they can say something positive to the student. They should try not to let anyone know whose name they have selected, and they should try to give their positive statements in a way that will be undetected. To help in this process, students should try to give positive statements to additional students.

At the end of the week, students can try to guess their secret supporter and discuss the difficulties they had in giving and receiving positive statements.

STRATEGY 6-9 *Continued*

Variations
Students can be encouraged to keep a record of their positive statements that can be reviewed at the end of the week. Near Christmas, elementary teachers might adapt this to a "Secret Santa." If students draw their own names, they can be given to the teacher to be placed back into the container (this avoids the desire to choose a name). After this activity, students can be encouraged to give positive statements to anyone they choose. Periodic discussions can help students determine if a relationship exists between the number of positive statements made to others and the number received from others.

STRATEGY 6-10

Success Lifeline

Purpose
This strategy uses students' previous positive experiences to enhance their sense of self-esteem. By identifying and sharing their past successes, students develop self-confidence, recognition, and a sense of identity.

TARGET Area
(R)

Grade Level
Can be used at all grade levels.

Procedure
Discuss the concept of self-confidence and how it is related to positive self-esteem. Help students realize that self-confidence is not a genetic trait that one is born with, but rather that it is developed through experiences of success in life and the way we think about ourselves. We can develop a negative image of ourselves by dwelling upon the unpleasant experiences in our lives, or we can choose to focus on our positive traits and successful experiences. This activity will help students focus on their positive characteristics and past successes by creating a personal "Success Lifeline."

The lifeline should begin with the year the student was born and continue to the present year. Students are asked to choose one major success from each year and then illustrate it with a picture from a magazine, a photograph, or an original drawing. A short explanation of each success might accompany the illustration.

Each student should be given an opportunity to share his or her Success Lifeline with the class and to display it in the classroom.

Continued

STRATEGY 6-10 *Continued*

Materials
Make markers, tape, magazines, construction paper, and scissors available. Students can also bring pictures from home. It may be useful to use a standard length of newsprint or poster paper for all students.

Variations
Depending on the grade level, the lifelines may cover a month, the school year, or every two years. It might be useful to spread this activity over the course of several months, so that all students are not required to present and discuss their lifelines at the same time.

Source: Chris Manke, elementary teacher.

7

Enhancing Student Autonomy

Most of us do not realize that no matter how much coercion we use,
we cannot consistently control other people. In fact, it is a axiom of
control theory that the only person any of us can consistently control
is ourselves. When others do as we ask, it is because they find it
more satisfying than anything else they can do at the time.

—GLASSER, 1990, pp. 72–72)

AS DISCUSSED IN chapters 2 and 4, students' need for a sense of autonomy or self-determination significantly influences their motivation to learn in the classroom. Regardless of grade level, students want the freedom to determine for themselves what activities to undertake and what behaviors to adopt. This need for control of the decisions that affect one's life lies at the foundation of the teacher empowerment movement. Many reformers have affirmed the importance of teachers' need for control over the selection of instructional objectives, educational methods, and evaluation and grading procedures used within their classrooms. Other reformers seem to have discounted this need in favor of standardized curricular objectives, methods, and testing procedures. While the debate continues, teachers can only imagine what it would be like to teach in a classroom where a district or state curricular guide spells out exactly what objectives are to be taught, has organized and structured the content so that each teaching activity is broken down into minute by minute instructions as to what the teacher is to say and what the students are to do, and requires that district or state tests be administered in order to assign predetermined grading distributions.

Although few educators advocate either extreme, most teachers feel insulted by the suggestion that they should have no control over what, when, and how education is to be conducted in their classrooms. As teachers lose autonomy, they often feel less and less responsibility about meeting curricular requirements, they become cynical about teaching, they blame others for their cynical attitude, and they may even try to undermine the system if given an opportunity. When given reasonable control over their teaching environment, teachers are likely to become committed to what they do, responsible for the outcomes of their behavior, and devoted to the improvement of student learning.

And so it is with students, regardless of age. Their desire to maintain reasonable control over what, when, and how they learn is no different from teachers' desires for the same sense of autonomy over their teaching. As discussed in Chapter 2, students begin to assert this need as toddlers, and then again as adolescents. The need for self-determination is satisfied when both teachers and students are reasonably free to act of their own volition, rather than being repeatedly coerced to behave according to the wishes of some higher authority.

Some students—and teachers, too, for that matter—seem reluctant to affirm their desire for self-determination and prefer having decisions made for them. This apparent abdication of autonomy often results from feelings of incompetence and a longstanding tendency to be totally dependent on the behavior and decisions of others (see Chapter 2). On the other hand, students who are given complete freedom to do as they choose, with little guidance or direction, often become frustrated by not knowing what choices to make; feelings of insecurity and incompetence soon follow. In both situations, a sense of autonomy can be nurtured by allowing these students to experience reasonable choices within a context of structure and guidance.

As discussed in Chapter 4, cognitive evaluation theory proposes that the intrinsic motivation of individuals is built on a foundation of self-determination. While teachers may have the power to control student behavior with rewards and punishments, it is apparent that when these controls subvert students' sense of autonomy, they increase the likelihood that students will choose to avoid participation when possible. The chapter also discusses how organismic integration theory explains the process by which individuals learn to regulate or control their own behavior. In both situations, informational rather than controlling limit setting and the use of minimally sufficient controls are important strategies for enhancing students' sense of autonomy.

As described in Chapter 4, informational limit setting is based on providing students with clear explanations of the reasons that limits may be needed; fostering and supporting students' choices wherever possible; using logical consequences rather than punishment when external control is necessary; and acknowledging student feelings, especially when behavior must be restricted for the good of the student or the class.

Minimally sufficient control is based on the principle that when it becomes necessary to control a student's behavior, teachers should be sure that external control is needed, should select the smallest reward or punishment possible to meet their objective, and should wean students from the use of rewards and punishments as soon as they are no longer necessary.

Although these suggestions are useful for allowing students to experience a sense of self-determination when their behaviors must be stipulated or restricted, the single most important strategy for building a sense of autonomy in students is to provide them with *choices*. It is learning to make choices, according to deCharms (1977), that leads to commitment, and it is commitment that leads to responsibility. In turn, it is responsibility, or the willingness to be held accountable for one's decisions, that leads to feelings of self-determination and autonomy.

As indicated in Chapter 4, teachers can provide students with scores of opportunities to experience small choices within the classroom each day. These choices might range from deciding whether to work on math before starting spelling, to where to place one's name on assignments.

On a broader level, providing opportunities for students to determine their individual learning goals can establish a framework in which they can experience significant and meaningful choices. This chapter will consider how helping students develop individual goal-setting skills can help them experience meaningful choices within the classroom and thereby foster their sense of autonomy. The following chapter will examine how individual goal-setting skills can contribute to helping all students experience a genuine sense of competence in the classroom.

Goal-Setting Conferences

In a review of research dealing with the influence of goal setting on academic performance, Raffini (1988) reported that many studies were designed to measure the achievement effects of individual goal-setting conferences between teachers and students. A number of studies indicated that goal-setting conferences were especially effective in increasing student academic achievement in the classroom (Raffini, 1988).

Klausmeier and his associates (1973) described a four-step procedure for helping teachers conduct goal-setting conferences. They warned, however, that while goal-setting conferences are reasonably easy to plan and conduct in classrooms that individualize instruction, traditional classrooms are likely to impose time and structural constraints that will frustrate attempts to initiate such conferences. Nevertheless, they offer the following suggestions (Klausmeier et al., 1973):

1. Help students concentrate on a single goal for a short period of time so that they can measure their progress and maintain interest.

2. Encourage students to state their goals clearly so that each knows exactly what must be done.

3. Although the teacher may suggest many possible objectives, each student should select those he or she chooses to work toward and attain by a specific date.

4. While reaching short-term goals is important, learning self-directedness and prosocial behavior is a long-term process.

One of the clearest examples of how individual goal-setting can offer students opportunities for autonomy is demonstrated by deCharms (1977) in his suggestions for a revised spelling bee. Invented by teachers attending one of deCharms' Origin Training Workshops, the modified spelling bee divides the class into two teams, with each participant, regardless of spelling ability, contributing equally to the team score. Strategy 8–10 describes the procedure for implementing this autonomy-supporting activity.

In regard to goal setting, Borba (1989), quoting McCollum, reports that the 87 percent of individuals have no specific goals or plans for their lives, and only 3 percent of the population have specific written goals. It is this group, according to Borba, "who accomplish 50 to 100 times more than those who have goals but do not write them down" (1989, p. 231).

Since many students have difficulty with the process of goal setting, the following five goal characteristics, adapted from Borba (1989), can be useful for teaching students the skill of goal setting:

- *Conceptualized.* After explaining to students that goals are something we try to achieve in life, it is helpful to encourage students to picture in their minds what it is they would like to accomplish. The process of mental imagery, discussed in Chapter 4, can be useful here. Students can focus on long-range goals, like career choices, or they can conceptualize weekly or monthly goals.

- *Measurable.* It is important that students be able to measure progress toward attaining their goals. This requires some type of evaluation procedure that will provide students with feedback regarding goal achievement.

- *Achievable.* Goals need to be challenging but attainable. Teachers need to help students examine this aspect of their goals and, if necessary, have them estimate their probability of reaching the goal they have selected. According to Borba, "the most successful goals are usually set *slightly higher than the last goal*" (1989, p. 231).

- *Sequential.* It is important that students learn that there are incremental steps in the process of goal attainment. Helping them define these steps is a valuable component of goal setting.

- *Personal.* Autonomy is fostered when students are encouraged to select goals based on their own interests, rather than being pressured by the expectations and performances of others. Students should be encouraged to avoid comparisons and focus on their own commitment and progress.

Recommendations for Enhancing Student Autonomy

The following recommendations are designed to help teachers at all grade levels find opportunities to foster student autonomy within the classroom. When students feel a sense of control and self-determination in regard to what happens to them in school, they are more likely to become actively involved in the learning process.

1. *When several learning activities meet the same objective, allow students to choose from among them.* Instructional objectives that deal with precise content or skills, like solving simultaneous equations, often allow little flexibility in how they are to be accomplished. When they deal with broader skills, like writing paragraphs or improving reading comprehension, there are usually many instructional opportunities that allow for choice; it is necessary that teachers keep a constant lookout for these opportunities. Although this suggestion may make the teacher's job a bit more difficult, it is a powerful method for building student self-determination and commitment to learning.

2. *When classroom procedures are not critical, allow students options in determining how to implement them.* Although it may be convenient for teachers to have all students place their names in the upper left-hand corner of their papers, allowing them the choice of placing their names in either corner, or even at the end of their papers, provides a small opportunity for self-determination. At first glance, such small choices appear insignificant. Yet any choice, regardless of size, contributes to student autonomy.

3. *When possible, provide opportunities for students to determine when, where, and in what order to complete assignments.* While many instructional activities may be required of all students, allowing some choice in determining when, where, and in what order these activities can be completed, while creating a bit more work for the teacher, can make a significant contribution to student autonomy. If, for example, students are required to finish a math assignment and a map project before the end of the day, allowing them the choice of which to complete first can contribute to their sense of self-determination. Likewise, when assigning practice problems, rather than assigning the odd-numbered problems or the first ten of twenty problems, letting them choose to complete the odd *or* even or any ten will support a sense of autonomy. (Some will do more than required to ensure that they have found solutions they believe are correct.) When faced with these choices, students are required to make a commitment; it is this commitment that leads to autonomous, goal-directed behavior.

4. *Try to create a psychologically safe environment in which students are willing to risk choices.* Feelings of insecurity and lack of self-confidence make it difficult for some students to choose from alternatives; they often prefer to be told exactly what to do and in what order activities must be completed. Building student autonomy requires that teachers are sensitive to these insecurities and attempt to create a classroom atmosphere that supports risk taking. Protecting students from the ridicule and criticism of others and reminding them that mistakes are a necessary and natural part of the learning process can help create a psychologically safe classroom.

5. *When student behavior must be restricted or limited, take time to provide clear and logical explanations of the reasoning behind the limits.* Students cannot be given a choice whether to run or walk in the hallways; for the safety of all, it is necessary that we restrict hallway behavior. When we must impose such limits, it is important that we provide students with clear and logical reasons for these restrictions. "Because I said so" is simply not good enough.

6. *When behavior must be restricted, acknowledge conflicting feelings.* As suggested by Ginott (1961), acknowledging students' feelings when their behavior must be restricted helps them accept restrictions without undermining their intrinsic motivation and sense of self-determination (Koestner et al., 1984). Acknowledging conflicting feelings lets students know that their thoughts and emotions are being understood. Statements like "I know it is sometimes more fun to run rather than walk in the hallways, but walking is necessary because some students can be injured when others are running" or "I know it is difficult to concentrate on algebra when the weather outside is so beautiful, but becoming a skilled equation solver requires complete attention to detail" can help students accept necessary restrictions without completely subverting their sense of autonomy.

7. *When behavior must be required or restricted, use minimally sufficient controls.* While on occasion it may be necessary for teachers to use external rewards or logical consequences to control certain student behaviors, using the least control possible can help teachers meet their objective while increasing the likelihood that students will eventually internalize the necessity for the restriction or requirement. (See Chapter 4 for a review of research on the minimal-sufficiency principle.)

8. *Use logical consequences rather than punishment when a student's behavior makes it difficult for you to teach others.* Chapter 4 provides a discussion of the differences between logical consequences and punishment. Since logical consequences emphasize the reality of the social order, rather than the personal power of the teacher, they are more likely to enhance a sense of autonomy by helping students assume ownership for their choices. Most importantly, they enable students to assume responsibility for changing their behavior; punishment places this responsibility with the authority.

9. *When possible, encourage students to use the skills of individual goal setting to define, monitor, and achieve self-determined objectives.* Helping students verbalize and affirm realistic goals puts them in control of their aspirations and behaviors. When students are encouraged to seek alternatives, identify consequences, and make decisions, they are acting autonomously. Having influence over the decisions that affect one's life gives a sense of empowerment that lies at the heart of all intrinsically motivated behavior. For verification we need only examine the elements that influence our own decisions.

10. *Try to avoid making students feel right, wrong, good, or bad for their actions. Rather, hold them accountable for the consequences of their choices.* Assigning value judgments to students' choices undermines their autonomy. They learn to evaluate alternatives more clearly when they are held accountable, rather than judged, for the consequences of their choices. Jimmy is not bad or wrong for failing to complete his English assignments; he is, however, accountable for the consequences of his behavior. Most likely, this means that he has not demonstrated a mastery of the objectives being measured by the assignment, and he has lowered his chances for earning a passing grade in the class. Jimmy's teacher can try to control Jimmy's behavior with bribes or punishments, but unless Jimmy learns to acknowledge *all* of the consequences that follow from his choices, he will not learn to assume the responsibility that comes with self-determined behavior.

Strategies for Fostering Student Autonomy

―――――― STRATEGY 7-1 ――――――――――――――――――――――――――

Control Coupons

Purpose
This strategy can provide opportunities for students to experience feelings of control and autonomy in regard to certain classroom procedures or activities.

TARGET Level
(A)

Grade Level
Useful for all grade levels.

Procedure
At the beginning of each grading period, the teacher gives each student one or two numbered coupons redeemable for one late homework assign-

Continued

STRATEGY 7-1   *Continued*

ment, one trip to the lavatory, one trip to the water fountain, or similar privileges to be used during the period under consideration. Each student is given a class number for the year, and control coupons are numbered correspondingly to prevent the exchanging or selling of coupons. Students are told that they can redeem their coupons anytime they choose during the semester or year.

Materials
Coupons can be as elaborate or as simple as desired. Using a 3 × 5 index card with a special ink stamp works well. Computer-generated designs are also useful. However, the paper should be durable enough to last for the semester or year. Some teachers may want to laminate the coupons with clear plastic and use them for several semesters.

Variations
Depending on the grade level or subject, coupons can be used for a variety of purposes. Examples might be arriving a few minutes late for class, eliminating one low test score from the grade book, or using independent study time to work on another subject. Occasional problems like tardiness or late assignments are often reduced or eliminated with the use of control coupons. Many students are reluctant to redeem their coupons and make a special effort to complete homework assignments or arrive at class on time to avoid using a coupon. In such cases, you may want to allow students to redeem their coupons for extra credit at the end of the semester, or bring some cookies and sell them for coupons.

STRATEGY 7-2

The *A* Exchange

Purpose
While somewhat contrary to test and measurement theory, this strategy is designed to foster student autonomy by empowering them with control over at least one of their test grades.

TARGET Areas
(A), (E)

Grade Level
This strategy is useful in all grades and subjects where periodic tests are given.

STRATEGY 7-2 *Continued*

Procedure

Assuming that the teacher gives periodic tests throughout the grading period, this strategy enables students to change any one test grade that they receive to an *A* within 24 hours of receiving it. This apparently simple gift allows students to feel a sense of control over the grading process.

Some students may choose to use the exchange on an early test, thereby forfeiting flexibility in all later tests. Others may decide to wait until late in the grading period before making the exchange. In either case, it is always a difficult choice for the student: "Do I exchange this *C* for an *A* now, and assume I can work hard to avoid a lower grade in the future, or do I wait because I might get a lower grade in the future?"

When using this strategy, it is important that the teacher downplay the emphasis on grades and support the self-determination and control that are generated by the strategy.

Variations

Teachers may choose to use the *A* exchange on homework assignments rather than, or in addition to, test grades.

Source: Kevin McKinnon, high school science teacher.

STRATEGY 7-3

You Rule

Purpose

This strategy enables students to experience a sense of control and self-determination in the classroom as they set standards of acceptable behavior for themselves and their peers.

TARGET Area

(A)

Grade Level

Useful for all grade levels.

Procedure

At the beginning of the school year or semester, students are asked if they would like to make a set of rules for the room. They are given instructions to limit the number of rules to five or less and to use positive wording in their construction. For example: "Treat others with kindness, courtesy, and decency," rather than "Don't put others down." After each student writes his or her list of rules, the class can break into groups of three or four and

Continued

STRATEGY 7-3 *Continued*

share their results. Repeated rules are eliminated, and each group's final list is presented to the entire class and recorded on the chalkboard. The five rules that students feel are most important are adopted by the group. The teacher should have input in this process but should be careful not to dominate the discussion or decision.

After the rules are decided upon, it is useful to encourage each student to copy the list inside the cover of his or her notebook, and a copy should be posted in the room. When students set the rules for acceptable behavior, they are more likely to feel a sense of ownership and control over the classroom atmosphere, and they often monitor themselves without reminders from the teacher.

Variations
The number of rules can be increased or decreased, and it might be useful to have students rank the rules from most important to least important when deciding on the rules that will be used in the class. After the rules are established, the class can discuss suggestions for enforcement, without relying on traditional punishments like staying after school or forfeiting recess.

Source: Vera Anderson, junior high school English teacher.

STRATEGY 7-4

Writer's Block

Purpose
This strategy is designed to help students enhance their feelings of self-determination by giving them some control over their writing choices.

TARGET Areas
(T), (A)

Grade Level
This strategy is useful for all grades and subjects in which writing skills are emphasized. It is particularly useful in classrooms that emphasize a writer's workshop approach to the teaching of language.

Procedure
At the beginning of the year, after students have been introduced to the importance of daily and weekly writing exercises or to the writer's workshop format and procedures (see Nanci Atwell's book, *In The Middle,*

STRATEGY 7-3 *Continued*

for a detailed discussion of this procedure), the teacher should describe the concept of "writer's block" and discuss how it can occasionally affect all writers.

The teacher should then present to the class a large block of wood with the words "Writer's Block" written on it. Students are told that this is to be the class's writer's block, and students may use it on a day when they have too much on their mind to write. They may, for example, have had an argument before they left home that morning, received a low test grade, or had an altercation with a classmate. Students are told that in situations such as these, they need only take the block from the teacher's desk and place it on their own. Whenever a student has placed the writer's block on his or her desk, the rest of the class, including the teacher, will not talk to or bother that student for the remainder of the period. Students are informed that they may use the writer's block once per quarter (or any other period established by the teacher).

Materials
One large block of wood, possibly varnished, with the words "Writer's Block" written on it.

Variations
Rather than allowing the student to simply sit without being bothered, some teachers may decide that students should be encouraged to write about their feelings that they are experiencing. It is important to tell students that they may write about anything they wish, and at the end of the period they may rip it up and throw it away without anyone reading it.

Another variation is to give students a small wood block of their own to be turned in to the teacher on the day that they feel the need to use it. Students could also make a block of their own from a cube shape that has been photocopied on paper (see Figure 6-1, page 158). They could then cut out words from magazines to show the feelings they may have and glue these to the cube.

Source: Nora Judd, elementary teacher.

STRATEGY 7-5

Celebrity Tea at the White House

Purpose
This strategy will enhance students' motivation by building their sense of autonomy and by enhancing their feelings of competence.

Continued

STRATEGY 7-5   *Continued*

TARGET Areas
(T), (A), (R)

Grade Level
This strategy is primarily useful for third to sixth grade, but can be adapted to other grades.

Procedure
Encourage students to brainstorm a celebrity list of past presidents, scientists, inventors, athletes, writers, actors, explorers, or entertainers and record the list on the chalkboard. After a brief discussion of each celebrity, students are asked to choose one celebrity they are interested in studying.

Students are encouraged to do library research about the person they have selected, since they will write a biography of their celebrity and "become" this person at a special Tea at the White House.

After discussing the nature and form of a biography, several class periods can be devoted to gathering information, taking notes, and writing rough drafts. Students should be continually encouraged to discover all they can about their famous person so they can answer questions and act like the person when they attend the White House Tea.

Students then write a final copy of their biography and practice answering questions as though they were the person they have just written about. They should be encouraged to use the pronouns *I*, *me*, and *my* when answering others' questions.

Parents and other classes are invited to attend a Tea at the White House to honor famous people from the past. During the tea, guests move around the room introducing themselves to students who are wearing costumes of the people they represent. Guests are encouraged to ask the celebrities questions about their accomplishments, hobbies, family, and so on.

This activity is an enjoyable way to bring history to life by allowing students choices in expressing their creativity.

Materials
You will need encyclopedias, biographies, autobiographies, costumes, tea (soft drinks or fruit punch are a good substitute), and cups.

Variations
You may want to skip the written biography with younger children and just have them read about and then act out their roles. You can use current celebrities or restrict choices to individuals who are no longer living.

Source: Tracy Baron and Kristine Carlson, elementary teachers.

—————— **STRATEGY 7-6** ——————————————————————

Contract Grading

Purpose
This strategy is designed to enhance feelings of self-determination and autonomy in students.

TARGET Areas
(A), (E)

Grade Level
Useful at all grade levels in which students are evaluated with letter grades.

Procedure
For a designated unit of study the teacher informs the students that they can choose to be evaluated with the conventional grading procedure typically used in the class, or with a contract grading procedure.

Contract grading systems can take many forms. Usually the teacher constructs a list of activities that can be used to meet the unit objectives. It is important to vary the nature of these activities in order to provide as much choice as possible, while still satisfying the unit objectives. Each activity is then evaluated on a "satisfactory" (S) or "not yet satisfactory" (NYS) basis. NYS means the work on the activity did not adequately demonstrate a mastery of the unit objective or reflect a reasonable amount of effort on the task. Students are informed of the work or ideas missing from the assignment and what additional work would be necessary to satisfactorily meet the activity objective. With encouragement and follow-up, most NYS papers can be resubmitted and earn an *S* evaluation.

At the start of the unit, the teacher determines the number of satisfactorily completed activities required to earn each letter grade. Students are then free to choose what grade they would like to achieve.

Variations
Within these broad guidelines it is possible, based on the unit's objectives, to earmark one or two activities and require them of all students. It is also possible to give a test at the end of the unit and use the same *S* and *NYS* evaluation. This requires that the teacher construct a parallel version of the test for those who did not achieve an S during the first administration.

━━━━━━━ **STRATEGY 7-7** ━━━━━━━━━━━━━━━━━━━━━━━━━━━━━━━━━

Grade Grid

Purpose
This strategy allows students an opportunity to experience a sense of self-determination and autonomy in regard to the grades they receive for a particular class or unit. It is an especially useful strategy for rewarding effort in supplementary activities in any course in which periodic tests are given.

TARGET Areas
(A), (E), (T)

Grade Level
This strategy is particulary useful in middle school and high school.

Procedure
Many academic courses involve activities such as optional laboratories, filmstrip loops, auxiliary problems, films, videotapes, and magazine articles that supplement the instructional objectives of the unit. The use of a Grade Grid is one way to acknowledge and reinforce students' effort on these activities.

The Grade Grid shown in Figure 7-1 is composed of two axes, with the total number of activity points earned during a specific grading period

FIGURE 7-1 Grade Grid

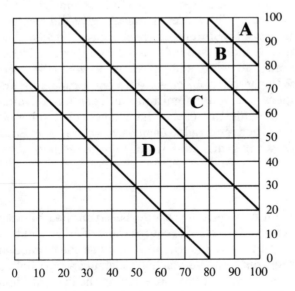

STRATEGY 7-7 *Continued*

on the horizontal axis and a student's average test and quiz scores on the vertical axis. Diagonal lines are then used to separate the area into different course grades.

Students use the Grade Grid by identifying their test and quiz scores on the vertical axis and then following horizontally to determine the total number of activity points necessary for a specific grade. This requires that teachers give students a list of the optional activities and their corresponding point values for each unit or grading period.

Materials
The Grade Grid and optional activity and point list should be duplicated and made available to all students.

Variations
Teachers can adjust the slope of the diagonal grade lines and the number and value of activity points to suit the objectives of their classes.

Source: Ed Sadler, high school physics teacher.

STRATEGY 7-8

Goal Journals

Purpose
This strategy can foster autonomy by encouraging students to set goals for themselves at the beginning of the semester and monitor their own progress toward achieving these goals.

TARGET Areas
(T), (A)

Grade Level
This strategy is useful for upper elementary, middle and high school.

Procedure
At the beginning of the semester each student is asked to keep a notebook that will be used as a personal writing journal during the class. The students will be asked to write in the notebooks for the first fifteen minutes of the class each Monday. Their first entry will focus on what they hope to achieve in the class during the semester. As a guide to the first entry, the following questions may be written on the chalkboard:

Continued

STRATEGY 7-8 *Continued*

What are my expectations for this class?
What grade am I going to work for?
What are some English skills that I think I lack?
What English skills have I mastered?
What three goals do I have for this class?
What must I do to achieve the goals I have stated?
Are my goals realistic for me?

During the following Mondays, students can reflect on their progress toward reaching their goal and can discuss their reactions to the class. The teacher can read the journals periodically and write encouraging remarks. The teacher can also use the journals to provide individual instruction to students who are having difficulty in certain areas.

Materials
Journal notebooks.

Variations
This activity can be adapted to other courses like math, social studies, or science. The teacher may want to collect the journals after every Monday entry and then return them the following Monday. This will ensure that all students will have their journal each week.

Source: Vera Anderson, middle school English teacher.

STRATEGY 7-9

Show Time

Purpose
This strategy provides opportunities for students to experience autonomy and competence. It can also build student self-confidence and self-esteem.

TARGET Areas
(T), (A), (R)

Grade Level
This strategy is useful for instrumental music classes in grades five through twelve. It is also useful for vocal or general music classes at the same grade levels.

STRATEGY 7-9 *Continued*

Procedure
Once a week for about ten minutes near the end of band period, individual students are given an opportunity to perform for the rest of the group. Students may choose any song they would like to play; it might be a tune from their lesson book, band music, or a piece they have written themselves. Students may choose to perform a solo or they may perform with other students. Students should also have the freedom to choose to pass, since this is not a required activity. Students should give prior notice of their desire to perform, so that the teacher can maintain a schedule.

Variations
Depending on the reactions of the group, you may want to select one day a month when you use the entire period for Show Time. Instead of performing on their instrument, some students may want to have an opportunity to be a "Guest Conductor" during part of the band period.

Source: Ron Peterson, middle school band director.

STRATEGY 7-10

Power Notes

Purpose
This strategy can build autonomy and control by offering students choices. It can also build feelings of competence in all students.

TARGET Areas
(T), (A), (E)

Grade Level
This strategy is used in a high school biology class, but it is useful in all grades and subjects where assigned reading is required.

Procedure
This strategy is designed to help students improve their textbook note-taking skills by giving them the choice to learn a different note-taking strategy called "Power Notes." Unlike traditional outlining, this approach uses the numbers 1, 2, 3, or 4 over and over as the student progresses through the material.

The Power Note strategy emphasizes the identification of main ideas, new concepts, and vocabulary. Many science textbooks lend themselve

Continued

STRATEGY 7-10 *Continued*

to Power Notes because of their various vocabulary items, topic headings, and subheadings.

The Power Note outline takes the following form (repeated as many times as necessary until the reading is complete):

1 Heading
   2 Subheading
      3 Main Idea
      3 Vocabulary (may be underlined or highlighted)
         4 Additional ideas or supporting information
1 Heading
   2 Subheading
      3 Main idea
         4 Support information for the main idea

When teaching the outlining skill, the teacher models the technique on the overhead projector or chalkboard, outlining the initial pages of a chapter. For the remaining part of the chapter, students can be given a worksheet with the Power 1s and Power 2s provided, with Power 3s to be constructed by the students. For the next chapter, the Power 1s can be given, with the students providing the Power 2s and 3s. Using this process, the Power Note technique can be learned quickly.

Once learned, students can be given a choice to use their Power Notes on both weekly quizzes and chapter tests. Having the freedom to choose to use Power Notes or not increases student autonomy and effort.

Variations
Some teachers may decide to allow students the choice of using their Power Notes on weekly quizzes but not chapter tests. Students can be given class time to begin their Power Notes at the beginning of each chapter. They can also choose to work by themselves or with another student.

Source: Adapted from Minnick Santa (1988).

8

Enhancing Competence in All Students

How Can the Testing Industry Survive
*When There's Nothing Left to Measure?**

"If there were more of him to measure,"
Said the testers of the child,
"How we'd expand our treasure!"
And the notion drive them wild.

"We've standardized his reading gains,
And measured how they grew.
We've probed into his psychic pains,
Confirmed his last IQ."

"A computer disk on file shows up
His every life decision.
What will he be when he grows up?
We'll tell you with precision."

"We've stanined, averaged, Likert-scaled;
We've standard-deviated,
Guilt from claims that we have failed
Profit alleviated."

"We've sliced his mind in quartiles,
We've ink-blotted his soul.
As for profits, there are more piles
In parts than in the whole."

"Mother love? Shoe size? Bad Breath?
We need more things to count,
So we can measure him till death
And watch our riches mount."

"There's wealth in it, if you've the nerve
To test until it kills;
Please help us find more bell curves—
There's gold in them thar hills!"

RICHARD LARSON (1979)

*From R. Larson (1979), "How Can the Testing Industry Survive When There's Nothing Left to Measure?" *Phi Delta Kappan, 60,* p. 653. Copyright 1979. Reprinted by permission of the publisher and author.

THERE APPEARS TO BE wide agreement among students, parents, and educators that the grades of *A* and *B* are the only valid designators of school achievement; they are also used to reward the behaviors that produce it. Given that the distribution of these two grades, along with the pluses and minuses that accompany them, is primarily determined by evaluation procedures that compare one student's performance against that of others (i.e., "Jimmy is spelling below average"; "Carol is in the top 10 percent of her algebra class"; or "I usually reserve *A*'s for the top 25 percent of the students"), we should not be surprised when large numbers decide to either physically or psychologically withdraw from participation. Structures that must inadvertently produce academic losers as a byproduct in the creation of academic winners motivate only those who believe they have a reasonable chance of ending up near the top.

To increase the academic motivation of *all* students, it is necessary to create an environment in which students can discover that their serious effort toward learning makes it possible for them to attain a sense of academic competence. While the amount of time and effort required for content mastery will vary considerably among students, they all need to have access to the official rewards for achievement.

This chapter will examine two classroom practices that can make it possible to ensure effort–outcome dependency for all students. The first practice is based on the goal-setting strategies discussed in Chapter 7, and the second focuses on the use of an outcome-based classroom learning and evaluation paradigm.

Goal Setting and Competence

As discussed in Chapter 7, goal-setting strategies can be useful in helping students experience a sense of autonomy and self-determination in the classroom. When they are free to select from alternatives, students begin to assume ownership for the consequences of their actions. In short, student commitment results from choice, which, in turn, leads to responsibility.

In addition to supporting autonomy, however, goal-setting strategies allow students to establish individual performance standards based on their own current skill and achievement levels. These personal standards make it possible for concentrated effort to lead to genuine feelings of success. In one of the first research studies to explore this phenomenon, Ferdinand Hoppe presented subjects with the simple task of hanging rings on hooks that passed by them on a rapidly moving conveyor belt. When interviewing subjects in regard to the degree of success or failure they experienced during the task, Hoppe discovered that feelings of success or failure were related to the individual goals of each subject, rather than to the actual number of rings that were placed on the hooks (Barker, 1942). A person with limited goals, for example, might experience success by placing six or seven rings on the hooks, while another who had higher goals might experience failure by placing ten or twelve rings correctly. Hoppe also discovered that individuals adjusted the number of rings they needed for success as they became more skilled at the task. Setting six rings, for example, may have been considered a success at an earlier trial, but that number would likely be considered a failure at a later trial when the individual's skill level had improved. Hoppe referred to these individual goal expectations as the *level of aspiration* for each person. He concluded that feelings of success or failure were independent of actual achievement; they were determined by the goal or aspiration of the individual at the time of performance.

Bandura (1989) proposed that students' perceptions of self-efficacy, or their belief in having the ability to exercise control over the events that affect their lives, significantly influence their motivation and level of aspiration. "After people attain the standard they have been pursuing," according to Bandura, "those who have a strong sense of efficacy generally set a higher standard for themselves" (1989, p. 1180).

Research by Raffini (1988, 1984) replicated Hoppe's findings regarding the relationship between success and goal–outcome performance and examined how this relationship is influenced by competitive, norm-referenced contingencies. Students enrolled in eight sections of a graduate course met individually with the instructor during the first class session and were asked to throw ten beanbags into a basket ten feet away. At the start of each of three trials, students were asked to estimate how many of the ten beanbags they thought they could get into the basket. After each trial, students were asked to count the number of baskets they made and to rate the degree of satisfaction they felt from their performance on a 5-point scale that had been drawn on the chalkboard (1 indicating disappointment, 5 indicating satisfaction). At the beginning of the second class session, each student was asked to throw ten more beanbags, this time in front of the entire group. Students were instructed to make as many baskets as they could, and at the completion of the throws, their names and the number of baskets were placed on the chalkboard. When all students had finished throwing, each score was placed into a frequency distribution and the class determined the median and upper and lower quartile scores. Finally, using the same 5-point scale as the previous week, the students were asked on a questionnaire to indicate their degree of satisfaction with their throws. They were also asked to indicate whether they preferred throwing alone with the instructor or in front of the class.

As Hoppe's results would predict, when throwing alone, student satisfaction ratings were significantly related to achieving their estimate of how many beanbags they thought they could make at the start of each trial; regardless of actual number of baskets, when students met or exceeded their estimate, they rated their satisfaction higher than if they had not reached their estimate. Indeed, the further students were from attaining their actual goal (level of aspiration), the greater was their dissatisfaction. Also consistent with Hoppe's findings, students tended to raise or lower their goal relative to their past performance: If performance fell considerably short of the goal, students tended to lower their estimate for the next trial; if performance reached or exceeded estimates, the goal was raised for the next trial. On the other hand, when students were asked to throw in front of the class, their satisfaction rating was significantly related to their class rank; those in the upper half of the distribution were more pleased with their performance than those in the lower half. Furthermore, those in the upper half preferred throwing in front of the group, while those in the lower half preferred throwing alone with the instructor.

In addition to allowing students an opportunity for self-determination, it seems that when they are free to determine their own goals, their level of aspiration operates as a type of governing mechanism that ensures a reasonable chance of attaining success, regardless of skill level or previous achievement. This is why the weekend duffer and Greg Norman can each experience success or failure on any given golf outing, although one is trying to break 100 and the other is trying to break par. It is this self-governing mechanism that protects against the possibility of repeated failure on the one hand, and against easy achievements on the other. When all students have the opportunity to raise or lower their goals relative to their performance, it is possible for all to have a reasonable chance to experience feelings of success and competence. When students are free to establish goals autonomously, most will prefer reasonable challenges rather than sure things (Ryan & Stiller, 1991). Inherent in challenges is the risk of failure, yet it is only by risking failure that genuine success can be experienced.

As lobbying groups increase pressure for a national curriculum and standardized national achievement tests, educators are forced to restrict students' individualized goal-setting opportunities. Society's demand that standards for successful performance be related to the relative performance of others or to absolute performance standards eliminates the protective aspects of the level of aspiration process. In these situations, satisfaction becomes more a matter of class rank or of meeting teacher expectations than of achieving one's goals. Faster-learning students who have confidence in their ability to achieve in competitive situations are often willing to risk the possibility of failure that comes with challenges and are likely to set realistic goals for themselves. Slower-learning students, however, often avoid this risk by selecting unrealistically high or low goals (Covington & Beery, 1976; Weiner, 1980).

Locke and colleagues (1981) conducted an extensive review of both laboratory and field studies on the use of individual goal-setting procedures for improving task performance. They concluded that goal setting improves task performance by focusing attention, mobilizing effort, and increasing worker persistence. They also found that in about 90 percent of the studies analyzed, specifically defined goals led to higher performance that did vague goals.

The previous chapter presented several suggestions for helping students learn to set realistic goals. These suggestions are useful only to the extent that teachers are willing or capable of allowing students some choice within the learning process. It is only when students have the freedom of choice within the context of raising or lowering their goals that they are capable of selecting goals relative to their current ability levels, a process that ensures that reasonable effort can lead to success. Yet even within highly restrictive and structured curriculum models, teachers can find some opportunities for allowing students to establish personal goals. Such simple inquiries as "How many of these problems can you finish before tomorrow?" or "How many days will you need to complete your history project?" are first steps toward realistic, individual goal setting.

Outcome-Based Education

In addition to individual goal setting, outcome-based learning practices represent a second major classroom procedure that can make it possible for most students to experience genuine success from reasonable effort. By replacing norm-referenced instructional and evaluation standards with standards of absolute performance on clearly stated instructional objectives, outcome-based education (OBE) avoids artificial limits on the number of students who can feel successful and competent. With norm referencing, it is possible for only *half* of the students to perform "above average" in their math class; with OBE it is possible for *all* students to successfully solve simultaneous equations or add mixed fractions with 90 percent accuracy.

The term *outcome-based education* has been primarily used to describe the philosophy of an educational program that bases instructional practice on the specific outcomes desired by teachers and parents. According to Spady:

> *Outcome-based practitioners start by determining the knowledge, competencies, and qualities they want students to be able to demonstrate when they finish school and face the challenges and opportunities of the adult world. Then, with these "exit outcomes" clearly in mind, they deliberately design curriculums and instructional systems with the intent that all students will ultimately be able to demonstrate them successfully. OBE, therefore, is not a "program" but a way of designing, developing, delivering, and documenting instruction in terms of its intended goals and outcomes. (p. 5)*

The term *mastery learning* is often used to describe the instructional implementation of OBE. Based on John Carroll's hypothesis that students will succeed in learning a task to the extent that they are able or willing to spend the amount of time necessary (see Chapter 3), mastery learning is founded on the fundamental assumption that given enough time on task and a willingness to expend concentrated effort, almost all students can attain mastery of the school's curriculum. This assumption contradicts the traditionally held belief that only a limited number of students have the aptitude and learning ability necessary to master the complexities of a given discipline. In its traditional form, mastery learning is usually designed around the following instructional procedures (Raffini, 1986):

1. The teacher establishes instructional objectives based on specific content and skill outcomes. These objectives are designed to reflect exactly what all students should learn and should be important enough to require that all students master them.
2. Two- and three-week instructional units are designed around the course objectives.
3. Whole-group instruction is used for teaching the units.
4. Formative tests determine who needs enrichment and who needs additional instruction and more time on task. These tests are part of the learning process and are not to be used for grading.
5. Students who have attained mastery of the objectives are provided with enrichment activities or "extensions."
6. Additional instruction or "correctives" are provided to those students who did not achieve mastery.
7. A second, parallel formative test is given to those who did not achieve mastery the first time.
8. All students move on to the next instructional unit and repeat the cycle.
9. Periodic criterion-referenced summative tests are used to determine grades.

Bloom (1976) has argued that if differences in student ability are viewed primarily as differences in the amount of time required to master content objectives, it may be possible for 95 percent of the student population to achieve academic success from reasonable effort. Research with individual tutoring seems to support Bloom's contention. Results of two separate studies on the topic revealed that "the average tutored student outperformed 98 percent of the students in the conventional classes, while the average student under the mastery learning condition was above 84 percent of the conventionally taught students" (Bloom, 1986, p. 7). Bloom contends that this research with tutoring demonstrates that *most* students have the *potential* of attaining the high levels of achievement that are often believed achievable by an exceedingly small percentage of students.

Nevertheless, there seems to be some disagreement among researchers about the actual achievement effects obtained in mastery learning studies. In a meta-analysis of findings from more than a hundred controlled research studies of master learning, Kulik, Kulik, and Bangert-Drowns (1990) concluded that, on the average, mastery learning programs "raise final examination scores by about .5 standard deviations, or from the 50th to the 70th percentile, in colleges, high schools, and the upper grades of elementary schools" (p. 285). They also report that although both high- and low-aptitude students gain from mastery learning programs, low-aptitude students gain more. It seems that mastery learning programs have the effect of reducing the achievement differences between high- and low-aptitude students.

Earlier meta-analytic reviews of mastery research all report that mastery learning provides significant increases in student achievement. Block's review of forty studies comparing mastery and nonmastery instructional approaches found that mastery students learn more *effectively* and more *efficiently* than their nonmastery cohorts (Block, 1980). In addition, Block reports that students in mastery classes had a more positive attitude toward the subject matter and instruction, more positive self-concepts, and higher levels of academic self-confidence.

Any structural change that can increase students' academic self-confidence will significantly affect their motivation to learn. As Bandura (1989) has so clearly stated, ". . . it is partly on the basis of self-beliefs of efficacy that people choose what challenges to undertake, how much effort to expend in the endeavor, and how long to persevere in the face of difficulties" (p. 1180).

Guskey and Gates, according to Kulik, Kulik, and Bangert-Drowns (1990), reported that their review of mastery learning studies indicated that the examination scores of students receiving mastery learning instruction improved an average of .78 standard deviations, or from the 50th to the 77th percentile. Chandler's review of 97 evaluation studies of mastery learning reported results similar to those of Guskey and Gates (Chandler, 1982). Students at the 50th percentile in nonmastery groups, according to Chandler, could expect to achieve at the 80th percentile using a mastery approach.

Bloom (1981) reports that mastery learning can result in even greater academic achievement: "The typical results of mastery learning studies in the schools is that about 80 percent of students reach the same final criteria of achievement (usually *A* or *B*+) as approximately the top 20 percent of the class under control group instruction" (p. 134).

Slavin (1987, 1990a) argues, however, that these reviews exaggerate the effects of mastery learning. He concluded that "in studies of at least four weeks' duration, mastery learning had essentially no effect on standardized achievement measures and a small effect on experimenter-made measures . . ." (1990a, p. 300). In response, Kulik, Kulik, and Bangert-

Drowns (1990) argue that Slavin focuses on only a limited area of the research. As a final word, they suggest:

> *Until more studies are conducted, researchers should keep in mind the current results: LFM [learning for mastery] students clearly do better than other students on tests developed to fit local curricula, and they do only slightly better than others on standardized tests that sample objectives from many school systems and many grade levels. There is no evidence to suggest that LFM has any negative effects on any type of student learning. Finally teachers and researchers can learn much more about mastery learning by looking at the full picture rather than the small corner of the research on which Slavin focuses.* (pp. 304–305).

As researchers continue to debate the magnitude and restrictions of mastery learning results, educators must be careful to avoid viewing mastery learning and OBE as panaceas for the problems of student apathy. Effective mastery learning programs are likely to require more time, effort, and creativity from teachers than does traditional instruction. Clearly stated instructional objectives provide the foundation for all mastery learning programs. However, without creativity and vigilance, these objectives can be inappropriately implemented through the introduction of insignificant and isolated pieces of information that students are asked to memorize and then regurgitate.

Cohen (1981) warns that many schools have not organized their curriculum to facilitate continuous progress and mastery. He believes that attempts at implementing outcome-based learning will fail if they are forced—like a square peg into a round hole--to conform to a traditional time-based and norm-referenced curriculum.

Yet an even greater threat to OBE may be the paradox created by its implementation. After monitoring more than 300 master learning projects, Cohen (1981) warns that the successful implementation of OBE on a systemwide basis requires the continuous support of educational leaders. Many attempts at implementing large scale mastery learning programs have been unsuccessful, and Cohen (1981) concludes that "in about 96 percent of the failures, the problem was a principal who would not take responsibility for the curriculum or who would not lead the teaching staff" (p. 37).

Changing the traditional, time-driven school curriculum in order to accommodate instructional extensions and correctives will require considerable administrative support; it will also require a delicate balance between educational leadership and administrative control in order to ensure that OBE doesn't become another "educational innovation" to be shoved down the throats of competent but powerless teachers who have been repeatedly force-fed on what others think is good for them. When teacher autonomy and self-determination are dismissed or disregarded by well-meaning administrators and politicians, educational reform is doomed. Like students, teachers need to feel in control of the contingencies that determine their behavior. Their intelligence and experience must be *respected* in the development and implementation of OBE—both as a signal of esteem and as a way of providing them with ownership. Unless teachers are allowed to fully participate in the decisions that determine their behavior, the hopes and promises of outcome-based education will end up in the overcrowded graveyard of educational reform.

Strong leadership is necessary to implement the changes required by an outcome-based view of instruction; it will require innovative time allocations and flexible teaching assignments to provide the necessary instructional correctives and extensions. More importantly, it will require a major change in the competitive educational philosophy that dominates our schools and has had as its major goal the differentiation and rewarding of those who excel. There is and will likely continue to be much resistance to the higher grades produced by mastery learning. Some erroneously perceive the distribution of higher grades as indicative of "grade inflation" or a lowering of standards, which would be true if grades were meant to indicate relative performance. However, when grades are used to indicate the attainment of absolute achievement standards, it is difficult to imagine any educational practice that will increase student achievement without producing higher grades. Nevertheless, the winners under the current structure are likely to feel deflated and resentful of an educational philosophy that has competence and success for all as its primary goal. "After all," they reason, "what value is an *A* if most people can earn one?" Until educators can answer this question directly and honestly, they will be unable to move toward the structural changes required to implement an authentic outcome-based educational philosophy.

Even without system- or schoolwide implementation of an OBE philosophy, teachers can find mastery learning a useful tool for increasing a sense of competence in greater numbers of students. Research conducted at the University of California at Berkeley (Covington, 1984) examined the effects of a criterion-referenced grading system that substituted absolute performance standards for norm-referenced grades, thus making it possible for all students to receive the grade of *A* or *B* if they achieved the performance criterion. In addition, students were randomly assigned to a one-try or two-try exam sequence, thus allowing half of the sample an opportunity to retake a parallel form of an exam without penalty. The researchers hypothesized that the retesting option would strengthen the causal linkage between effort and outcome and would therefore lead to higher student achievement. Throughout the semester, researchers measured student attitudes toward several key motivational dimensions, including system fairness, confidence that goals would be attained, and grade aspirations.

Results from this complex array of data indicated that students assigned to the prototypic mastery group (absolute performance standards combined with multiple tests) scored significantly higher on test performance and on all the motivational measures than did students assigned to the conventional paradigm (norm-referenced standards combined with a single test). Further analysis revealed that this performance superiority, which resulted from higher grade aspirations and increased confidence, depended exclusively on the presence of a retest opportunity. It seemed that the retesting option increased the amount of effort expended by students and contributed directly to improved future test performance. This upward cycle of successful performances supported effort–outcome linkage and undermined the ability–outcome linkage that sabotages self-worth and contributes to student apathy. In addition, despite many initial failures, a majority of mastery students eventually succeeded in attaining their personal grade goals through persistent effort. "Indeed, approximately 60 percent of all initial mastery failures were followed by successful second-test performances" (Covington, 1984, p. 104).

The Berkeley study also found that students' perceptions of the value of successful performance did not decrease even though the number of students attaining success was greater. According to Covington (1984), competition still exists in a mastery system, but the focus shifts from peer-group competition to competing against the objective standards of the instructor.

Although Covington's research was conducted in a university setting, it has significant implications for teachers at all grade levels. Most importantly, teachers need not wait for systemic, outcome-based educational changes in order to help more students experience competence. By establishing significant and clearly stated objectives, setting criterion-referenced grading standards, and then allowing students multiple testing opportunities, teachers can increase student achievement and improve student motivation and attitude toward learning.

Recommendations for Enhancing Competence for All Students

1. *Evaluate achievement against the attainment of clearly stated instructional objectives.* If all students are to experience academic success, they need to know exactly what knowledge and skills they are required to master. Test questions should not come as a surprise; students need to know exactly what is required of them. It is especially useful if each student receives a copy of the instructional objectives they are required to master.

2. *Wherever possible, achievement should be the constant and time the variable in the class.* Many traditional classrooms provide all students with the same amount of instruction and the same amount of time to master learning objectives. Biology, for example, is typically a discipline all 14- to 16-year-olds attempt to master one hour per day, five days per week, for thirty-six weeks. As a result, achievement in biology varies considerably. Since some students learn at faster rates than others, it seems advisable to allow slower-learning students the time they need to attain the same level of content mastery as faster-learning students. Making time the variable, however, requires major changes in how we view education. After-school time, weekends, and summers offer students opportunities for additional instructional and practice time. It is important that students not be penalized or stigmatized for taking additional time to attain high levels of achievement.

3. *Use individual goal-setting strategies to allow students to define their own personal criteria for success.* Allowing students the opportunity to determine their own task and content goals empowers them to define their own standard for success. When students are free of threats to their self-worth, they can raise or lower their goals relative to their current abilities. Some students, for example, are elated with getting 80 percent of an assignment correct, while others are disappointed by such performance. Allowing them to focus on their own goals increases the likelihood that all students will be able to experience success.

Many teachers fear that when students are free to choose, they will set minimal goals. While this is a common failure-avoiding strategy in competitive environments, it is less likely to occur when students realize that they are competing against their own goals or those of the teacher, rather than against the performance of others.

4. *After initial instruction, use formative tests to identify the specific objectives not yet mastered by each student.* Students will vary in the amount of time they will require to master the instructional objectives. Slower-learning students are likely to require more time and additional instruction. Using diagnostic tests ensures that each set of learning tasks is thoroughly mastered before subsequent tasks are inaugurated. According to Bloom (1981), "Formative evaluation tests should be regarded as part of the learning process and should in no way be confused with the judgment of the capabilities of the student or used as part of the grading process" (p. 170).

5. *Use criterion-referenced rather than norm-referenced evaluation procedures to determine student grades.* Specific standards of excellence can and should be identified by teachers. If we want all students to experience success in the classroom, then it is necessary to evaluate students against these standards, rather than against the performance of others. While some teachers find it useful to establish that the score of 90 percent or above is an *A*, and between 80 and 89 percent a *B*, there is more to criterion-referenced grading than the percentage of items correct. Most teachers are capable of developing a test on which almost all students can earn 100 percent; they can also develop one on which almost no student can achieve over 80. The key to developing a criterion-referenced exam is the selection

of items that measure mastery of specific learning objectives, rather than the creation of items designed specifically to discriminate among students.

6. *Allow students to retake, without penalty, parallel forms of exams that cover clearly stated objectives.* This suggestion may be one of the clearest ways for all students to realize that their increased effort can lead to higher levels of success. It is, however, a difficult suggestion to implement in a classroom of thirty students. While there may be some value in allowing students to retake a test as many times as necessary, for example, more than one retake places an almost overwhelming burden on the teacher. To assist with implementation, Strategy 8.9 will examine this suggestion in more detail.

7. *Design learning and evaluation activities so that performance outcomes are related to the level of effort expended.* Students will expend effort toward learning to the extent that they believe that a relationship exists between the attainment of desired goals and the amount of effort expended. In order to ensure effort–outcome dependence, it is necessary for teachers to structure learning tasks so that meaningful and reasonable effort of students is reinforced by goal attainment. When students know that they will be evaluated against clearly defined objectives, then it is possible for their increased effort toward the mastery of these objectives to lead to desired grade outcomes. The use of contracts that encourage students to correct and resubmit written projects without penalty is helpful to this purpose.

8. *Match learning tasks and the pace of learning to the skill level of individual students.* There is no single pace or level of challenge that is appropriate for all students. Instructional objectives, therefore, need to be task-analyzed to ensure that each student is working at a task appropriate to his or her skill level. This will enable slower-learning students to gradually, but systematically, progress along the path toward mastery.

Providing optimal levels of challenge for twenty-five or thirty different kids every day (or a hundred, at middle and high school levels!) is an impossible task for any teacher. Yet multi-level instructional material, enrichments, extensions, correctives, retesting, and flexible grouping are realistic options a teacher can employ to challenge most students. In fact, just talking to students on a one-to-one basis can help in this process.

9. *Provide faster-learning students with challenging opportunities to enrich and extend their content mastery.* When students are forced to progress through content at speeds considerably slower than their learning rates, they become bored and do not experience a sense of success. True success comes when students are challenged and risk nonsuccess. All students deserve learning experiences that provide reasonable challenges.

10. *Increased achievement requires an increase in higher grades.* When the rewards for content mastery are limited, only a limited number of students will expend effort. Some teachers worry that if they give too many A's and B's they cheapen the value of these grades. Viewing grades as a measure of student ranking fails to acknowledge the goal of content mastery and academic competence for all. High standards are desirable and necessary; their attainment, however, need not be artificially limited or restricted to faster-learning students.

Strategies for Fostering Competence in All Students

───────── **STRATEGY 8-1** ───

BUG Honor Roll

Purpose
This strategy can provide an opportunity for all students to experience a sense of competence and success.

TARGET Areas
(R), (E)

Grade Level
Appropriate for all levels and subject areas in which grades are used to evaluate student progress.

Procedure
At the end of the first grading period, students are introduced to the BUG Honor Roll. They are told that BUG stands for "Bring Up Grades," and that the BUG Honor Roll can be achieved by students who show improvement during the next grading period.

In order to become a member of the BUG Honor Roll, students must improve one class or subject an entire grade without letting any other grade drop. Students who have received the grade of A in all of their courses will be included if they do not let any grades drop. The BUG Honor Roll is a goal that all students can attain, and it is not overwhelming since improvement is required in only one class per grading period.

It is helpful to ask students to examine their report cards and select a subject in which they plan to improve by one letter grade. In elementary and middle school, enthusiasm for the Bug Honor Roll can be generated by having each student draw a picture of a bug with their name and goal subject identified on it. The bugs can be hung throughout the class along with posters and slogans such as, "Look Out for BUGS," "Warning, This Class is Full of BUGS," or "Beware, There are BUGS in This Room."

At the end of the grading period, student names can be sent to the

Continued

STRATEGY 8-1 *Continued*

local newspaper to be published, letters of recognition can be sent to parents, BUG certificates can be presented to students, and the BUG Honor Roll can be read during school announcements just like the traditional GPA Honor Roll. Teachers should be aware, however, that the idea of having one's name announced—particularly at the high school level—as having improved may in fact be a *disincentive* for students who have decided that academic achievement isn't "cool." With these students, teachers may want to emphasize making the recognition more personal and private.

This process can continue during each grading period, although students will find that it becomes increasingly more difficult to continue to improve each time.

Materials
Art materials are needed to make the BUGs, and BUG certificates can be designed and produced on the school computer. A list of requirements for membership might also be helpful.

Variations
This strategy can be used by a single classroom teacher or it can be implemented for the entire school. Physical education classes that utilize the President's Physical Fitness Tests can adapt a similar strategy to reinforce student improvement in selected areas.

Source: Bonnie Jenko, middle school English teacher.

STRATEGY 8-2

Sentence Success

Purpose
This strategy provides a nonthreatening learning activity that can generate feelings of competence and success in all students.

TARGET Areas
(T), (R)

Grade Level
Useful in upper elementary, middle school and high school language arts and English classes.

Procedure
This strategy requires that the teacher write two sentences on the chalkboard before every class period. Each sentence should contain several errors in spelling, usage, syntax, punctuation, or grammar.

STRATEGY 8-2 *Continued*

When students come to class each day, the first thing they are asked to do is write down the two sentences as they appear on the chalkboard. When they have finished writing, they are asked to find the grammatical errors and make the necessary corrections. When they have had enough time, the teacher leads the class in identifying the errors. Reluctant students can be called on first as they can usually find some of the easier errors like punctuation and capitalization. As the more sophisticated corrections are made, students can discuss the reasons for the changes. Students seem to enjoy this strategy because it isn't graded, and they like the structure of knowing exactly what is expected at the beginning of class. It also reduces the "down time" while the teacher takes attendance and gets the class ready for the day's activity.

Material
A good source for sentences is *Daily Oral Language, Levels 1–12*, published by McDougal, Littell & Co., Evanston, Illinois, 1990.

Variations
It may be helpful to encourage students to use one notebook to keep all of their daily sentences for reference in their own writing and editing.

This strategy lends itself to cooperative group work by providing a clear goal. Each group can keep a record of their successes with finding all of the errors.

Source: Patricia Mamerow, high school English teacher.

STRATEGY 8-3

Criterion Grading

Purpose
This strategy is designed to enhance feelings of competence by allowing students to experience effort–outcome dependence in the classroom.

TARGET Areas
(E), (T)

Grade Level
Useful at all grade levels at which students are evaluated with letter grades.

Procedure
Criterion grading is based upon three important assumptions: First, test questions are designed to measure clearly stated course or unit objectives

Continued

STRATEGY 8-3 *Continued*

with which students are familiar; second, the grading criteria are established and have been explained to students; and third, slower students have been given adequate time to achieve the criterion chosen.

In practice, this means that the teacher needs to select test items that clearly measure the stated course or unit objectives rather than trying to discriminate between fast and slow learners. The difficulty level of items should be related to the complexity of the objective being measured, and it is hoped that all students would get all items correct.

A universal set of evaluation criteria does not exist. Variations in the selection, wording, and difficulty of test items and course objectives makes this impossible. Many educators find the following evaluation criteria satisfactory: 100–90 percent = *A*; 89–80 percent = *B*; 79–70 percent = *C*; and below 70 percent = nonmastery. Others advocate the use of an *A* and *B* grading system in which an average of less than 80 percent correct indicates nonmastery.

Probably the most important aspect of criterion grading is that slower students are allowed to retake a parallel test, without penalty, to achieve mastery of the criterion desired. It is equally important that they get time and help to master the content and to correct their errors.

Variations
Given the busy schedules of both teachers and students, retaking exams is difficult to schedule. It may be necessary for students to give up some of their out-of-school time for this purpose and for receiving extra help to master the unit objectives. Faster-learning students often enjoy helping others in this process. Some schools have added an unscheduled period to each school day to create the time for teachers and students to work individually.

Source: Block and Anderson (1970), Bloom (1976), Guskey (1985).

STRATEGY 8-4

Chain Link

Purpose
The absence of predetermined answers makes this strategy useful for helping all students experience feelings of competence. Interest and involvement are generated as students are encouraged to link their prior knowledge to the topic under discussion.

TARGET Areas
(T), (R)

STRATEGY 8-4 *Continued*

Grade Level
Useful for all grades and all subjects.

Procedure
Select a key term or concept from the unit being studied that can encapsulate several related ideas. Since the word chosen will be used to trigger other words, select one that will be familiar to most students. Depending on the content, terms like *health, pollution, fractions,* or *conflict* might be useful.

Print the word on the chalkboard, and ask your students to print the word in their notebooks. Then ask them to identify other words that are related to the topic that begin or end with each of the letters in the key term. The chain link is constructed by writing these words down or up from the key word. Other links can now be developed from the letters of these new terms. As in the game of Scrabble, each new word adds possibilities for additional words.

After students have had ample time to work on their chain links, the class can construct a group chain on the chalkboard, with each student, in turn, offering words from his or her own chain that may fit into the class chain link.

Variations
As the class constructs its chain link, you might want to print the key word on the chalkboard several times to allow for more possibilities in the construction of chains. Using the words from the chain links, students can be encouraged to develop a crossword puzzle of the unit vocabulary terms. Chain links can also be a useful cooperative learning activity with each group developing its own chain.

Source: Jerry Schliem, health and physical education teacher.

STRATEGY 8-5

Concept Blocks

Purpose
This strategy is useful for enhancing feelings of competence in all students by providing a visual reference for organizing and comprehending difficult material.

TARGET Areas
(T), (G)

Continued

STRATEGY 8-5 *Continued*

Grade Level
This strategy is useful for upper elementary, middle school and high school students in most subject areas.

Procedure
Explain the use of a concept block by drawing the grid identified in Figure 8-1 on the chalkboard, numbering and labelling the quadrants. Next, take a one- or two-word concept from a current lesson and write it in quadrant I. Then ask each student in turn to offer an idea related to the concept that can be added to any of the remaining three quadrants. An example using the concept of a dangling modifier is provided in Figure 8-1.

Concept blocks should not be overused, as they can easily become viewed as busywork. They should be seen by students as useful ways to help organize and understand difficult material.

Variations
Self-determination can be enhanced by allowing students to choose which concepts they would like to organize into a concept block. The teacher may mention three or four concepts from the unit or lesson and ask students to vote on which one they would like to use.

This strategy is particularly useful in cooperative groups; Each student or group works on a different concept and then shares results with

FIGURE 8-1 Dangling Modifier Concept Block

I Concept: Dangling Modifier	II Examples: Mixing the eggs, the salt was added. After practicing for weeks, the musical was a success. I saw many trees walking down the road.
III Nonexamples: Mixing the eggs, I added the salt. After practicing for weeks, we had a successful musical. I saw many trees as I walked down the road.	IV Definition: A phrase or clause that does not clearly make more definite the meaning of another word.

STRATEGY 8-5 *Continued*

the group or entire class. It can also be combined with the Jigsaw procedure identified in Strategy 9-1, with different students specializing in each quadrant and then sharing their results.

STRATEGY 8-6

Penquin Parents

Purpose
This strategy generates feelings of competence by inviting students to participate in an activity that fosters responsibility and independent research skills, making it possible for all to succeed.

TARGET Areas
(T), (R)

Grade Level
Elementary school.

Procedure
This strategy requires that the teacher draw or paint several penguins on a large sheet of white butcher paper and display the drawing in the classroom before the students arrive. The teacher can start by mentioning a few facts about penguins and then asking the students to share what they know about these rare birds. After generating some initial interest, the teacher can discuss ways in which the class can find out more information.

The teacher can then set aside one area of the classroom where students can search through materials from the library to learn more about penguins. Children can add newly discovered facts and information to a master list that can be used to develop Penguin trivia questions every few days.

After a week or two of fact gathering, students choose partners and become Penguin Parents for a day. The class will have discussed the responsibilities that male and female penguins share in the task of caring for a penguin egg. On the "parenting day," the teacher brings in hard-boiled eggs and the class pretends they are specially shipped South Pole penguin eggs. Each pair of students cares for one egg for the remainder of the day. They might want to use a felt pen to dress up their penguin egg so that they can distinguish it from the others.

The teacher can also inform the class that he or she will play the role

Continued

STRATEGY 8-6 *Continued*

of the skua and will steal any unattended penguin eggs (students will have learned about the skua during their research). "Responsible Penguin" certificates can be given to each parent who helps his or her egg make it through the day uncracked.

The activity might culminate with egg salad sandwiches or deviled eggs served as a treat on the following day.

Materials
Hard-boiled eggs and library books about penguins.

Variations
The research on penguins can be done in cooperative learning groups. It is also possible to use the same Penguin Parents format when studying other animals.

Source: Diane Miley, third-grade teacher.

STRATEGY 8-7 ━━━━━━━━━━━━━━━━━━━━━━━━━━

Reaction Guide

Purpose
This strategy can provide opportunities for enhancing feelings of competence in all students by encouraging them to express their opinions in a critical thinking activity.

TARGET Areas
(T), (E)

Grade Level
Useful for any grade level or subject area.

Procedure
Before presenting a new unit, the teacher should analyze the significant concepts and identify from five to ten thought-provoking statements regarding the topic to be studied. Next to each statement, construct two columns of blanks, one labelled "Before" and the other labelled "After." Distribute

STRATEGY 8-7 *Continued*

a copy of the statements to each student. Working with a partner, students should take turns reading each statement and putting a (+) to show agreement or a minus (−) to show disagreement in the Before column. Students should be encouraged to discuss with their partners the reasons for their responses, although they do not need to agree on every statement. The teacher can then take an informal poll of the class's opinion regarding each statement. Results should be saved until students have completed the unit.

After students have had an opportunity to study the unit, they can meet with their partners to discuss each statement again. Students should be asked to find evidence from the unit that supports their answers and to explain whether they have changed their views. A large-group discussion of the concept statements can then follow.

Figure 8-2 shows an example of a reaction guide taken from a chapter segment on "Air" from a seventh-grade earth science unit.

The reaction guide in Figure 8-3 was used with remedial reading students in a language arts unit designed around a story on O. J. Simpson. According to Wood (1986), the guide helped provide a lively, thought-provoking discussion both before and after the reading.

Figure 8-4 presents a reaction guide that can assess middle school students' knowledge of factoring. Since reaction guides often assume some prior knowledge of the topic, they can be useful for reviewing previously studied material.

Materials
Reaction guides for each student or each pair of students. Placing a copy on the overhead projector can also help focus group discussion.

FIGURE 8-2 Air Reaction Guide

Before	After	
_____	_____	1. The earth's atmosphere is made up of gases and liquids.
_____	_____	2. Nitrogen is taken in directly as a food source for plants and animals.
_____	_____	3. Without carbon dioxide, plants could not produce oxygen.
_____	_____	4. The atmosphere is made up of two layers.
_____	_____	5. The ozone layer keeps ultraviolet radiation from reaching the earth's surface.
_____	_____	6. The coldest layer of the atmosphere is the stratosphere.
_____	_____	7. Barometers measure the force and direction of air.

From K. D. Wood (1986), "How to Improve Critical Thinking," *Journal of National Middle School Association, 18.* p. 25. Copyright 1986. Reprinted by permission of the publisher.

Continued

STRATEGY 8-7 *Continued*

FIGURE 8-3 Language Arts Reaction Guide

Before   After

_____   _____   1. If you are poor, chances are you will never be able to get very far.

_____   _____   2. People who have been in a lot of trouble probably never change.

_____   _____   3. Sometimes a person has to defend himself no matter what the cost.

_____   _____   4. A mean attitude is necessary if you want to play good football.

_____   _____   5. The ability to play a sport really well is something you are born with.

_____   _____   6. You can do almost anything if you put your mind to it.

_____   _____   7. People who are successful in sports are usually very lucky.

From K. D. Wood (1986), "How to Improve Critical Thinking," *Journal of National Middle School Association, 18,* p. 25. Copyright 1986. Reprinted by permission of the publisher.

Variations

Reaction guides can be used for a variety of purposes in almost any subject. One option is to include a column entitled "Author," which allows the students to differentiate between their opinion and that of the author's. Statements may represent both convergent and divergent aspects of the unit.

FIGURE 8-4 Mathematics Reaction Guide

Before   After

_____   _____   1. The equation $2X^2$ is a quadratic equation.

_____   _____   2. The equation $X^2 - 2X + 1$ can be factored.

_____   _____   3. There is no solution to an equation that has a variable with a higher value than X.

_____   _____   4. It is possible for $(2X - 4)(X + 4)$ to equal $X + 8$.

_____   _____   5. The solutions to $2X - 13X + 15$ are $[+3/2 +5]$.

From K. D. Wood (1986), "How to Improve Critical Thinking," *Journal of National Middle School Association, 18,* p. 25. Copyright 1986. Reprinted by permission of the publisher.

Source: Adapted from Wood (1986). Suggested by Bernadine Butt, middle school English teacher.

_____ **STRATEGY 8-8** _____

Nonverbal Day

Purpose
This strategy is useful for allowing all students to experience success and competence and for developing group identity and relatedness.

TARGET Areas
(T), (G)

Grade Level
This strategy is appropriate to all grade levels. It is particularly useful in middle and high school instrumental music, art, physical education, typing, computer, and industrial arts classes.

Procedure
Announce to the students that on a particular day during the term, the class will be challenged to go through an entire class period without saying a single word. Each student will be asked to focus his or her complete attention on the teacher (conductor) without speaking.

Announcing the event several days in advance allows students to anticipate the challenge and look forward to the new experience. Most students enjoy the feelings of success and pride that come from meeting the challenge and look forward to additional nonverbal days. The activity is also appealing because it is something out of the ordinary routine.

Variations
Elementary teachers might try this during a special activity in which students are involved in individual work.

With a somewhat different purpose in mind, the author has used a similar strategy called the "nonverbal camping weekend" with graduate students enrolled in a course for improving communication skills.

Source: Jerry Borchart, middle school instrumental music teacher.

_____ **STRATEGY 8-9** _____

Second Chance Testing

Purpose
This strategy is designed to allow students an additional opportunity toward achieving competency and mastery of specific content objectives.

TARGET Areas
(E), (T)

Continued

STRATEGY 8-9 *Continued*

Grade Level
Suitable for all grade levels and content areas in which tests are given.

Procedure
At one time or another, most students have finished an exam knowing that if they had another opportunity to retake a similar or parallel form of the test, they could perform much better. This feeling often results from the fact that they did not have a clear understanding of the concepts, knowledge, or skills they had been expected to master. In these situations, testing becomes a game of guessing what content the teacher believes is important. Those who guess wrong get no credit for their effort. On the other hand, many slower-learning or slower-reading students simply do not have sufficient time to master the required material in the time allocated. This strategy allows all students the time they need to demonstrate mastery of the instructional objectives by retaking a parallel form of a unit exam.

Before they retake any test, students should be provided with opportunities to analyze the causes of their unsatisfactory performance on the initial form of the test. Additional instruction may be needed to be sure that all students understand the concepts being tested. Some may simply need more time to absorb the material or to practice a skill, and this need can be accommodated by allowing students additional time after school or on weekends to attain mastery.

Constructing parallel forms of an exam requires additional teacher time, but only minor changes may be necessary when the instructional objective involves mastery of a particular skill such as solving simultaneous equations or learning the appropriate use of semicolon and comma. In these cases, the same questions can be used with different problems. If the objective involves mastery of a specific body of knowledge—such as a spelling test or the five reasons the Union won the Civil War—identical questions can just be readministered. On the other hand, when test items measure only a sampling of the content students are expected to master, then a completely different sampling of test items may be required for the retest.

Some teachers decide to average the results of the original test with those of any retests in order to determine a student's final test grade. This procedure has the effect of punishing slower-learning students; after all, why should it matter that it takes some students a few days longer to learn to spell a list of twenty words correctly, if they eventually master the list? While there are inevitable disadvantages to being a slower-learning student, punishment in the form of lower grades for taking longer to master prescribed objectives need not be one of them.

Some teachers fear that allowing students to take a retest without

STRATEGY 8-9 *Continued*

penalty will encourage them to expend little effort preparing for the initial test. Although some will occasionally take advantage of the retest option by blowing off the initial test, most students discover that it actually requires more effort on their part to take the test twice. They soon learn that by putting in the higher levels of effort for the first test they can avoid the additional burden of the retest.

Retesting does not mean that students who master the material the first time should have to be stifled or bored as they wait around for their slower-learning peers to master the content. On the contrary, these students need challenging and stimulating enrichment and extension activities to broaden and deepen their understanding of the content. For these reasons, retesting may be most effective when combined with a total mastery learning instructional program of the type advocated by Guskey (1985) and Block, Efthim, and Burns (1989).

Variations

To avoid the stigma that may accompany a retest, teachers can use formative tests for their initial testing procedure. These diagnostic tests identify which students have mastered the objectives and which students need additional instruction. Because these formative tests are not graded, students will come to see them as simply another part of the learning process. Occasional summative tests can be used for grading purposes.

Source: Block (1990), Bloom (1976), and Guskey, (1985).

STRATEGY 8-10

Stingerless Spelling Bee

Purpose

This strategy allows all students to experience success and competence by enabling them to contribute equally to a team spelling bee, regardless of their current spelling ability.

Grade Level

Any grade or subject in which mastery of spelling is a major objective. The strategy can also be adapted to other content areas.

Procedure

Students are given a pretest on a list of spelling words to be studied during the week. After allowing a few days for the students to review and practice their spelling list, the class is divided into two teams to begin the Stingerless Spelling Bee. During each round, the teacher calls on each team

Continued

STRATEGY 8-10   *Continued*

member, asking if the student would like to choose an easy word for one point, a moderately difficult word for two points, or a hard word for three points. Since the teacher has each student's original pretest in hand, the difficulty of the words is adjusted to each student's spelling level. An easy word is one that the student spelled correctly on the pretest, a moderately difficult word is one a student had spelled incorrectly on the pretest but had had time to review, and a difficult word is drawn from an unseen spelling list suited to the student's spelling level. One student for each team can serve as a scorekeeper and keep a running total of each team's score on the chalkboard.

While team members confer with one another over the number of points they need and the difficulty level they will choose, each student experiences a sense of autonomy by being free to make his or her choices. By keeping a folder for each student, the teacher can develop a file of words at each difficulty level over the course of the year or semester. The sense of competence, success, and autonomy experienced by students during this activity contributes to their effort and enjoyment in spelling and helps them learn to make realistic choices (deCharms, 1976).

Variations
This procedure can be used in almost any subject area in which it is possible to give students pretests of the material to be studied. It has been used in science classes in which students are required to learn definitions and in English classes where students work with grammar.

Source: deCharms (1976).

9
Facilitating Students' Need for Relatedness

AS DISCUSSED IN Chapter 2, all human beings have a basic psychological need to relate to others in ways that reinforce their feelings of emotional security and belonging. Confronted with the existential realities of life and death, all individuals strive to establish contact, support, and a sense of community with others (Ryan & Powelson, 1991). These emotional bonds foster and maintain feelings of cohesion and connectedness, and it is through this relatedness that individuals come to know themselves as worthy and capable.

Many of the group activities students undertake in school support their sense of relatedness, although this support is often a byproduct of the activity's major goals. Designed primarily for attaining academic objectives, group activities also can foster a sense of relatedness and mutuality among participants. Cohesion, however, is not a natural or inevitable result of group activities. Its development requires an interdependence among group members and the employment of social interaction skills that support each member of the group. Many students learn these social skills at home, while others, unfortunately, arrive at school with a strong need to relate to their peers but without the skills they need to do so.

Experienced teachers have observed socially inept students respond to their sense of isolation and rejection in ways that intensify their ostracism from the group. Feeling spurned and frustrated, they either withdraw into themselves or are compelled to boast or show off as desperate but futile attempts to satisfy their need for belonging. These behaviors, of course, only serve to increase rejection and stifle connectedness.

Most students need help in learning to relate to others in ways that are mutually beneficial. According to Ryan and Powelson (1991), students who feel connected to and supported by significant others within an educational context are more likely to be highly motivated to learn. When they feel socially alienated and disconnected, they disengage from learning. In addition, unpublished research by Ryan, Stiller, and Lynch (reported by Ryan & Powelson, 1991) revealed that the quality of student relatedness with teachers and parents was in large part a function of the degree to which these adults were supportive of student autonomy.

> *It thus appears that autonomy support and involvement facilitate a positive relationship with adults in the social context of learning, which in turn promotes more active engagement, volition, and confidence. It also appears that the experience of relatedness is at least in part founded on one's sense that the other respects and supports one's autonomy. (Ryan & Powelson, 1991, p. 24)*

Furthermore, these authors argue that, in addition to promoting one's psychological well-being, the presence of emotional and personal bonds among students and between teachers and students also supports the process of internalization discussed in Chapter 4. It appears that helping students satisfy their need for relatedness is inextricably intertwined with helping them satisfy their need for self-determination and is a prerequisite for helping them identify with school goals.

Cooperative Learning

Cooperative learning strategies are designed to help students build a sense of relatedness within the classroom while increasing their academic achievement; few instructional approaches are as ambitious. The term *cooperative learning* has come to mean a variety of systematic instructional methods and procedures that bring together from two to five students of varying achievement levels to work collectively in mastering instructional objectives. Although most teachers have used group activities in the past, the current focus on cooperative learning embodies the systematic application of specific group strategies that have been found to increase student achievement and involvement with learning. Robert Slavin and his colleagues at Johns Hopkins University and David Johnson, Roger Johnson, and their associates at the University of Minnesota have independently developed cooperative learning models. Both models are useful for helping students build a sense of relatedness within the classroom, although the Johnson and Johnson model seems to place a greater emphasis on teaching students the specific skills necessary to advance productive group interaction. It is useful to examine the five major elements of the Johnson and Johnson cooperative learning model (1984, 1987):

1. For effective cooperative learning to take place, teachers must structure activities so that they *create positive interdependence* among students. This "we-are-all-in-this-together" atmosphere develops from the belief that each individual's success is based on the mutual success of all group members; this in turn contributes to a group identity based on team membership. It is only by sharing a common fate that all individuals learn that they are interconnected and that they must cooperate for their mutual benefit.

2. Abundant opportunities for *face-to-face interaction* among students are essential for successful cooperative learning and for satisfying students' need for relatedness. Not only does this interaction help students develop personal meanings for the content under discussion; it also fosters a sense of emotional attachment as students express their ideas and have them heard and accepted by others.

3. Activities should be designed so that students are *individually accountable* for their contributions. Each member of the group must be responsible for pulling his or her own weight; "slackers" and "hitchhikers" who try to let others do all of the work cannot be tolerated in an effective cooperative learning lesson.

4. Students need *collaborative skills* for successful group work and for improving their ability to develop relationships that support personal relatedness. Systematic instruction in interpersonal social skills is an essential component of any program that uses cooperative learning to support group productivity and cohesion.

5. *Group processing* or assessment of how well students are working together and meeting each others' needs is a fifth element in the Johnson and Johnson cooperative learning model. By assessing progress and problems, individuals can improve their relationships with their peers and further satisfy their need to belong.

Similarly, Slavin (1990b) maintains that two essential features are necessary if cooperative learning activities are to substantially affect the achievement levels of elementary and secondary students. First, all group members must work together to achieve *group goals*. Second, the group's success must depend upon the achievement of each group member such that each is *individually accountable*. According to Slavin (1987), "[S]imply putting students into mixed ability groups and encouraging them to work together are not enough to produce learning gains: students must have a reason to take one another's achievement seriously, to provide one another with the elaborate explanations that are critical to the achievement effects of cooperative learning" (p. 104).

When a teacher is implementing a cooperative learning instructional model, Kagan (1990) argues that he or she should develop a structural orientation that concentrates on the use of content-free ways to organize group social interaction.

Cooperative *activities,* Kagan notes, are content-bound and limited; making a team bulletin board, demonstrating the potential use of superconductivity, or conducting a group writing exercise are a few examples. Cooperative *structures,* on the other hand, provide teachers with a core of cooperative learning lessons that can be used repeatedly within a wide range of subject matter or grade levels (see strategies 9-1 and 9-2). Such a repertoire of cooperative learning structures is necessary, he argues, since different structures have different functions or objectives (such as team building, improving communication, or fostering content mastery).

Integrating cooperative learning into traditional classrooms requires patience and perseverance. Students may be accustomed to working alone, or they may struggle to maintain an individually competitive orientation when teachers introduce cooperative activities. Using cooperative learning strategies also requires that teachers value the development of student relatedness as an important objective in its own right. According to Johnson and Johnson (1987), teachers should keep in mind that the students who are the most difficult to integrate into cooperative groups are often those most in need of peer support to build their sense of belonging. By starting slowly and by encouraging these students to discuss their reasons for resisting, the teacher and the group may find ways to facilitate increased involvement by reluctant students. The teacher might also design groups so that the more supportive and encouraging classmates can bolster their apathetic and alienated cohorts. It is only through positive interdependence and total group effort that the entire group can experience success.

Although some students may intuitively know how to interact effectively with others, most need specific training in these skills. If teachers assume that students can work together without having been taught the requisite social group skills, positive achievement and interpersonal interactions will be unlikely. This task, however, is not always easy; there are many effective communication and group skills, and a teacher must identify and emphasize those that match the age level, maturity, and competence of the individuals or group in question. Johnson and Johnson (1986, 1987) Johnson, Johnson, and Holubec (1990), Raffini (1980), and Gordon (1974) provide detailed suggestions about how teachers can help students learn and practice the many skills necessary for effective communication and collaboration.

In particular, skills in the following four areas are integral to developing and maintaining productive relationships: (1) accepting and trusting others, (2) sharing thoughts and feelings clearly, (3) listening actively and reflectively, and (4) negotiating conflicts constructively.

The first prerequisite of effective communication is building acceptance and trust. As mentioned in Chapter 6, acceptance is demonstrated by empathetic listening, which illustrates that the listener is trying to understand the speaker's feelings and concerns. Some students assume incorrectly that acceptance and empathetic listening require them to agree with the views or ideas of the speaker. Instead, acceptance means only that the listener accepts others' statements as real for *them*—not for the listener. When students realize that agreement is not necessary for acceptance, they feel less compelled to argue with others or to try to change their views.

Trust, on the other hand, means a willingness to risk self-disclosure. To build relationships, students need to let others know what they are thinking and how they feel. This is never easy, since disclosing one's ideas, opinions, and feelings is always a risk. For most, however, it is a risk worth taking; in the words of one anonymous observer: "To risk is to be vulnerable. To be vulnerable is to live on the edge of pain, but not being vulnerable is not being fully alive."

The skills of active and facilitative listening, also examined in Chapter 5, involve communicating understanding and empathy through paraphrasing and reflection of feelings. Although some students feel artificial or mechanical when they practice active listening skills, reflecting back the speaker's message or feelings can be a far more effective way to express empathy than simply saying, "I understand what you mean" or "I know how you're feeling." Telling someone that they have been understood may or may not communicate effectively; proving understanding through reasonable paraphrasing and reflection of feeling leaves no doubt.

Communicating thoughts and feelings clearly requires a willingness to self-disclose and the skills that involve descriptive confrontation and "I" messages discussed in Chapter 5. Like teachers, students need to learn to express their feelings and opinions without attacking or name calling, especially when these feelings are strong and concern the behavior of others. It is also important that they learn to communicate warmth and support for others in ways that are easily understood. This is a difficult skill for some students to learn, especially given their experience that statements like "Hi, Ugly" or a punch in the arm can also be used to convey acceptance or recognition. It is necessary, therefore, to encourage students to err on the side of clarity and to avoid the possibility of mixed messages.

Conflicts arise as a natural part of human interaction, and it is important for students to learn to resolve them in ways that protect rather than destroy relationships. The skills of conflict negotiation, presented in Chapter 5, were offered as suggestions to help teachers resolve conflicts with students; these skills are also useful for helping students resolve conflicts with one another.

In addition to the communication skills previously discussed, Johnson, Johnson, and Holubec (1990) offer the following four levels of *cooperative skills* necessary for students to work effectively in groups:

1. *Forming skills.* This set of skills includes the organizational and management skills necessary for students to move into groups and conduct their work without disturbing others. Logistical considerations such as desk arrangement and movement in the classroom must be discussed and understood.

2. *Functioning skills.* This level of skills deals with helping students maintain effective working relationships so that they can complete their tasks. Students need to be encouraged to use the previously discussed communication skills in order to keep all group members on task while maintaining a friendly and supportive working environment. All participants must learn to contribute to the leadership responsibilities necessary for obtaining a comfortable balance between task and supportive roles.

3. *Formulating skills.* This stage of development is concerned with helping groups use higher-level reasoning and processing skills to build a deeper understanding of the issues being studied. Johnson, Johnson, and Holubec (1990) offer the following models to assist in this process:

- *Summarizer:* Students should be asked to summarize verbally the material that has just been read or discussed as completely as possible without referring to notes or texts. All the important ideas and facts should be included in the summary. All members of the group must summarize from memory often if their learning is to be maximized.
- *Corrector:* Student should be asked to check for accuracy by correcting other students' summaries, adding important information they did not include and pointing out ideas or facts that were summarized incorrectly.
- *Elaboration Seeker:* Students can seek elaboration by asking other members of the group to relate the material being learned to earlier material and to other things they know.
- *Memory Helper:* Members of the group can identify clever ways of remembering the important ideas and facts by using drawings, mental pictures, and other memory aids.
- *Checker:* Students should vocalize their understandings as a way of making explicit the reasoning process being used by group members and thus open to correction and discussion.
- *Explanation Checker:* The group should plan out loud how to teach another student the material being studied. Planning how best to communicate the material can have important effects on quality of reasoning and retention.

4. *Fermenting skills.* This level of skills help students confront controversial material and challenge the arguments and reasoning of others in ways that maintain group productivity and cohesiveness. Students need to agree to disagree in ways that attack ideas rather than people, so that when they ask for justification or clarification others do not take their probes personally. This allows all members to integrate and extend the ideas of others so that a group position can be formulated and clarified.

To assist in helping students acquire these and the other skills necessary for effective interpersonal and group relationships, Johnson and Johnson (1990) offer the following five suggestions:

1. Students must perceive a need for using the skill. This requires that teachers take the time necessary to help students realize why they will be more effective in meeting their goals if they will practice the skills being discussed. Students can easily identify situations in the past where group productivity has broken down. By processing the causes of these breakdowns, they can begin to realize how the use of effective interpersonal skills may have prevented these difficulties.

2. Students must be able to understand and recognize the specific characteristics of the skill and when it is most effectively used. Johnson and Johnson (1990) suggest that teachers use a factor analysis or T-chart to help students become thoroughly familiar with the skill. Figure 9-1 provides an example of a T-chart for the skill "encouraging participation." T-charts allow the teacher to list individual skills and then ask the class to help generate a list of what the skill looks like or what can be observed when students are practicing the skill. After generating these observational aspects are listed, the other side of the T-chart is filled in with student-generated phrases describing what the skill sounds like when students are

FIGURE 9-1   T-Chart

SKILL: Encouraging Participation	
Looks Like	Sounds Like
Smiles	"What is your idea?"
Eye Contact	"Awesome!"
Thumbs up	"Good idea!"
Pat on back	"That's interesting"

From D. W. Johnson and R. T. Johnson (1990), "Social Skills for Successful Group Work," *Educational Leadership, 47* (4), p. 30. Copyright 1990. Reprinted by permission of the publisher.

practicing it. The teacher can then model the skill until all class members have a clear understanding of its specific behavioral aspects.

3. The third step of the skill development process involves creating opportunities for students to practice until they have thoroughly mastered it. Role playing each skill with a partner is a useful first step in this process. The teacher can also secretly assign skill roles to specific members of a group and have them play these roles while the group is dealing with a simulated topic. The roles can then be rotated so that each student has an opportunity to practice each skill.

4. Students should be encouraged to evaluate how well they are using their interpersonal skills during actual cooperative learning projects. The teacher should provide regularly scheduled time during each group activity for students to discuss and reflect on their use of interpersonal skills. Johnson and Johnson suggest that teachers ask the group to name three things they did well and to identify one skill that the group could do better during the next activity. They report that such group processing not only fosters student skill development but also increases student academic achievement and improves the quality of the interpersonal relationships developed among students (Johnson & Johnson, 1990).

5. Students should be encouraged to practice group skills until their use becomes fully internalized. During the first stages of skill development, students will feel phony and mechanical. They should be encouraged to discuss these feelings and to accept them as a natural part of the learning process.

Learning and using effective communication and cooperative skills are difficult processes for many students, and it may require the friendly support and encouragement of teachers. Figure 9-2 presents a four-step process that can help students understand and identify with the stages

FIGURE 9-2 Phases in Communication Skill Development

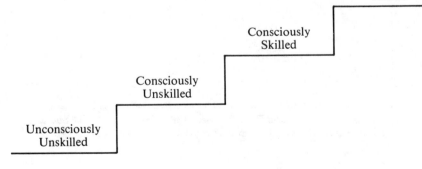

they may experience when learning effective communication and group skills. The first stage, labelled *unconsciously unskilled,* describes individuals who demonstrate poor listening skills by disregarding the feelings of others, interrupting others to change topics, using put-downs, and generally interacting in ways that close off effective communication. During this phase, individuals are unaware of the negative effects that these poor listening skills have on others or on their own need to relate in supportive ways. This lack of awareness causes people to blame others for their isolation or for break-downs in communication. This step can be characterized as the "ignorance is bliss" stage of verbal intercourse.

The second phase, *consciously unskilled,* is when individuals become aware of the negative impact of their communication style but feel helpless to change. They are either ignorant of alternative approaches for responding, or they repeatedly forget to use the skills they have been taught to improve communication. In either case, this is the guilt stage of skill development in which individuals often reflect back on interactions and realize that they "should" have responded differently.

The third phase on the path to effective communication is called *consciously skilled,* and it is reached when individuals decide to consciously and systematically practice the skills of effective interpersonal and group communication. Although their responses may seem rehearsed and mechanical, they begin to see improvements in group productivity or in the quality of their relationships with others. Yet the mechanical nature of their responses often generates feelings of phoniness; they respond as they "should," but they don't feel authentic in doing so. The student thinks, "I'd like to tell Jimmy to stop being such a jerk, but I know I should say, 'Jimmy, when you interrupt others when they are speaking, I get frustrated because I can't hear or understand what they are saying.'"

If individuals persist in using theie effective communication skills through the third step, they may eventually become *unconsciously skilled.* It is at this step that individuals no longer need to question or premeditate their responses. Effective communication, based on the integration of previously practiced skills, becomes their natural way of responding in interpersonal and group interactions. Attaining this phase is a life-long process, and one that is supported by repeated practice during phase three.

Group Rewards in Cooperative Learning

To help students perceive the need for interpersonal and small-group skills, Johnson and Johnson (1990) advocate the use of a bonus point system that rewards students with academic credit or special privileges when they use targeted cooperative skills. Slavin (1991a) also argues that if teachers want to encourage students to expend the necessary effort to master a subject, they will need to use external rewards like praise, high grades, or recognition to reinforce these efforts. As indicated in Chapter 4, however, there is considerable evidence to indicate that when rewards are used to undermine student autonomy, they may actually decrease student interest in the tasks at hand. As Kohn (1991) says, "If bribing individuals to learn is so demonstrably ineffective and disadvantageous, what makes us think that bribing groups to learn is productive and benign?" (p. 85). Although Kohn agrees that group goals are a necessary part of the cooperative learning process, he worries that bribing groups with certificates, bonus points, or privileges may be counterproductive and, in fact, minimize student motivation.

In summarizing the debate over group rewards in cooperative classrooms, Graves (1991) offers several proposals that are consistent with the research, as well as suggestions on the controlling versus informational aspects of rewards discussed in Chapter 4:

1. When teachers believe that the use of rewards is necessary, they should avoid the appearance of manipulation by involving students as much as possible in setting their own goals. Rewards should then be given when students achieve these agreed-upon goals.

2. Symbolic rewards like certificates of group achievement that communicate the teacher's appreciation of students' efforts are more useful than tangible rewards like small gifts and treats that may become ends in themselves.

3. Unanticipated rewards like a class party or free time at the end of the day after the class has worked hard are useful for enhancing student motivation.

4. Try to help students make the pleasure of working together in cooperative groups a reward in itself. Many teachers find that students who enjoy working together no longer need external incentives. Weaning students away from extrinsic rewards may not be as difficult as some authors suggest. "In fact," as Graves points out, "it may be more difficult to wean *teachers* away from routinely using these rewards even when they are no longer necessary."

Cooperative Learning Research

A substantial amount of research has been conducted on the effects of cooperative learning methods on student achievement. Slavin (1990b, 1991b) has analyzed more than sixty studies that contrast the achievement outcomes of cooperative learning and traditional instructional methods in elementary and secondary schools; Johnson and Johnson (1981, 1987), using different inclusion criteria, have analyzed many more. Both analyses have concluded that when cooperative learning methods provide for group goals and individual accountability, the effects on student achievement are marked and consistent. A synthesis of research on cooperative learning by Joyce, Showers, and Rolheiser-Bennett (1987) concluded that on standardized achievement tests, cooperative learning models generated an average effect size greater than 1 standard deviation, meaning that the average student in cooperative learning groups performed above the 90th percentile of students in the control groups.

In addition to achievement gains, cooperative learning has been shown to have a significant impact on the attitudinal and motivational levels of students. The Joyce, Showers, and Rolheiser-Bennett analysis indicated that cooperative learning environments substantially increase students' feelings of empathy toward others, reduce anti-social behavior and intergroup tensions, and increase positive feelings toward others. Slavin reports similar noncognitive outcomes of cooperative learning. Specifically, cooperative learning has been shown to increase student cooperation, favorable attitudes toward school, self-esteem, and autonomy or internal locus of control (Slavin, 1983).

McDaniel (1984) found that although cooperative learning groups focus primarily on academic achievement, they can promote higher levels of self-esteem in students by fostering a sense of group belonging. He concludes, "When students learn the joy of working productively together toward common goals, motivation inevitably improves" (p. 47).

In summarizing some of the areas of agreement and controversy in the cooperative learning research, Slavin concluded:

> *In every area of research there are debates about what the research means. Cooperative learning, a topic studied by many researchers from different research traditions, is certainly no exception. However, after nearly two decades of research and scores of studies, a considerable degree of consensus has emerged. There is agreement that—at least in elementary and middle/junior high schools and with basic skill objectives—cooperative methods that incorporate group goals and individual accountability accelerate student learning considerably. Further, there is agreement that these methods have positive effects on a wide array of affective outcomes, such as intergroup relations, acceptance of mainstreamed students, and self-esteem. (1990b, p. 54)*

Recommendations for Building Student Relatedness

1. *Help students learn the skills of empathetic listening.* If students are to satisfy their need for relatedness, they must learn to listen to their peers in ways that communicate an understanding and acceptance of feelings. Only by listening and accepting the feelings of others does one come to expect that one's own feelings will be heard and understood. It is a mistake to assume that students know instinctively how to listen and to understand each other; listening skills must be learned and practiced.

2. *Help students learn to express their feelings in ways that don't attack or injure others.* All individuals need to assume ownership of their feelings and to express them in ways that do not judge others (see Chapter 5's discussion of confrontation). Although it may be easier for Jimmy to call Johnnie an inconsiderate jerk for interrupting him, communication is maintained and feelings of relatedness are fostered if Jimmy simply acknowledges his anger or frustration with the interruption without labelling the character of the interrupter.

3. *Take time to systematically help students learn to communicate acceptance and support for one another.* Students need help in learning the skills of acceptance and interpersonal support; T-charts and role playing can be helpful in this process. In addition, students need opportunities to discuss and reflect on the value of interpersonal support in the classroom. Cliques and intolerance of others are the norm in many classrooms, and students need a supportive environment in which to discuss the causes and effects of such behavior. They do not need lectures on the importance of cooperation and the ills of intolerance, although open discussions where the integrity and esteem of all participants are valued and protected can be beneficial. Individual identities should be protected in discussions of rejection or discrimination. Rather than focusing on specific incidents of put-downs or rejections, feelings of rejection and belonging can be discussed in broad terms that protect all participants.

4. *Help students learn and practice the skills of conflict resolution.* Chapter 5 presents a systematic approach for helping teachers resolve conflicts with students. Teachers may want to discuss this approach with students and help them learn the skills necessary to use it when dealing with conflicts among themselves. Students often turn to the teacher to "solve" their conflicts, rather than working to resolve them on their own. Yet students cannot be expected to settle conflicts without the prerequisite skill training.

5. *Attempt to develop group goals and positive interdependence in the classroom.* In addition to designing small-group activities around the goal of positive interdependence, it is useful for teachers to work to establish interdependence among all class members. Each student must be made to feel that he or she is an important contributor to the group's identity. In this environment, the success of each person is strengthened and reinforced when others in the group are successful. Competitive classrooms create both winners and losers and undermine a sense of esprit de corps and relatedness among their members. When cooperation replaces competition, group goals become mutual and individuals identify and relate with one another.

6. *Foster individual accountability for contributing to class and group goals.* Each person in the class must be helped to realize that his or her achievement and contributions are important to the success of others in the class. Students can relate to one another primarily by contributing to the group's goals. If the content objective is to learn to add fractions, for example, then each member is responsible for his or her achievement in the process of getting everyone to a level of content mastery. When students are competing to be and to do better than others, group identity and individual relatedness are sacrificed.

7. *Avoid penalizing some students for the behavior of others.* While group goals build positive interdependence, no one should be penalized for the behavior of others. When a student lets a group or class down by failing to fulfill an obligation or complete an assignment, penalizing others only serves to increase resentment among students. This suggestion does, in part, contradict the objective of building positive interdependence. Some teachers find that they can meet both objectives by focusing on the *bonus* benefits of group contributions. With this approach, individuals are not directly penalized for a group's failing to achieve its goal, although they may receive an extra benefit from group success.

8. *Avoid forcing students to compete for a limited number of rewards.* Forced competition can contribute to detachment and alienation from the losers and can create jealousy and resentment toward the winners. It is probably the most powerful factor undermining group relatedness in the classroom. Group competition can, however, soften these negative effects. When groups compete against each other, the pain of defeat and the elation of victory are shared among team members. Both experiences can foster a sense of relatedness.

9. *Affirm the importance of affective goals within the classroom.* As pressures to attain cognitive outcomes increase, a commitment to affective goals may easily be swept aside. The algebra teacher, for example, may be so concerned that all of her or his students achieve at a certain level that little time is available for helping students improve interpersonal skills or establishing a sense of group relatedness. Yet 90 percent of workers who have been fired from their jobs have been dismissed because of poor attitudes or poor interpersonal relationships rather than for lack of basic and technical skills (Johnson & Johnson, 1990). Even in highly technical jobs, the ability to work effectively with others is one of the skills necessary for success. To assume that students will learn these skills on their own or that someone else will take responsibility for teaching these skills is shortsighted and unfair. Although cooperative skills may have been taught elsewhere, students need extensive practice with these skills in order to reinforce their importance and to increase the likelihood that they become internalized; all teachers have a responsibility to provide these opportunities and reinforce those skills.

10. *Use feedback procedures to assess and discuss the interpersonal* *climate and personality of the classroom.* Classes as well as small groups need opportunities to assess how well they are doing in meeting their academic and interpersonal needs. A useful procedure is to occasionally distribute 3 × 5 cards to all class members and have them anonymously answer questions like, "Identify two things about this class that make you feel like you belong, and two things that separate you from others in the class" and "What suggestions do you have for improving the way that the class works together?" Small groups can also discuss these topics, and their conclusions can be reported to the entire class. In either case, it is the teacher's commitment to helping students meet their interpersonal needs that makes this feedback productive.

Strategies for Building Student Relatedness

―――――― STRATEGY 9-1 ――――――――――――――――――――――――――――

Jigsaw

Purpose
This structural strategy is designed to foster a sense of group relatedness by making the contributions of each participant necessary for achieving a group goal.

TARGET Areas
(T), (R), (G)

Grade Level
This strategy is multifunctional and can be adapted to almost all grade levels and content areas.

Procedure
This strategy involves structuring a classroom learning project so that several small groups of equal size (four to six students each) work independently to master new material. The topic being studied is divided into a number of subtopics to equal the number of members for each group. Each participant is then expected to become an "expert" on the assigned subtopic so that he or she can teach it to the other members of the group. Each group member thus represents a part of a jigsaw puzzle that takes shape when all the pieces come together; the total becomes greater than, but dependent on the sum of the parts.

   After the subtopics have been assigned to group members, it is useful to have students work with members from other teams assigned the same

STRATEGY 9-1 *Continued*

topic. (These new expert groups become equal in size to the number of original or home groups. If this number is too large, these expert groups can be split into two or even three subgroups.) It is important that the teacher serve as a resource to each of the expert groups, helping them find more information on their topics, analyze the important concepts, and devise visual and creative methods for teaching the concepts to their home groups.

Upon returning to their home groups, each student in turn presents the information on his or her subtopic and helps each group member understand and master it. Since students will be assessed on all aspects of the topic, each expert has an important obligation to help others with his or her portion.

Variations
It is sometimes helpful to have each group member fill out anonymous feedback forms for each expert's presentation. Both strengths and weaknesses of the presentation can be identified, and suggestions can be offered on how the presentation might have been made more effective.

Source: Aronson et al. (1978).

STRATEGY 9-2

Numbered Heads Together

Purpose
This structural strategy is designed to foster a sense of group relatedness by utilizing the contributions of all members to help each master the content objectives.

TARGET Areas
(T), (R), (G)

Grade Level
Useful for all grade levels and content areas.

Procedure
This relatively simple four-step strategy builds positive interdependence and individual accountability while fostering a sense of relatedness and belonging within each participant. The first step is to number each student in the group; all groups should have approximately equal numbers, usually four or five. The teacher then provides the class with a question

Continued

STRATEGY 9-2   *Continued*

or problem based on the unit objectives. Groups are then told to "put their heads together" to solve the problem or find the answer to the question posed. They are also told that each member of the group must know the answer to the problem and be able to demonstrate the procedure for deriving it. If it was a conceptual question, students must know the reason or reasons why their answer is correct. The final step in the process is for the teacher to call a number and for students with that number to explain their answers or carry on a discussion of the problem in front of the entire class.

This simple question-answer procedure can involve all class participants in the academic content of the class, and it builds a sense of group identity and relatedness by encouraging each member to contribute to the learning of others.

Variations
The teacher can use this strategy to create a learning tournament or group contest where different test questions are given to each number and then a total group score is determined by adding member scores. Special bonus points can also be distributed to the entire team when each team member has obtained mastery. Other bonuses or celebrations might be used when members of all groups have obtained mastery.

Source: Kagan (1990).

STRATEGY 9-3

Epidemic

Purpose
This strategy is useful for building group relatedness while getting students actively involved in problem solving.

TARGET Areas
(T), (G)

Grade Level
Middle or high school general science, biology, or chemistry classes.

Procedure
This activity is described by using a group of twenty-four students, although it can be adapted to almost any number. Students are to work in pairs, with each pair given a sterile petri dish containing a piece of hard red

STRATEGY 9-3 *Continued*

candy. The dishes are numbered, and the piece of candy in dish 9 should be treated with 2 ml of 24 hour nutrient broth culture of *Micrococcus roseus*, a bacterium that produces a red pigment. The remaining pieces of candy can be treated with 2 ml of sterile water. One student in each pair is instructed to avoid the temptation of eating the candy, but to pick it up and roll it around in the nondominant hand. The candy is then to be returned to the dish.

Next, the teacher calls out the pairs of numbers indicated in the first set, and students with those numbers who held the candy are instructed to shake hands, making sure to make a good contact with their nondominant hands that held the candy. As the numbers are called, the partners are to record the numbers of each pair of students shaking hands. The teacher then calls out the numbers in set two, and these students shake hands as in the first set, with their partners recording the pairings. This procedure is continued through set three.

After the handshaking is completed, partners of the shakers are instructed to moisten a sterile cotton swab with a sterile nutrient broth and to roll the swab over the hand of their partner that was used in the shaking. They are then instructed to streak a plate of nutrient agar with the cotton swab, making sure to roll the swab while streaking. The swabs and nutrient broth should then be discarded, and the students should wash their hands with soap and water and, as an added precaution, clean their workstation with an antiseptic. *It is important that students wash their hands and workstations thoroughly.*

The agar plates should be incubated for twenty-four to forty-eight hours and then examined for red colonies of bacteria. The results of each student's agar test are to be indicated on the record sheet.

After the agar tests, students are instructed to use the data on their record sheets and decide who started the "epidemic" and to trace its progress throughout the class. (They will be able to narrow it down to either student number 9, or student number 4.)

First Set	*Second Set*	*Third Set*
1–12	1–2	3Λ–9*
2–10	3Λ–4Λ	2–11
3–11	5–6	1Λ–10Λ
4Λ–9*	7–8	4Λ–5Λ
5–8	9*–10Λ	8–12
6–7	11–12	6–7

* = starter of the epidemic
Λ = bacteria obtained by shaking

Continued

STRATEGY 9-3   *Continued*

Materials

1. Sterile, numbered petri dishes for each pair of students
2. A piece of hard red candy for each pair of students
3. *micrococcus roseus* broth culture
4. one sterile test tube containing a sterile cotton swab for each pair of students
5. one tube of sterile nutrient broth for each pair of students
6. sterile plate of agar for each pair of students

Variations

Red marbles can be substituted for the candy, and if the class is small enough, students could work individually rather than in pairs.

Source: Recommended by Jim Barnstable, high school biology teacher. Adapted from Mangino (1975).

STRATEGY 9-4

Kids on Camera

Purpose

This strategy provides an opportunity for students to become actively involved in an activity that generates a sense of group relatedness and identity.

TARGET Areas

(T), (R), (G)

Grade Level

Upper elementary, middle, and high school.

Procedure

This strategy invites students to plan, write, and perform a class television program. Possibilities include talk shows with host and guests, similar to Arsenio Hall or the Church Lady; game shows such as "Jeopardy"; talent shows such as "Star Search"; or news shows such as "60 Minutes" or "20-20."

Once the class decides on a format and title, they discuss the various roles that might be needed, including production crews and actors. Plans can also be made for the inclusion of two or three commercials. After the format for the show has been established, students divide into cooperative

STRATEGY 9-4 *Continued*

groups and each group chooses an aspect of the program for which they will be responsible. Possibilities include camera and videotape crew, teams for commercial production, program and script writers, interviewers, make up and costumes department, hosts, guests, and so on, depending on the nature of the production. It is important that the teacher attempt to get all students significantly involved in some aspect of the production. If several students prefer the same roles, random selection may be the fairest approach.

The school's audiovisual coordinator can help the technical crew arrange the necessary production equipment. Parents are also good sources for video cameras, recorders, lights, and other help. A director or production team can coordinate the writing, rehearsing, and videotaping schedule. It is also important that all students appear on camera during some part of the program. With some of the behind-the-scenes roles, this can be accomplished during the "rolling of the credits" following the program.

The actual airing of the program can be shared with parents, local cable stations, or other classes within the school. This activity can generate high levels of enthusiasm and involvement and a sense of pride and identity with the total production. Many students will want to have their own copy of the videotape, and the video crew can establish a procedure for making these.

Variations

There are many variations possible with this strategy. Topics for the show can be directly related to the content being studied, such as a roving reporter interviewing members of the Lewis and Clark expedition, or investors during the stock market crash. Regardless of variation, it is important that all class members be actively involved in the program's production.

Source: Adapted from Laurie Marx, elementary teacher.

─────── **STRATEGY 9-5** ───────────────────────

Accomplishment Hunt

Purpose

This strategy is useful for developing a sense of group relatedness and group identity during the ice-breaking stage of a new class. It also serves to enhance a sense of competence by focusing on students' accomplishments.

TARGET Areas
(T), (R)

Continued

STRATEGY 9-5 *Continued*

Grade Level
Upper elementary through high school.

Procedure
At the beginning of a new year or semester, ask students to list two of their personal accomplishments for which they feel most proud, regardless of how insignificant they may appear to others. Encourage students to select accomplishments that are likely to be original and unique, such as being the best banjo player in his or her family, having the cleanest room in the house, being able to spit watermelon seeds farther than anyone in his neighborhood, having gone white-water rafting or sailing on a square-rigger during a vacation, etcetera. Ask students not to mention these two accomplishments to others in the class since they will be used in a special activity during the next class period.

Before the next class meeting, make a random list of the two accomplishments for each student in the class. Next to each item leave a blank where a student's name can be written in during the accomplishment hunt.

At the start of the next class, hand out the list of accomplishments to the students, informing them that the object of the activity is to discover which class member has achieved each of the accomplishments. By browsing around in a large group, they are to interview as many students as they can and ask them if they ever have. . . . The interviewee can only respond by answering "yes" or "no." Once the two accomplishments have been identified, the two students can discuss them for a few moments before they switch roles.

The teacher should try to play down the competition to be the first finished. Encourage students to use the accomplishment hunt to meet every other class member and get to know a little about them.

Variations
In addition to accomplishments, the teacher might focus on states or countries visited by students or on students' previous places of residence as topics for the hunt. The teacher might also decide to use more than two accomplishments, depending on the size of the group.

STRATEGY 9-6

The Crusher

Purpose
This strategy is a particularly useful cooperative learning activity for building relatedness and for stimulating interest in math classes. It has

STRATEGY 9-6 *Continued*

a clear outcome goal and offers an exciting challenge for groups to work together to resist the devastating force of the "Crusher."

TARGET Areas
(T), (G), (R)

Grade Level
Particularly useful for middle and high school math, technical drawing, and science classes.

Procedure
Working in cooperative groups, students are asked to construct a geometric structure, a minimum of five inches in height, using a maximum of forty straws, forty paper clips, and forty straight pins that have been made available by the teacher. Each group is challenged to build the strongest structure possible using the least amount of weight.

It is important that each group member be given a specific role in the structure construction. The following are examples of possible roles:

- *Designer:* This person is responsible for designing the group's structure. All group members should be encouraged to contribute ideas, but the designer is the person who completes the final sketches before construction and has the final word on any suggestions or changes during the construction process.
- *Paper clipper:* The paper clipper is in charge of monitoring paper clips and physically placing them into the structure when they are needed.
- *Strawboss:* The strawboss is in charge of monitoring straws and physically placing them into the structure when they are needed.
- *Pinboss:* The pinboss is in charge of monitoring pins and physically placing them into the structure when they are needed.
- *Project expediter:* The project expediter can work with the designer to coordinate the structure's construction.

Prior to using this strategy the teacher must construct the "Crusher" (see materials section). When students have completed the design and construction of their geometric object, they are ready to confront the Crusher. To start, each structure is accurately weighed and the weight recorded on the chalkboard. The structure is then placed in the center of the crusher base and the platform is set on top. Weights of various sizes are added one at a time to the Crusher platform to determine the total weight necessary to crush a particular structure (crushing can be defined as the weight needed to bring the platform to within two inches of the base). This number is placed alongside the structure weight on the chalkboard. After all structures have been crushed, each group is given a score based on the ratio

Continued

STRATEGY 9-6   *Continued*

of the load weight withstood by their structure to the total weight of the structure.

In addition to building a sense of group identity and relatedness, this activity shows the application of ratios in the construction industry and provides opportunities for students to calculate these ratios.

Material
To construct the "Crusher," one-foot square pieces of 1/4- or 1/2-inch plywood can be used for the base and for the platform. Four 1/2 inch by 18 inch wooden dowels are attached to each corner of the base, using screws and glue. Four corresponding 5/8-inch holes are drilled into the platform (see Figure 9.3). To add to the challenge, the Crusher can be painted and decorated to look intimidating.

Small dive weights, science lab weights, or assorted stones or pieces of metal that have been weighed and marked can be used to determine the total weight withstood by each structure. An accurate scale will be necessary to weigh each structure.

Variations
In art or drawing classes, students could be asked to construct a scale drawing of their model before it meets the Crusher. Using both standard and

FIGURE 9-3   "The Crusher"

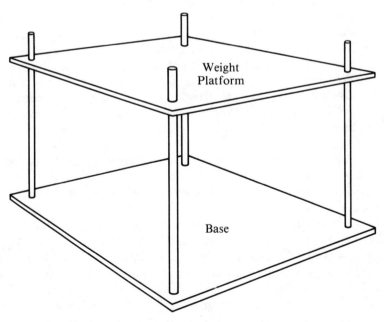

STRATEGY 9-6 *Continued*

metric measures of weight provides students with an interesting and practical comparison between these two methods of measurement. Additional construction material such as rubber bands, thumbtacks, or thread might be used in the construction of each group's structure.

Source: Adapted from Chris Pavlotos, math teacher.

STRATEGY 9-7

New Kid on the Block

Purpose
This strategy is useful for helping new students develop a sense of belonging and relatedness with members of an existing class.

TARGET Areas
(R), (G)

Grade Level
Adaptable to all grade levels and content areas.

Procedure
When new students join an existing class, they often feel isolated and alone. While most teachers recognize this problem, it is necessary for them to devise ways to ensure that all new students become systematically integrated into the group. This strategy is designed to assist new students in the transition from being an "outsider" to becoming a productive and accepted class member.

In elementary and middle schools, "welcome coupons" can be used to help new students feel accepted. These coupons can be designed on a school computer and need only include a large "Welcome to Our Class" heading followed by blanks that each class member can complete when a new student arrives. After the new student is introduced to the class, all class members are given a blank welcome coupon to be completed and presented to the new member while shaking hands and introducing themselves. Redemption possibilities could include:

- I will introduce you to a student in another class.
- I will play a game with you at recess.
- I will show you where the (office, bathroom, lost & found, telephone) is located.
- I will sit with you at lunch.

Continued

STRATEGY 9-7   *Continued*

- I will save a space for you at my group's lunch table.
- I will help explain what we have been studying in (math, reading, language arts, science, etc.).
- I will share my books with you until you get your own.
- I will sit with you on the bus.
- I will walk home with you after school.

It is important not to embarrass new students during their introduction to the class. With older students, subtle but systematic efforts must be made to assist the student with his or her transition to the new school and to invite the student to participate in class activities.

Materials
Welcome coupons can be graphically designed and duplicated on small pieces of paper, or construction of coupons can be used as a writing assignment on lined paper.

Variations
Rather than students' composing their own coupons, typed and laminated coupons can be constructed by the teacher and students can choose one to present to the new student. Prior to the arrival of new students, discussion of what it feels like to be an outsider or a new member of a group can be quite useful for sensitizing students to the plight of new class members.

Source: Sharon Gresens, elementary art teacher.

___

STRATEGY 9-8

Belonging Bag

Purpose
This strategy reinforces feelings of belongingness, affiliation, and security in students who must move during the school year. It provides these students with a tangible reminder of support and relatedness that they can hold on to during the difficult time of establishing a sense of belonging with a new group.

TARGET Areas
(T), (G), (R)

STRATEGY 9-8 *Continued*

Grade Level
Used in primary through middle school, but can be adapted to high school.

Procedure
When students move from one city or school to another, they usually experience a great deal of sadness about losing their friends and a familiar teacher and classroom. The Belonging Bag is a gift from the class to their departing classmate that can serve as a reminder of the friendship and community they shared together. It can serve as a source of support and as a bridge between the old and new school communities.

On or near the student's last day at school, classmates decorate a large paper bag with their friend's name, words of encouragement, designs, pictures from magazines, yarn, sparkle, etcetera. Each class member is then given a piece of colored paper on which to write an affirming message to the person who is leaving. They might include things like:

- I'm glad you were in my class.
- I hope you make many new friends at your new school.
- I will miss your . . . .
- One of the things I will remember about you is . . . .
- Something I really like about you is . . . .
- I really appreciated it when you . . . .

The students can plan a going-away party for the departing classmate and present the Belonging Bag as a gift at the party. Most students pass up eating ice cream and cake or playing party games until they have read every warm message in their bag. It becomes a treasured gift for those who receive it.

Materials
Grocery-sized paper bag, decorating supplies, and note-sized colored sheets of paper.

Variations
High school teachers might forgo the decorated paper bag and party, but they will find that taking a few minutes for classmates to write encouraging messages on a card, in a notebook, or on pieces of paper will provide an important and valued gift for the departing student and will support a sense of cohesiveness among the group.

Source: Sally Rossmiller, elementary teacher.

—————— **STRATEGY 9-9** ——————————————————————————

Mystery Problems

Purpose
This strategy builds group cohesiveness and relatedness by helping the students realize that the contributions of each member are necessary if groups are to work effectively.

TARGET Areas
(T), (G)

Grade Level
Adaptable to all grade levels and subject areas.

Procedure
Mystery problems are a useful strategy for helping each member of a group realize that he or she has a responsibility to actively contribute to group cohesiveness and problem solving. Once a mystery problem has been determined, the group is arranged in a circle and each class member is given a clue to the solution of the problem typed on a 3 × 5 card. Depending on the size of the group, some students may be given two clues, or two students may have to share a clue. Students are then given the problem and encouraged to work together, sharing the information on the cards to find a solution. A time limit can be established, and students are told that they can take notes but cannot pass cards around.

After completion of the time limit or when the solution is obtained, students should discuss the factors that helped or hindered the problem-solving process.

The following are examples of mystery problems:

1. *The Mountain Bike Mystery* This mystery has 16 clues. With smaller groups, some participants may receive more than one clue. It may be necessary to subdivide larger groups and provide duplicate sets of clues. After distributing clues and explaining the above instructions for mystery games, read the following problem: "Lee Vernon is a senior at George Washington High School. His new, uninsured mountain bike was stolen from the school bike rack during a Friday afternoon basketball game. Your task is to determine which of the suspects questioned by the school principal is most likely to be the thief."

Clues

- The principal knows that Chuckie Parker has a police record for shoplifting.
- The principal, Mr. Deming, narrowed the list of suspects to 5 students.

STRATEGY 9-9 *Continued*

- Lee Vernon's bike lock was cut through with a hacksaw.
- Jean Seidl is dating a rock singer and once called Mr. Deming a male chauvinist.
- The rock singer's girlfriend told the principal that when she left the basketball game during the third quarter, she saw a boy with brown hair riding on a mountain bike with a hacksaw in his hand.
- The parents of the reformed shoplifter picked up their son after the basketball game.
- Georgie Kean's sister celebrated her birthday on the day of the basketball game.
- Georgie Kean and Ken Cornell were given a 3 day suspension by Mr. Deming for sawing down the goal posts before the homecoming football game.
- The birthday girl and her brother were attending a birthday party during the afternoon of the basketball game.
- Ken Cornell has brown hair, is interested in auto mechanics, and cannot afford to buy a mountain bike.
- The student who could not afford to buy a mountain bike was seen in the shop classroom about 30 minutes before the start of the basketball game.
- The student interested in auto mechanics operates the scoreboard for all basketball home games and sells popcorn at halftime.
- Barbara Koala is a member of a street gang that steals hubcaps from teacher's cars.
- The gang member and her friend Joan were attending a motorcycle rally in another state during the day of the basketball game.
- The police reported that several street gangs have been stealing bikes and selling them in another cities.
- Joan's friend has an Australian sheep dog that once attacked the school principal.

Answer: Jean Seidl is most likely to be the thief. All other suspects have alibis.

2. *Who's the Freshman?* (Useful for small groups). Give the following explanation: "Steve, Paul, Art, Don, and Bruce are a freshman, a sophomore, a junior, an senior, and a graduate student in chemistry, engineering, medicine, law, and mathematics, but not necessarily in that order. Your task is to find out who is the freshman and who majors in engineering."

- The engineering student graduated from the same high school as Paul and Art.

Continued

STRATEGY 9-9   *Continued*

- Bruce graduated from the law school last year with honors.
- Steve will become an intern next year.
- Paul and the sophomore mathematics students room together.
- Don is in a higher class than Paul.

Answer: Paul is the freshman. Don majors in engineering.

From Stanford (1977, p. 98).

Materials
Clues typed on 3 × 5 cards.

Variations
Mystery problems can be devised with any number of clues, and can deal with any content area. Students enjoy solving mystery problems and can be encouraged to write their own.

Source: Stanford (1977).

STRATEGY 9-10

Group Consensus

Purpose
This strategy is useful for building a sense of group belonging and cohesion by providing students with a graphic representation of the effectiveness of group consensus relative to majority rule and individual effort.

TARGET Areas
(T), (G)

Grade Level
This strategy is useful for upper elementary through high school.

Procedure
This activity is designed to have students solve a problem individually, using group voting, and by group consensus. In most cases they will discover the power of group consensus relative to individual and voting approaches.

Give each student a list of the following equipment and then read the following directions:

STRATEGY 9-10   *Continued*

Imagine that a friend stops by your home on a Saturday morning in October and suggests that you go with him for a day-long drive in the mountains to try out his new Jeep. You quickly pull on jeans, a sweatshirt and sneakers to go along. By late afternoon you are on a trail in the remote part of the Rockies when a severe snow storm blows up. The trail soon becomes almost impassable, and you can hardly see where you are going. Suddenly the Jeep starts to skid, and you plunge several hundred feet down a steep mountainside. Your friend is killed instantly and the Jeep is completely wrecked, but fortunately you have only a few scratches. By your best estimate you are thirty to forty miles from the nearest source of help. Luckily you discover a summer cabin nearby. Although it has no heat other than a wood burning fireplace and no telephone, it does offer shelter and about a week's supply of food. You soon realize that you cannot hope to stay in the cabin until you are rescued, for no one has any idea where to start looking for you. Therefore, when the storm starts to abate, leaving almost three feet of dry powder snow, you decide to try to follow the trail back to civilization. You are fortunate that the cabin is well stocked with camping equipment and other supplies and you can take almost anything you want, but you know that your survival over the three days that it will probably take you to reach help will depend partly on how carefully you select what equipment to take. You have been given a list of the materials the cabin contains and their weight. Decide which of the following items you will wear or carry, not exceeding a total of 50 pounds.

Equipment List

A. _____ wool hat (1 lb.)
B. _____ heavy wool mittens (2 lb.)
C. _____ axe (8 lb.)
D. _____ 50 feet of 1/8″ rope (1 lb.)
E. _____ saucepan (3 lb.)
F. _____ folding camp saw (1 lb.)
G. _____ rock climbing gear, including rock hammer, piton, etc. (10 lb.)
H. _____ 150 feet of 7/16″ rope (8 lb.)
I. _____ gasoline camp stove and fuel (10 lb.)
J. _____ plastic canteen filled with water (2 lb.)
K. _____ one large can of beef stew (10 lb.)
L. _____ fire-starting kit, including matches (1/2 lb.)
M. _____ heavy wool jacket with hood (10 lb.)
N. _____ pack frame and bag (6 lb.)
O. _____ pound cans of soup and vegetables (10 lb.)

Continued

STRATEGY 9-10   *Continued*

P. _____ sleeping bag (5 lb.)
Q. _____ downhill skis, boots, bindings, and poles (10 lbs.)
R. _____ air mattress (3 lb.)
S. _____ down-filled jacket without hood (3 lb.)
T. _____ high-top hunting boots (6 lb.)
U. _____ snowshoes (5 lb.)
V. _____ canvas tent (15 lb.)
W. _____ plastic tarp (2 lb.)
X. _____ eight boxes of high protein dry cereal (4 lb. total)
Y. _____ first-aid kit with splints and other equipment for setting bones (4 lb.)
Z. _____ first-aid kit without splints, etc. (1 lb.)
AA. _____ heavy wool pants (4 lb.)
BB. _____ knife with can opener (1/2 lb.).

First, ask students to make a list of the items they will take (not to exceed 50 pounds) without consulting other members of the group. When finished, ask them to write their names on their papers and hand them in for scoring. Then give each a new copy of the equipment sheet, and instruct them to do the task again, as a group of six to ten students, recording the items that the majority of the group thinks should be taken (adjusting the list to keep it under 50 pounds). Suggest that they use a minimum of discussion in getting their group vote (when students are voting, score their individual answers according to the answer key below). Then have each group turn in one sheet labelled with a group number.

Finally, making sure everyone has a copy of the equipment sheet, instruct the group to try to arrive at consensus on which items to take. The following directions will be helpful:

> *In trying to arrive at your answers, be sure to use reasoning and factual information instead of simply trying to get the group to see things your way. You should neither refuse to compromise nor give in just to make things easier. Try hard to understand the suggestions of other members, even when they disagree with your own choices. Don't change your mind just to avoid conflict; make sure that you can support any decision the group comes to. Do not use majority rule to decide on an answer; strive for complete agreement by all members of the group.*

Answer Key

Answers are based on the opinions of Bill May, author of *Mountain Search and Rescue* and member of the Rocky Mountain Rescue Group, and Bob Bruce, Merchandise Manager of Holubar Mountaineering, Ltd. and a member of the Certification Committee of the United States Ski Association.

STRATEGY 9-10 *Continued*

- wool hat (1 lb.)
- heavy wool mittens (2 lb.)
- 50 feet of 1/8″ rope (1 lb.)
- saucepan, for melting snow for drinking (3 lb.)
- folding camp saw (1 lb.)
- plastic canteen filled with water (2 lb.)
- fire-starting kit, including matches (1/2 lb.)
- pack frame and bag (6 lb.)
- sleeping bag (5 lb.)
- air mattress (3 lb.)
- down-filled jacket without hood (3 lb.)
- high-top hunting boots (6 lb.)
- snowshoes (5 lb.)
- plastic tarp (2 lb.)
- eight boxes of high protein dry cereal (4 lb. total)
- first-aid kit without splints, etc. (1 lb.)
- heavy wool pants (4 lb.)
- knife with can opener (1/2 lb).

To score individual answer sheets, penalize the student one point for each item on his or her list that does not appear in the key and one point for each item in the key that does not appear on the list. Total these points; this gives an overall score of the individual's performance. (The lower the score, the more accurate the student's answer.)

Separate answer sheets according to the groups students are working in. When the groups are trying to arrive at consensus, score the choices made by the voting, following the same procedure.

Prepare a summary sheet for each group that includes the score of the most accurate member, the score resulting from majority rule, and the score resulting from consensus (make sure to offer groups ample time for this part of the activity). Then tell students the choices that the experts made and let them compare their individual scores with the group scores. (In most cases the consensus scores will be lower than almost all individual and voting scores.)

Materials

Two equipment lists for each students and two for each group. Copy of the answer key for the overhead projector or written on the chalkboard. Summary sheet for each group member.

Variations

Similar activities are available in Pfeiffer and Jones (1969).

Source: Reprinted with permission from G. Stanford and A. E. Roark (1974), *Human Interaction in Education* (Boston: Allyn and Bacon), pp. 117–120.

10

Stimulating Student Involvement and Enjoyment in Learning

He had had a nice, good, idle time all the while-plenty of company—and the fence had three coats of whitewash on it! If he hadn't run out of whitewash, he would have bankrupted every boy in the village.

Tom said to himself that it was not such a hollow world, after all. He had discovered a great law of human action, without knowing it—namely, that in order to make a man or a boy covet a thing, it is only necessary to make the thing difficult to attain. If he had been a great philosopher, like the writer of this book, he would have comprehended that Work consists of whatever a body is obligated to do, and Play consists of whatever a body is not obligated to do. And this would help him understand why constructing artificial flowers or performing on a treadmill is work, while rolling tenpins or climbing Mount Blanc is only amusement.

MARK TWAIN—*The Adventures of Tom Sawyer*

PSYCHIATRIST WILLIAM GLASSER (1984, 1985) argues that the need for fun is basic to all human beings. Although the word *fun* has many interpretations, it implies the desire of people to seek activities that provide either physical, social, cognitive, or psychological pleasure. While most people, according to Glasser, do not feel as driven by the need for fun as they are by other needs, some will make drastic alterations in their lives, even risking death, as they attempt to satisfy this need; the current interest in sky diving and mountain climbing certainly supports his point.

Intertwined with the need for fun is an individual's desire to laugh, which Glasser believes is an indicator that one's need for fun has been temporarily satisfied. He also points out that events or comments

239

that cause people to laugh provide a quick and powerful insight into a truth, or they identify a falsity of an old tradition.

> *The punch line of a joke always contains a valuable lesson delivered in a new, quick, and usually irreverent manner. The reason adults do not laugh at children's jokes is that they do not usually teach us anything new, and children do not laugh at our jokes because they are not ready to learn what we find funny. (Glasser, 1984, p. 15)*

To demonstrate his point, Glasser quotes the late comic Joe E. Lewis's famous line, "I've been rich and I've been poor and, believe me, rich is better," which completely contradicts the "virtues of poverty" illusion. It's difficult not to laugh, or at least break out with a broad smile, when we encounter the simple truth of this uncomplicated statement.

Glasser also believes that educators often fail to consider students' need for fun when they design their curriculum and lesson plans. With increasing pressures to produce clearly defined outcomes, it's understandable why the emphasis on the product of learning can supersede and occasionally obliterate the process. If teachers, however, truly want to motivate students to devote large amounts of effort to learning, then they must design the process of learning to meet or at least recognize students' need for fun; failing to do so makes learning drudgery and the results superficial.

By definition, intrinsically motivating activities provide individuals with fun or enjoyment, although fun and enjoyment need not be limited to intrinsically motivating activities. Many activities undertaken for external goals can also satisfy inner needs. Large numbers of teachers, for example, find considerable enjoyment and fun in their jobs, although it seems likely that few would continue to teach if a paycheck did not accompany the activity.

Middleton, Littlefield, and Lehrer (in press) use Kelly's personal construct theory to form a framework for developing a model of academic fun. They propose that, when deciding whether or not an activity will be fun to perform, individuals evaluate the activity in terms of the degree to which success in the activity will provide an optimum level of arousal and sufficient feelings of control—in short, whether the activity is meaningful. Their research with high-achieving third- through eighth-grade students, labelled "gifted" in their study, indicated that students' conceptions of fun in academics tend to be organized around their own interests and perceptions of arousal ("There are lots of choices of things to do") and control ("I get to do what I want"). These results appear consistent with the intrinsic motivation research discussed in Chapter 4. It is interesting to note that the two activities most frequently rated as being "most fun" by these "gifted" students were recess and physical education. Unfortunately, a control group was not available to determine what activities "average" students would rate as most fun.

It seems reasonable to conclude that all students seek fun and enjoyment in school activities. When asked to describe the teachers in whose classes they are motivated to work their hardest, students invariably describe teachers who are enthusiastic about their content and find ways to make the learning interesting and enjoyable. Yet, as Wlodkowski (1989) suggests, too often the word *enjoyable* has a bad reputation in schools. Apparently many educators believe that learning is supposed to be hard work, and if it's enjoyable, it can't be serious or significant. This argument, however, is repeatedly contradicted by students' descriptions of classrooms in which they were highly motivated to do their best. It is in these classrooms that students are most willing to spend many hours learning content and meeting course objectives.

When teachers reflect on their own experiences as students, they usually confirm the assertion that stimulating and enjoyable learning need not be frivolous; enjoyment and hard work often go hand in hand. As John Dewey wrote many years ago, "When a child feels that his work is a task, it is only under compulsion that he gives himself to it. At every let up of external pressure his attention, released from constraint, flies to what interests him" (1913, p. 2).

Clearly, learning that is enjoyable stimulates the interests of the student. This process often happens naturally, in accordance with the developing interests of the individual. The ritual that surrounds the Sunday newspaper in many homes is one example. Parents, teenagers, relatives, and younger children scan the pages of the paper for headlines that will stimulate their interest to learn more about the topic by reading further. Family members with narrow interests may look at only one section of the paper, ignoring all others; they have learned from previous experiences that other sections simply do not contain articles of interest to them. Others in the family peruse the entire paper, section by section, finding that most headlines stimulate them to read further. These individuals often take three or four hours with this task, while others in the family take ten minutes. In either case, enjoyable, intrinsically motivated learning is being controlled by the personal interests of the reader.

Some newspapers believe that if they write headlines that capture a broader spectrum of interest, they can sell more copies. This technique is readily apparent on the front pages of the tabloids near the check-out counter at most supermarkets. Most readers, of course, quickly discover that these headlines rarely deliver what they promise; nevertheless, circulation data would indicate that they still buy the paper. Reputable newspapers, however, use headlines to convey the content of articles, rather than to simply attract the uninterested. Although Dewey probably never saw a tabloid of the type grocery shoppers are bombarded with today, he was certainly concerned that educators might use similar tactics to sell education:

> *I know of no more demoralizing doctrine—when taken literally—than the assertion of some of the opponents of interest that after subject-matter has been selected, then the teacher should make it interesting. This combines in itself two thorough-going errors. On one side, it makes the selection of subject-matter a matter quite independent of the question of interest—that is to say of the child's native urgencies and needs; and, further, it reduces method in instruction to more or less external and artificial devices for dressing up the unrelated materials, so that they will get some hold upon attention. In reality, the principle of "making things interesting" means that subjects be selected in relation to the child's present experience, powers, and needs; and that (in case he does not perceive or appreciate this relevancy) the new material be presented in such a way as to enable the child to appreciate its bearings, its relationships, its value in connection with what already has significance for him. It is this* bringing to consciousness of the bearings of the new material *which constitutes the reality, so often perverted both by friend and foe, in "making things interesting." (1913, pp. 23–24)*

Dewey, of course, never experienced the impact of modern television. When the previously described family later sits down to watch their favorite Sunday evening TV programs, a phenomenon different from their newspaper-reading behavior seems to occur, particularly when commercials are aired. Now all members find themselves attending to and learning about automobiles that they have no intention of purchasing, detergents and fabric softeners that they have no intention of using, colas and fruit punches that they have no intention of drinking, and gender-specific hygiene products that they have no possibility of using. Yet, in each case, almost the entire family is attentive and attracted to the information being provided, especially when it is their first viewing of a particular commercial. It is true that some will leave the room when a familiar commercial is being aired, but it is surprising how many individuals will continue to attend to a commercial they have observed scores of times.

Contrary to Dewey's admonition, it appears that the advertising industry has learned that it can, indeed, stimulate attention and learning about products or topics in which individuals have little initial or subsequent interest. By utilizing movement, novelty, color, sound variations, and two- to four-second image cuts, they can generate interest and attention toward topics that hold little or no prior appeal or personal association.

For educators, however, stimulating student interest is more than just exciting their visual or auditory senses. At the heart of enthusiastic teaching is the ability to select instructional procedures and activities that relate "to the child's present experience, powers, and needs." Television exploits the passive receptivity of viewers and uses visual and auditory stimulation and repetition to implant images and build product recognition. As educators, however, we need to remind ourselves continually that significant learning requires that students actively construct a personal meaning of what is being taught through the dynamic and interactive processes of analyzing and dissecting new information and then integrating one's interpretation of this information into that which is already understood. Significant learning generates involvement, and involvement is a prerequisite to commitment and enjoyment of the learning process. In short, when product recognition is the goal, passive receptivity is all that is required; when comprehension and application are the goals, the mind must be actively involved in the construction of meaning.

In addition to engaging students' brains, educators must articulate the relevance of the material they're teaching if they hope to help students appreciate "its value in connection with what already has significance" for them. Teaching the relevance of subject matter is a difficult task since content, in itself, is never relevant or irrelevant. One cannot say that the five reasons for the spread of Christianity in the Roman Empire, for example, are either relevant or irrelevant; the students decide that for themselves. If Jimmy enjoys reading about historical facts, then details about the Roman Empire might be very relevant for him. If he has no interest in the Roman Empire at the stage in his life that it is presented, then it probably is irrelevant to him. On the other hand, if getting a good grade on his history exam is of importance to him, the reasons for the spread of Christianity in the Roman Empire become relevant to that particular purpose. Many students, however, are no longer willing to learn information just to get good grades; they demand that learning have more meaning to their lives.

Relevance is a function of the motives and goals of each individual. It has been said that "the fatal error in education is that we throw answers, like stones, at the heads of those who haven't yet asked the questions." While this position is consistent with Dewey's, district- or statewide mandates make it almost impossible to design curricula solely around the questions and current interests of students. As Brophy (1987) clearly describes, "If teachers were recreation program directors, they could solve motivation problems merely by finding out what their clients like to do and arranging for them to do it. Instead, like supervisors in work settings, teachers must find ways to motivate their students voluntarily to try to do what is required of them" (p. 41). It follows, then, that one of the most difficult problems facing teachers is how to select, structure, and present content in ways that help students identify their own personal values in it. It is both inconceivable and unnecessary that teachers ensure that all students find personal value in everything being taught. Fortunately, when students, as well as teachers, believe that *most* of what they do in a given situation contributes to their self-enhancement, they will often become actively involved in the not directly valuable tasks that enable them to maintain "what already has significance" for them.

Wlodkowski (1989) suggests that educators should endeavor to help students value the process of learning as well as its intended benefits. Valuing the process of learning suggests that students are motivated to integrate information in ways that enable them to actively construct meaning from it; valuing the benefits of learning suggests that the product that was acquired has utility and meaning. Brophy (1987) uses the terms *learning* and *performance* to distinguish between the motivation to process information by actively constructing meaning from knowledge, and the motivation to demonstrate or exhibit that knowledge or skill after it has been acquired. He believes that many of the strategies designed to encourage student motivation in the classroom ignore learning and are primarily concerned with performance, especially on tests or assignments. According to Wlodkowski (1989), "When students value both *how* they learn as well as *what* they learn, motivation has a unity which is more continuous and dynamic. Like a wonderful adventure, both the journey and the destination have much to offer" (p. 8).

Although willing to use external controls to bribe or threaten students to perform in certain ways, many teachers believe they are helpless in influencing the informational-processing aspects of students' motivation to learn. The old adage "You can lead a horse to water, but you can't make him drink" seems to describe this helplessness. This conceptualization views motivation to learn as a motivational *trait*, or a consistent and enduring disposition to strive to either attain or avoid content mastery in most learning situations. On the other hand, Brophy (1987) suggests that motivation to learn can also be viewed as a motivational *state*, which exists when students are actively involved in mastering a particular skill or concept. This view suggests that teachers are not mere reactors to the motivational dispositions that students bring to their classrooms. They are, as Brophy (1987) suggests, "*active socialization agents* capable of stimulating the general development of student motivation to learn and its activation in particular situations" (p. 41).

As "active socialization agents," teachers can wield considerable control over the likelihood that students will enjoy learning, or, as Madeline Hunter has suggested, although we can't *make* the horse drink, we certainly can increase the likelihood of it drinking if we feed it large amounts of salt before bringing it to the trough. Rather than using salt, however, motivating teachers are constantly on the lookout for ways to maintain student attention and to stimulate their involvement with the learning process. Creating suspense, curiosity, and challenges to cognitive assumptions are useful ways for helping students become active participants in the creation of their own experiences (Wlodkowski, 1984). This does not mean that teachers need to act like vaudeville entertainers, albeit those who do certainly cause students to sit up and take notice. Nevertheless, although their routines, like television commercials, can temporarily command student attention, the effects are usually short-lived. It is only when teachers use instructional activities that are capable of stimulating student minds that active involvement with learning is initiated, and it is then that the process of learning becomes enjoyable.

Teacher enthusiasm is an obvious prerequisite for stimulating learning. According to Wlodkowski (1989), two functional criteria define teacher enthusiasm: First, teachers must be committed to and value what they teach; and second, this commitment must be expressed with reasonable emotion, animation, and energy. Students seem to have an intuitive sense for when teachers are committed to what they are teaching and when they are not. Yet, caring for and valuing content is not enough. While it may be a necessary precondition to enthusiastic teaching, it is irrelevant unless it is accompanied by an equal commitment to helping students acquire these feelings. English or science teachers, for example, may find personal excitement and enjoyment from literature, poetry, or the beauty and intrigue of the double helix, but unless they are equally committed to helping students discover this same excitement and enjoyment, their own dedication to the content is of little instructional value.

This desire of teachers to share the commitment that they have for their content triggers the animation and enthusiasm they display in the classroom. This enthusiasm is as contagious as a newly discovered flu virus, and students are capable of absorbing it with little conscious effort.

Although most individuals can remember at least one soft spoken, dead-pan, monotonistic teacher who was capable of providing academic expositions with words that provoked passionate excitement, they can remember many others with similar presentation styles who put them to sleep. There is no doubt that the content of what one says is far more important that how one says it, yet "how one says it" it still important. All things being equal, (which they seldom are), teachers who convey information and express ideas by varying the pitch, volume, and speed of their speech, maintain eye contact with students, and move freely around the classroom using natural arm, face, and head gestures are more likely to stimulate enthusiasm and interest than are inanimate talking heads.

Recommendations for Stimulating Student Interest and Involvement

1. *Find ways to get students actively involved in the learning process.* This is probably the most powerful suggestion for fostering student motivation to learn. When students' minds or bodies are dynamically engaged in the construction of meaning and in the integration of ideas and skills, they become active participants in learning, rather than mere observers. Mindless worksheets that require low-level thinking and busywork do not promote active participation—they foster boredom. Although students need opportunities to practice newly acquired skills, they also need challenges and stimulation if they are to value both the process and product of learning.

2. *Relate content objectives to student experiences.* Personal experiences are factually concrete and emotionally valuable. As a result, acknowledging student experiences and using them in the learning process stimulate involvement. Using family recipes to learn to divide fractions or discussing personal experiences with anger and frustration when trying to understand international conflict can provide students with a basis for accommodating new understandings. The guided recall and imagery techniques discussed in Chapter 4 are particularly useful for engaging students' minds and for drawing upon a broad range of personal experiences to better understand and integrate abstract concepts.

3. *Assess students' interests, hobbies, and extracurricular activities.* If teachers are to relate content to student interests and experiences, then they need to be knowledgeable about them. A short questionnaire at the beginning of the year or a round-robin discussion about interests or out of school activities can be useful for obtaining this information. These assessments can also help teachers discover students' heroes and role models.

4. *Occasionally present information and argue positions contrary to student assumptions.* When students are challenged by contrary ideas and opinions, they are stimulated to explore justifications, clarify facts, or alter beliefs—all processes that require active involvement and participation. While the role of "devil's advocate" can frequently be overplayed, it can be useful for stimulating student interest and enjoyment.

5. *Support instruction with humor, personal experiences, incidental information, and anecdotes that represent the human characteristics of the content.* Students are highly receptive to the personal and humorous aspects of content since they help relate the material more directly to their own emotions and lives. Nevertheless, it is possible to overuse personal experiences at the expense of other instructional methods. After all, forcing students to sit through 400 slides of a family vacation because one stopped for a couple of hours at Fort Sumpter is simply a waste of valuable instructional time. Ten clear slides of your family at Fort Sumpter, however, can help stimulate student interest in the start of the Civil War. Likewise, knowing that George Washington had bad teeth may not help students remember why he crossed the Delaware, but such incidental information, usually not included in textbooks, can help students realize that President Washington was a fallible human being. This, in turn, can help stimulate their interest in his life and accomplishments.

6. *Use divergent questions and brainstorming activities to stimulate active involvement.* Questions without right or wrong answers encourage creative thinking and stimulate student involvement and risk taking.

Pondering the racial or economic consequences that might have resulted had the South won the Civil War, for example, allows all students opportunities to participate in class discussions or contribute to small-group activities. Most students enjoy the change of pace and the challenge provided by open-ended questions and activities.

7. *Vary instructional activities while maintaining curricular focus and structure.* Students enjoy and are stimulated by teachers who are not locked into predictable and limited instructional patterns. By implementing a variety of activities and approaches, teachers can help students look forward to the unexpected challenges and stimulation offered by each class. While many find security in structure and appreciate having clearly defined assignments and expectations, they also find that routines can become dull and stagnant. Novelty and variety stimulate curiosity and invite involvement.

8. *Support spontaneity when it reinforces student academic interest.* While sequential and clearly structured objectives and lesson plans are necessary for student achievement, teachers should be ready to stray occasionally from a lesson plan when student interest is sparked by a topic not directly included in the lesson. Although some students enjoy the challenge of intentionally trying to lead teachers off on tangents that slow the pace of instruction, pursuing an occasional tangent prompted by genuine student curiosity can stimulate academic involvement. Although discussions on topics to be developed later in a course may have to be postponed, there are times when it's better to sacrifice continuity and sequence in order to capitalize on student interest. When, for example, military action breaks out in the Middle East and a teacher feels compelled to postpone discussions about it because the Middle East will be covered next month or next semester, student curiosity and involvement are sacrificed; a spontaneous teachable moment has surfaced and the teacher should seek to take advantage of it.

9. *By making a conscious attempt to monitor vocal delivery, gestures, body movement, eye contact, and facial expression, teachers can evaluate the degree of enthusiasm conveyed in their teaching.* Attitudes toward learning are caught rather than taught, and students can't catch a positive and enthusiastic learning attitude from dull, boring, and negative teachers. Teachers who are cynical and burned out in their jobs need to renew their enthusiasm by changing either their beliefs, schools, grade levels, or professions—the academic future of too many students is being sacrificed by their personal disillusionment. On the other hand, even teachers who enjoy their jobs and are enthusiastic about helping students learn may not be conveying this commitment to their students. It takes courage to videotape one's teaching or to solicit anonymous student feedback. Both procedures, however, are useful for monitoring and evaluating the degree to which teacher enthusiasm is being conveyed.

10. *Instructional objectives should be reviewed and redefined to* *ensure that teachers recognize their value and are committed to ensuring that all students attain them.* Teachers need to value and be committed to what they are teaching if they hope to stimulate student interest and involvement in learning it. It seems difficult, for example, to be committed to having all students memorize the five reasons for the spread of Christianity in the Roman Empire, although some may find the task enjoyable. However, helping students appreciate the power and magnitude of the Roman civilization and understanding some of the factors that contributed to its development and decline may be an important enough objective to ensure that all students master it. Although state and national achievement testing may reduce individual teachers' professional judgments on these matters, it is incumbent upon all educators to work to ensure that achievement tests measure outcomes that have been determined by debate from a broad spectrum of professionals, with the greatest input provided by practicing classroom teachers.

Strategies for Stimulating Student Involvement and Enjoyment in Learning

_____ STRATEGY 10-1 _____

Things Are Not What They Seem

Purpose
This activity is designed to stimulate student interest and enjoyment in the "scientific method" of drawing conclusions from systematic observation.

TARGET Area
(T)

Grade Level
Upper elementary, middle school, and high school general science classes.

Procedure
After a discussion of the importance of careful observation of the scientific method, the teacher stands in the front of the classroom and use a match to light a "candle" that has been placed on a plate on the teacher's desk. As the candle burns, the teacher asks the students to list all of their observations on a sheet of paper. Several minutes are allowed for this. When students are finished listing their observations, the candle is blown out and volunteers read their observations. After all observations are presented, the teacher picks up the candle and bite off the wick and about

STRATEGY 10-1 *Continued*

an inch of the candle. This is chewed and swallowed as the teacher discusses the scientific method. Students are then asked to list additional observations they have made about the "candle."

Materials
Before the class begins, take a long potato and peel the ends. Then whittle it down until it is about one inch in diameter. Soaking it in a mixture of water and lemon juice for a few minutes will prevent it from turning too brown when used later. Next, cut the bottom flat so that it will stand on a plate. Shape the tip so that it looks like the tip of a real wax candle. Now take a piece of slivered almond, or slice a half of unroasted almond so that it is about 1/8 of an inch in diameter. Sharpen one end and push it into the tip of the potato so that it looks like the wick of a candle. The natural oils in the almond will cause it to burn for several minutes when lit with a match.

Variations
An apple can be substituted for the potato. You may want to time your chewing and swallowing of the "candle" just as the bell rings. This can generate suspense and student interest until the next science lesson.

Source: Dick Wolff, sixth-grade teacher.

STRATEGY 10-2

A Dozen Book Bangers

Purpose
While many students find reading books interesting and stimulating, traditional book reports can often become boring and mechanical. This strategy can generate interest and enthusiasm by getting students actively and creatively involved in the book reporting process.

TARGET Areas
(T), (A), (R)

Grade Level
Adaptable for all grades and classes where book reports are required or expected.

Continued

STRATEGY 10-2 *Continued*

Procedure
The following twelve Book Bangers can be used in a variety of ways to provide a higher level of interest and enjoyment to the traditional book reporting process.

1. *And the Winner is . . .* —Every year the Motion Picture Academy presents awards to people in the movie industry who achieve distinction in certain fields or artistic endeavors. Oscars are awarded for the best actor and best actress, best musical score, best cinematography, best director, best sound score, and so on. Assume that your book has been turned into a major motion picture with all of the book's sights and sounds transferred to the wide screen. Who or what in your book would be nominated for Oscars?

For this project, please make a list of possible award categories and likely contenders, and then make a statement about each nominee expressing why you think he or she is deserving of the honor sought.

2. *Wanted: One Invention* —An author often uses a very basic formula when writing a book: Invent some characters, develop a problem, solve the problem, and then tie up the loose ends. The handling of the problem is of critical importance to the book. Plots, subplots, and counterplots are written into the story to aid the explanation of the problem and to heighten interest in the book.

Where man labors very hard, a machine can often solve the problem in a snap. In your book the author might have had an easier time if the main character had found a machine that would have instantly solved the problem.

For this project, please invent a machine that could have helped one of the characters in your book. Draw a diagram of your machine and explain how it could have been used by your chosen character.

3. *Poster* —Most novels leave the picture making to the mind's eye. Think about the novel you have just read. Which events, places, or people are most vivid in your mind? Try not to think of them in words, only in pictures. Can you see one with all its details? Draw a poster to illustrate this picture you have in your mind and that might be used to advertise your novel.

4. *In Pursuit of Trivia* —When you read a novel, it is the plot line, the message of the author, and the use of language that generally hold your attention and capture your imagination. We often gloss over minor details in pursuit of the overall theme or story. There are some readers, however, who actually delight in finding the minor, the insignificant, the unnoticed, or the trivial. To these people, there's a joy in trivia, a pleasure derived from knowing what most other readers ignore.

Prepare a minimum of twenty trivia questions from your book and then incorporate these questions into a board game of your own design.

STRATEGY 10-2 *Continued*

5. *Time For Toys*—It is always interesting to watch children in a toy store as they scamper from aisle to aisle, investigating every shelf and display, determined to find the perfect toy. Choose a character from you book and, looking through toy catalogs, find a toy you know this character would be excited to receive. Discuss the reasons for your choice.

6. *You'll Never Forget Your Vacation to . . .*—When you visit a travel agency you are often bombarded with brochures enticing you to visit one place or another, tantalizing you with tales of things to see, hear, and experience. By the time you leave the agency you often want to go everywhere; they all sound so terrific.

Design a travel brochure advertising the setting in your book. Include pictures (either drawn or from magazines) and descriptions that will make your readers want to drop everything and travel there immediately.

7. *Diorama*—As previously indicated, most novels leave the picture making to the mind's eye. Think about the book you just read. What events, places, and people are most vivid in your mind? Can you see a situation with all of its details? On a piece of paper do some sketching of what you see. Then, using a shoe box, create this scene as a diorama.

8. *A Picture Scrapbook*—Looking through a picture album can stir up memories of old friends, special times, and special places. Often just a glimpse at a simple photograph can flood the mind with recollected images, ideas, and feelings. A book is a virtual scrapbook of people, old friends, events, special times, and special places.

For this project, recreate the magic moments of your book by developing a picture scrapbook of the story it told.

9. *One Hundred Years Ago*—Our modern lifestyle is often taken for granted. Many of the material things we value today did not exist one hundred years ago; this we tend to forget. Yet nearly everything we depend on today is the successor of an idea from the past or the improvement of an older, now outdated adaptation.

For this project, predate your book by one hundred years. Discuss how the plot, characters, and settings would change because of the time warp you've put them in.

10. *Dear Diary*—A diary is a daily record of the events that occur in a person's life. Famous people often keep diaries so historians would have dated reference material when writing that person's biography. Many people who do not think they will be famous also keep diaries to organize their schedules or to record their thoughts and feelings.

For this project, write a diary of one of the characters in your book. Instead of a daily sequence, yours can be a bits-and-pieces approach where you lift important dates and events out of your character's life and explain them in your diary entries.

11. *There Once Was a Limerick*—The limerick, originating in Ireland, is a five-line poem with a rhyming pattern of AABBA. It is usually a

Continued

STRATEGY 10-2 *Continued*

humorous story about a particular person and situation. The following is an example:

> *There was an old man quite wierd,*
> *Who said, "It is just as I feared!*
> *Two owls and a wren;*
> *Four larks and a hen,*
> *Have all built their nests in my beard!"*

For this project, select several characters from your book, and write a limerick about each one. You might also want to design a unique presentation for your collection of limericks.

12. *Crazy Crosswords*—Many students are looking for books to read during the summer. Many others enjoy spending time doing crossword puzzles. Here's a chance to assist your classmates.

For this project, construct a crossword puzzle from a minimum of fifteen ideas in your book. You can use a computer program for crossword puzzles or generate your own design. The teacher will duplicate your puzzle and make it available to others who choose to read the book.

Variations
Students who have read the same books can often work together in completing the above Book Bangers.

Source: Three bangers from Susan Moe, elementary teacher; nine bangers from *Blast Off with Book Reports* by Debbie Robertson, copyright © 1985 by Good Apple, Inc., reproduced by permission of the publisher.

STRATEGY 10-3

Through the Stomach to the Brain

Purpose
Stimulating student interest and enjoyment is easy with food—its a natural motivator. From toddler to adult, most are willing to get actively involved in an activity when the final product is eating. In such cases food is not used as bribery, but as a culmination to the learning activity.

TARGET Area
(T)

Grade Level
Useful for all grade levels.

STRATEGY 10-3 *Continued*

Procedure

Food preparation can be used to get students involved in a wide variety of subjects other than cooking and nutrition classes. The following are some examples in different content areas:

• *Language Arts*—The focus can start on using the correct terms, definitions, and spelling for each ingredient, piece of equipment, and cooking process. Some of the many examples are: *dissolve, squeeze, melt, boil, freeze, beat, knead, pare, bitter, sweet, hot, warm,* and *saute.* Young children can discover differences in textures and learn to describe them. They can also copy a recipe, write out a grocery list, alphabetize it, and so forth. Many foreign language teachers have found the value of these activities with getting high school students actively involved in the learning process.

• *Science*—Topics such as reproduction and nutrition can be taught with eggs and milk, or bread making can be used to get students involved with the study of spores and yeasts. Other concepts such as how solids turn into liquids or the nature of different heating methods can also be discussed.

• *Math*—Addition, subtraction, multiplication, and division of whole numbers and fractions can be taught in the process of pricing grocery items, measuring ingredients, figuring out cooking times, and dividing cooked food in portions or servings. The use of percentages and decimals can also be incorporated.

• *Social Studies*—Students can discover the diversity of cultures that have created our food heritage, and they can delve into the habits and food preferences of the ethnic groups that have contributed to the American cuisine. Students can also study how geography, transportation, and climate have influenced food production and eating habits. Cooking also provides an opportunity to discuss how changing male and female roles are affecting meal preparation in homes.

• *Health and Physical Development*—Kitchen safety, sanitation, and food storage methods are useful topics for class discussions. Small-muscle development and eye–hand coordination can be improved with activities such as kneading dough, stirring batters, pureeing liquids, opening packages, and handling an egg beater. Older students can work on more demanding tasks such as rolling out pie crusts or separating egg yokes and whites.

Variations

Using food preparation to achieve content objectives is easily adaptable to cooperative learning activities. The goal is always clearly defined, and the preparation process helps develop the skills of planning, following directions, and organizing.

It is particularly useful to design academic homework assignments

Continued

STRATEGY 10-3 *Continued*

around the process of family food preparation. Students seem to enjoy practicality of these activities, as well as the positive interaction it can generate with their parents.

Source: Carole Curts, high school home economics teacher.

STRATEGY 10-4

Mystery Box

Purpose
This strategy uses student curiosity to stimulate interest and enthusiasm in the topic, concept, or skill to be studied.

TARGET Area
(T)

Grade Level
Appropriate for all grade levels. It is particularly useful in science classes where topics change often.

Procedure
Paint or decorate a medium sized box that has a lid and write the words "MYSTERY BOX" across the front. Old hat boxes are particularly suited for the purpose. With each new concept, topic, or skill to be studied, place some simple demonstration, example, or focus picture in the box before the start of class. Place the box on your desk or in a conspicuous place in the classroom so that students will see it when they enter the class. When the class begins, open the box and use its contents to start a focus on the lesson being studied.

In science classes, use novelties such as a "radiometer" that spins by the power of light, a short chemistry demonstration, a balance display that has an odd center of gravity, or an apple to start a presentation on Newton's Law of Gravity. In history classes, for example, old war relics or a gas mask might be used to start a unit on World War I.

The item in the box does not need to be novel. All that is required is that it relates to the topic to be studied. Students often look forward to the start of a new topic in order to see what you have selected.

Materials
A decorated box with lid and an object relating to the topic being studied are all that are required.

STRATEGY 10-4 *Continued*

Variations
By informing students of the future topics to be studied, you can encourage them to secretly place their own items in the box before the start of class. You might also cut a lift up door in the side of the box and ask students to feel the item and try to guess what it is.

Source: Dave DeRemer, science teacher and planetarium director.

STRATEGY 10-5

Headline News

Purpose
This strategy can stimulate student interest and enjoyment in writing and can encourage creativity in students.

TARGET AREA
(T)

Grade Level
Useful for upper elementary, middle school, and high school language arts and English classes.

Procedure
Pick up a few copies of some of the outrageous tabloids available near most grocery store check out counters. *The National Enquirer, Star,* and *Sun* are three of the more popular publications. Cut out some of the more provocative headlines and throw away the accompanying stories. Place them in a box or large envelope and have each student pick one. Headlines can be duplicated to ensure one for each student.

Introduce the activity by discussing some of the questions usually answered in a news story (who, what, when, where, and how). Suggest that students pretend that they are reporters and have them create a story pertaining to their headline. Students especially enjoy reading their stories to the entire class.

Materials
News tabloids available in most grocery stores. You may be able to make arrangements with the owner to receive expired issues free or at a substantial discount.

Continued

STRATEGY 10-5 *Continued*

Variations

Speech teachers may want to use this activity to encourage students to practice their extemporaneous speaking skills. Students can also generate their own headlines and add them to the teacher's collection.

Source: Sharon Crooke, elementary school teacher.

STRATEGY 10-6

Geometric-Tac-Toe

Purpose

While contributing to student interest and enjoyment, this variation of the traditional tic-tac-toe game is useful for developing concentration and problem-solving skills. Although it is somewhat competitive in nature, students of varying abilities seem to enjoy the friendly challenge created by the activity.

TARGET Areas

(T), (R)

Grade Level

This strategy is useful for all grade levels.

Procedure

Distribute copies of the diagram shown in Figure 10-1 for students to use during transition times during the class or school day. Since most students are familiar with the rules of tic tac toe, little explanation will be necessary. This grid allows nine possible solutions for aligning three O's or X's instead of the traditional eight possibilities.

Materials

Copies of the diagram in Figure 10-1 can be duplicated on the back of discarded sheets of paper. Older students will enjoy the challenge of sketching their own diagrams, as is most often done with the traditional game.

Variations

After students have had practice with this grid, they can be encouraged to develop their own, more complicated variations of the game. Having these new variations duplicated and shared with classmates can provide a valuable source of pride, competence, and relatedness for students.

STRATEGY 10-6 *Continued*

FIGURE 10-1 Geometric-Tac-Toe

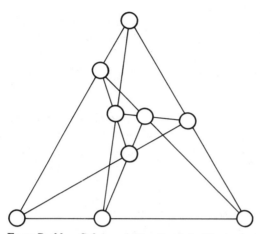

From *Problem Solving: A Handbook for Elementary School Teachers* by Stephen Krulik and Jesse A. Rudnick, copyright 1988 by Allyn and Bacon, Inc., reproduced by permission of the publisher.

STRATEGY 10-7

How Hot Is It?

Purpose
This strategy is useful for stimulating interest and involvement by helping students personally distinguish between heat and temperature.

TARGET Area
(T)

Grade Level
Upper elementary, middle, and high school science classes.

Procedure
On a table or desk in front of the room place four numbered one-liter beakers half filled with water at approximately the following temperatures: beaker No. 1 at 0 degrees Celsius; beakers No. 2 and No. 3 at 20 degrees Celsius (room temperature); and beaker No. 4 at 40 degrees celsius. Do not tell students the temperatures of the water in each beaker.

Continued

STRATEGY 10-7 *Continued*

Invite students to come to the front of the room and place one hand in beaker No. 1 and their other hand in beaker No. 4 for approximately ten seconds. Next have them remove their hands from these beakers and place the hand that was in beaker No. 1 into beaker No. 2, and the hand that was in beaker No. 4 into beaker No. 3. After about ten seconds, ask the students to dry their hands with a towel and then return to their seats and write down what they think were the temperatures of the water in each of the four beakers.

Students will be quite surprised to discover that beakers No. 2 and No. 3 are the same temperature, since almost all will believe that beaker No. 2 is warmer. Thermometers should be used to help students verify these results.

Materials
Four one-liter beakers, water at room temperature, ice water, and heated water, four thermometers, and one or two towels.

Variations
If the class is large, you may want to set up a second or third set of beakers in order to enable all students to participate in this activity. Students can also perform their own experiments using different temperatures in each beaker.

Source: David Magner, high school science teacher.

STRATEGY 10-8

Sinkers and Floaters

Purpose
This strategy is useful for stimulating student interest and involvement by providing a familiar and visual representation of the concept of density.

TARGET Area
(T)

Grade Level
Upper elementary, middle, and high school science classes.

Procedure
Build interest and suspense by telling students a story about two identical twins who were exactly the same in every respect except that when they went swimming one always floated and the other always sank. You might ask them to suggest some reasons why this might have happened.

STRATEGY 10-8 *Continued*

Continue the story by saying that although the twins appeared to be exactly the same, they had one small difference: One preferred regular soda and the other preferred diet soda. As they begin to think about this difference, set up your demonstration by moving to the front of the room where you have placed a glass container of water (a small aquarium is perfect for this).

Next set out a can of regular soda and a can of diet soda of the same brand. Ask students to speculate what might happen if you were to place each can in the water. Then gently place the regular soda into the water; it should sink. Remove the can and then place the diet soda into the water; it should float. You can then have students verify these results using different brands of regular and diet soda.

You can now continue the discussion of the twins and list reasons why one can of soda sinks and the other floats. Students will begin to realize that the sugar in the regular soda makes it denser than the water and therefore causes it to sink, while the artificial sweetener in the diet soda makes it less dense than the water and causes it to float.

Materials

Containers of water deeper than the length of the cans of soda. Small aquariums are useful for this purpose. Several cans of regular and diet soda of the same brands. Try to find as many different brands as possible.

Variations

This activity is particular adaptable to cooperative groups, with each group receiving two cans of soda, a container of water, and the story of the two twins. They can then be asked to asked to make and test hypotheses about the twins and about the sodas. Further examples are provided in Wiebe, Ecklund, and Mercier (1987).

Source: Ronda Hansen, elementary teacher.

STRATEGY 10-9

Word Puzzlers

Purpose

This activity is designed to stimulate student interest and enjoyment in language arts and in problem solving.

TARGET Area

(T)

Continued

FIGURE 10-2 Word Puzzlers

1 LO HEAD VE HEELS	2 WRITERS	3 JOBS IN JOBS	4 ego
5 SYMPHON	6 TIMING TIM ING	7 YOU JUST ME	8 I N W A I T
9 BEND DRAW DRAW	10 R E A D I N G	11 HE ART	12 CAR RE NATION
13 A T B H B T U	14 W R I T E I T	15 R ROAD I L	16 C E C O N N A T D T S E
17 ARREST YOU'RE	18 0 TV	19 MY A OWN PERSON HEART	20 A STINK
21 THERASINGINGIN	22 ENTURY	23 P NOANO Y	24 NE1410S

1. Head over heels in love   2. Writer's block   3. In between jobs   4. Inflated ego   5. Unfinished
symphony   6. Split second timing   7. Just between you and me   8. Lying in wait   9. Bend
backwards   10. Reading between the lines   11. Broken heart   12. Reincarnation   13. Bathtub ring
14. Write it down   15. Railroad crossing   16. Square dance contest   17. You're under arrest
18. Nothing on TV   19. A person after my own heart   20. Raising a stink   21. Singing in the rain
22. Long time, no see   23. Pay through the nose   24. Anyone for tennis

STRATEGY 10-9 *Continued*

Grade Level

Appropriate for use with upper elementary, middle, and high school.

Procedure

Figure 10-2 provides twenty-four Word Puzzlers. Before the beginning of class, put one puzzle on the board. As students enter the class, they are asked to think about the puzzle and try to determine the meaning. Students should be encouraged to avoid giving out the answer once they have discovered it. At the end of the period, randomly select someone to explain the meaning of the puzzle.

Although some teachers may be tempted to assign points or extra credit to those who answer the puzzle correctly, students seem to enjoy the puzzles more if they do them for their own sake rather than to improve their grade. This is a simple activity and takes little time away from the daily lesson. Yet students often look forward to the start of class and to trying to solve each new puzzle.

Variations

Rather than random selection, you may want to select students alphabetically or according to the seating arrangement to ensure that a different student is selected each day to offer the answer to the puzzle. You can also encourage students to devise their own puzzles for their classmates to decipher. You might use the word puzzles once a week, say on Monday or Friday morning. As you increase your supple of puzzles, you may have enough to start each class with this activity.

This strategy also lends itself to a cooperative group activity. You might duplicate a sheet of five to ten puzzles and let small groups work to solve them together. The common goal created by each puzzle fosters group identity and cooperation.

Source: Sherri Braun, elementary student teacher.

STRATEGY 10-10

The Cliffhanger

Purpose

This strategy is useful for stimulating student interest, involvement, and creativity, especially on gloomy days.

TARGET Areas

(T), (R)

Continued

STRATEGY 10-10   *Continued*

Grade Level
This strategy is useful for preschool through elementary school and can also be used in middle and high school language arts and English classes.

Procedure
On a dark, rainy day turn the lights off and have the students relax at their desks or tables. Then distribute drawing paper, crayons, pencils, and/or felt markers. Explain to them that they are famous authors and artists and are being asked to finish the story that you are about to tell or read them. (You can either make up an exciting mystery or science fiction story, or browse through the school library to find one that you don't think the students have read.) Tell or read the story to a critical moment of suspense before the story's climax. At this point, ask the students to finish the story with pictures and words.

Materials
Standard art material, including paper, crayons, colored pencils, or felt markers.

Variations
You might ask students to prepare their own mystery stories to the critical moment and have them ready for a rainy day. You could then randomly select one of these stories when you decide to use this strategy. This variation could also be used in cooperative groups, with each group selecting a different story.

Source: Unknown.

REFERENCES

Albert, L. (1990). *A teacher's guide to cooperative discipline.* Circle Hills, MN: American Guidance Services.

Allport, G. W. (1961). *Pattern and growth in personality.* New York: Holt, Rinehart, and Winston.

Ames, C. (in press, a). Achievement goals and the classroom motivational climate. In J. Meece and D. Schunk (Eds.), *Students' perceptions in the classroom: Causes and consequences.*

Ames, C. (in press, b). Achievement goals, motivational climate, and motivational processes. In G. Roberts (Ed.), *Motivation in sport and exercise.* Champaign, IL: Human Kenetics.

Ames, C. (1984). Competitive, cooperative and individualistic goal structures: A cognitive-motivational analysis: In R. Ames and C. Ames (Eds.), *Research on motivation in education* (vol. 1). New York: Academic Press.

Ames, C. (1990a). Achievement goals and classroom structure: Developing a learning orientation in students. Paper presented at the annual meeting of the American Educational Research Association, Boston.

Ames, C. (1990b). Motivation: What teachers need to know. *Teachers College Record, 91,* 409–421.

Ames, C. & Archer, J. (1988). Achievement goals in the classroom: Student learning strategies and motivation processes. *Journal of Educational Psychology, 80,* 260–267,

Aronson, E., Blaney, N., Stephan, C., Sikes, J. & Snapp, M. (1978). *The jigsaw classroom.* Beverly Hills, CA: Sage.

Association for Supervision and Curriculum Development. (1989). Issue: The sorting of students into ability groups. *Update, 31*(1), 4–5.

Association for Supervision and Curriculum Development. (1990). Computer "revolution" on hold. *Update. 32*(9), 1, 4–5.

Atkinson, J. W. (1957). Motivational determinants of risk-taking behavior. *Psychological Review, 64,* 359–372.

Atkinson, J. W. (1982). Old and new conceptions of how expected consequences influence actions. In N. T. Feather (Ed.), *Expectations and actions: Expectancy–value models in psychology.* Hillsdale, NJ: Erlbaum.

Atkinson, J. W. & Litwin, G. (1960). Achievement motive and test anxiety conceived as motive to approach success and motive to avoid failure. *Journal of Abnormal and Social Psychology, 60,* 52–63.

Bandura, A. (1977). Self-efficacy: Toward a unifying theory of behavior change. *Psychology Review, 84,* 191–215.

Bandura, A. (1981). Self-referent thought: A developmental analysis of self-efficacy. In J. H. Flavell & L. Ross (Eds.), *Social cognitive development: Frontiers and possible futures.* New York: Cambridge University Press.

Bandura, A. (1989). Human agency in social cognitive theory. *American Psychologist, 44,* 1175–1184.

263

Barker, R. G. (1942). Success and effort in the classroom. *Progressive Education, 19,* 221–40.

Bednarek, D. (1983, August 31). State students' scores exceed US Average. *The Milwaukee Journal,* pp. 1, 4.

Berglund, R., Raffini, J. P. & McDonald, L. (1992). Teacher characteristics in selected Australian and American classrooms: Fifteen years later. *Reading Research and Instruction, 31*(2), 31–48.

Bishop, J. H. (1989). Why apathy in American high schools? *Educational Researcher, 42,* 6–10.

Block, J. H. (1980). Promoting excellence through mastery learning. *Theory into Practice, 19* (1), 66–74.

Block, J. H. & Anderson, L. (1970). *Mastery learning in classroom instruction.* New York: Macmillian.

Block, J. H., Efthim, H. E. & Burns, R. B. (1989). *Building effective mastery learning schools.* New York: Longman.

Bloom, B. (1976). *Human characteristics and school learning.* New York: McGraw-Hill.

Bloom, B. (1981). *All our children learning.* New York: McGraw-Hill.

Bloom, B. (Ed.), (1985a). *Developing talent in young people.* New York: Ballantine Books.

Bloom, B. (1985b). On talent development: A conversation with Benjamin Bloom. *Educational leadership. 43*(1), 33–35.

Bloom, B. (1986a). Automaticity. *Educational leadership. 43*(5), 70–77.

Bloom, B. (1986b). What we are learning about teaching and learning: A summary of recent research. *Principal, 66* (2), 6–10.

Boggiano, A. K., Barrett, M., Weiher, A. W., McClelland, G. H. & C. M. Lusk (1987). Use of the maximal-operant principle to motivate children's intrinsic interest. *Journal of Personality and Social Psychology, 53,* 866–79.

Borba, M. (1989). *Esteem builders.* Rolling Hills Estates, CA: Jalmar Press.

Boyer, E. L. (1983). *High school: A report on secondary education in America.* New York: Harper and Row.

Brandt, R. (1988). On students' needs and team learning: A conversation with William Glasser. *Educational Leadership, 45*(6), 38–45.

Brophy, J. E. (1982). Classroom management and learning. *American Education, 18*(2), 20–23.

Brophy, J. E. (1986). *Socializing student motivation to learn* (Research Series No. 169). East Lansing: Michigan State University, Institute for Research on Teaching.

Brophy, J. E. (1987). Synthesis of research on strategies for motivating students to learn. Educational Leadership, 45(2), 40-48.

Cannell, J. J. (1989). *How public educators cheat on standardized achievement tests.* Albuquerque, NM: Friends For Education.

Carroll, J. B. (1963). A model of school learning. *Teachers College Record, 64,* 723–733.

Chandler, T. A. (1982, May). Mastery learning: Pros and cons. *NASSP Bulletin, 66,* 9–15.

Cohen, A. S. (1981). In defense of mastery learning. *Principal, 60* (5), 35–37.

Combs, A. W. & Avila, D. L. (1985). *Helping relationships.* (3rd ed.) Boston: Allyn and Bacon.

Combs, A. W., Avila, D. L. & Purkey, W. W. (1971). *Helping relationships.* Boston: Allyn and Bacon.

Combs, A. W. & Snygg, D. (1959). *Individual Behavior* (rev. ed.). New York: Harper & Row.

Connell, J. P. (1990). Context, self, and action: A motivational analysis of self-system processes accross the life span. In D. Cicchetti & M. Beeghly (Eds.), *The self in transition.* Chicago: University of Chicago Press.

Connell, J. P. & Wellborn, J. G. (1990). Competence, autonomy and relatedness: A motivational analysis of self-system processes. In M. Gunnar & L. A. Sroufe (Eds.), *Minnesota Symposium on Child Psychology* (vol. 22), Hillsdale, NJ: Erlbaum.

Connell, J. P. & Ryan, R. M. (1984). A developmental theory of motivation in the classroom. *Teacher Education Quarterly, 4,* 64–77.

Coopersmith, S. (1967). *The antecedents of self-esteem.* San Francisco: Freeman.

Covington, M. V. (1984). The self-worth theory of achievement motivation: Findings and implications. *The Elementary School Journa, 85* (1), 5–20.

Covington, M. V. & Beery, R. G. (1976). *Self-worth and school learning.* New York: Holt, Rinehart and Winston.

Covington, M. V. & Omelich, C. L. (1979). Effort: The double-edged sword in school achievement. *Journal of Educational Psychology, 71,* 169–182.

Covington, M. V. & Omelich, C. L. (1981). As failures mount: Affective and cognitive consequences of ability demotion in the classroom. *Journal of Educational Psychology, 73,* 796–808.

Csikszentmihalyi, M. (1978). Intrinsic rewards and emergent motivation. In M. R. Lepper and D, Greene (Eds.), *The hidden costs of reward: New perspectives on the psychology of human motivation.* New York: Wiley.

Csikszentmihalyi, M. & Nakamura, J. (1989). *The dynamics of intrinsic motivation: A study of adolescents.* In C. Ames and R. Ames (Eds.), *Research on motivation in education* (vol. 3). New York: Academic Press.

de Charms, R. (1976). *Enhancing motivation: Change in the classroom.* New York: Irvington.

deCharms, R. (1977). Pawn or origin? Enhancing motivation in disaffected youth. *Educational Leadership, 34,* 444–48.

deCharms, R. (1983). Intrinsic motivation, peer tutoring, and cooperative learning: Practical maxims. In J. M. Levin and M. C. Wang (Eds.), *Teacher and student perceptions: Implications for learning.* Hillsdale, NJ: Erlbaum.

Deci, E. L. (1972). Intrinsic motivation, extrinsic reinforcement and inequity. *Journal of Personality and Social Psychology, 22,* 113–120.

Deci, E. L. (1975). *Intrinsic motivation.* New York: Plenum.

Deci, E. L. (1986). Motivating children to learn: What you can do. *Learning 86. 14*(7), 42–44.

Deci, E. L., Nezlek, J., & Sheinman, L. (1981). Characteristics of the rewarder and intrinsic motivation of the rewardee. *Journal of Personality and Social Psychology, 40,* 1–10.

Deci, E. L. & Porac, J. (1978). Cognitive evaluation theory and the study of human motivation. In M. R. Lepper & D. Greene, *The hidden costs of reward: New perspectives in the psychology of human motivation.* New York: Wiley.

Deci, E. L. & Ryan, R. M. (1987). The support of autonomy and the control of behavior. *Journal of Personality and Social Psychology, 53,* 1024–1037.

Deci, E. L. & Ryan, R. M. (1985a). The general causality orientations scale: Self-determination in personality. *Journal of Research in Personality, 19,* 109–134.

Deci, E. L. & Ryan, R. M. (1985b). *Intrinsic motivation and self-determination in human behavior.* New York: Plenum Press.

Deci, E. L., Schwartz, A. J., Sheinman, L. & Ryan, R. M. (1981). An instrument to assess adults' orientations toward control versus autonomy with children: Reflections on intrinsic motivation and perceived competence. *Journal of Educational Psychology, 73,* 642–650.

Dewey, E. A. (1978). *Basic applications fo Adlerian psychology for self-understanding and human relationships.* Coral Springs, FL: CMTI Press.

Dewey, J. (1913). *Interest and effort in education.* Carbondale: Southern Illinois Press.

Dreikurs, R. (1968). *Psychology in the classroom* (2nd ed.). New York: Harper & Row.

Dreikurs, R., Grunwald, B., & Pepper, F. (1982). *Maintaining sanity in the classroom: Classroom management techniques* (2nd ed.). New York: Harper & Row.

Dweck, C. S. (1986). Motivational processes affecting learning. *American Psychologist, 41,* 1040–1048.

Erikson, E. H. (1963). *Childhood and society* (2nd ed.). New York: Norton.

Erikson, E. H. (1968). *Identity, youth and crisis.* New York: Norton.

Epstein, J. L. (1988). Effective schools or effective students: Dealing with diversity. In R. Haskins & D. MacRae (Eds.). *Policies for American's public schools: Teacher equity indicators.* Norwood, NJ: Ablex.

Epstein, J. L. (1989). Family structures and student motivation: A developmental perspective. In C. Ames & R. Ames (Eds.), *Research on motivation in education* (vol. 3). New York: Academic Press.

Feather, N. T. (Ed.). (1982). *Expectations and actions: Expectancy-value models in psychology.* Hillsdale, NJ: Erlbaum.

Fisher, R. T. & Ury, M. C. (1981). *Getting to yes.* New York: Penguin Books.

Foster, H. (1974). *Ribbin', jivin', and playing the dozens.* Cambridge, MA: Ballinger.

Friedenburg, E. Z. (1959). *The vanishing adolescent.* New York: Dell.

Gardner, J. W. (1961). *Can we be equal and excellent too?* New York: Harper & Row.

Ginnott, H. (1972). *Teacher and child.* New York: Macmillian.

Glasser, W. (1969). *Schools without failure.* New York: Harper & Row.

Glasser, W. (1977). Ten steps to good discipline. *Today's Education, 66,* 61–63.

Glasser, W. (1984). *Take effective control of your life.* New York: Harper & Row.

Glasser, W. (1986). *Control theory in the classroom.* New York: Harper & Row.

Glasser, W. (1990). *The quality school.* New York: Harper & Row.

Goodlad, J. I. (1984). *A place called school.* New York: McGraw-Hill.

Gordon, T. (1974). *Teacher effectiveness training.* New York: Wyden.

Graves, T. (1991). The controversy over group rewards in cooperative classrooms. *Educational Leadership 48* (7), 77–79.

Guskey, T. R. (1985). *Implementing mastery learning.* Belmont, CA: Wadsworth.

Guskin, S. L., Okolo, C., Zimmerman, E. & Peng, C. J. (1986). Being labeled gifted or talented: Meaning and effects perceived by students in special programs. *Gifted Child Quarterly, 30* (2), 61–65.

Hahn, A. (1987). Reaching out to America's Dropouts: What to Do? *Phi Delta Kappan, 69,* 256–267.

Harter, S. (1978). Pleasure derived from challenge and the effects of receiving grades on children's difficult level choices. *Child Development, 49,* 788–799.

Johnson, D. W. (1986). *Reaching out* (3rd ed.). Englewood Cliffs, NJ: Prentice-Hall.

Johnson, D. W. & Johnson, R. T. (1987). *Learning together and alone* (2nd ed.). Englewood Cliffs, NJ: Prentice-Hall.

Johnson, D. W. & Johnson, R. T. (1990). Social skills for successful group work. *Educational Leadership, 47 (4),* 29–33.

Johnson, D. W., Johnson, R. T. & Johnson Holubec, E. J. (1990). *Circles of learning* (3rd ed.). Edina, MN: Interaction Book Co.

Johnson, W. (1987). *Workforce 2000: Work and work for the 21st century.* Indianapolis: Hudson Institute.

Jones, V. & Jones, L. (1990). *Comprehensive classroom management: Creating positive learning environments* (3rd ed.). Boston: Allyn and Bacon.

Joyce, B., Showers, B. & Rolheiser-Bennett, C. (1987). Staff development and student learning: A synthesis of research on models of teaching. *Educational Leadership, 45* (2), 11–23.

Kagan, S. (1990). The structural approach to cooperative learning. *Educational Leadership, 47*(4), 12–15.

Kamali, C. (1984). Autonomy: The aim of education envisioned by Piaget. *The Kappan. 65,* 410–415.

Kangas, J. & Bradway, K. (1971). Intelligence at middle age: A thrity-eight-year follow-up. *Developmental Psychology. 5*(2), 333–337.

Kaplan, P. S. (1990). *Educational psychology for tomorrow's schools.* St. Paul, MN: West.

Katz, M. B. (1987). *Reconstructing American education.* Cambridge, MA: Harvard University Press.

Klausmeier, H. J., Jetter, J. T., Quilling, M. R. & Frager, D. A. (1973). *Individually guided motivation.* Madison: Wisconsin Research and Development Center for Cognitive Learning.

Koestner, R., Ryan, R. M., Bernieri, F. & Holt, K. (1984). Setting limits on children's behavior: The differential effects of controlling vs. informational styles on intrinsic motivation and creativity. *Journal of Personality, 53,* 233–248.

Kohn, A. (1991). Group grade grubbing versus cooperative learning. *Educational Leadership, 48*(5), 83–87.

Kozol, J. (1991). *Savage inequalities: Children in American schools.* New York: Crown.

Kulik, C. C., Kulik, J. A. & Bangert-Drowns, R. L. (1990). Effectiveness of mastery learning programs: A meta-analysis. *Review of Educational Research, 60,* 265–299.

Larson, R. (1979). How can the testing industry survive when there's nothing left to measure? *Phi Delta Kappan, 60,* 653.

Larson, R. (1991). *Why is a wild pig called a boar? Poems for kids growing up, and adults growing down.* (Available from R. Larson, 2740 N. 46th St., Milwaukee, WI 53210.)

Larson, R. (1992). Personal correspondence.

Lefrancois, G. R. (1988). *Psychology for teaching* (6th ed.). Belmont, CA: Wadsworth.

Lepper, M. R. (1981). Intrinsic and extrinsic motivation in children: Detrimental effects of superfluous social controls. In W. A. Collins (Ed.), *Aspects of the development of competence.* Hilsdale, NJ: Erlbaum.

Lepper, M. R. (1983). Extrinsic rewards and intrinsic motivation: Implications for the classroom. In J. M. Levin & M. C. Wang (Eds.), *Teacher and student perceptions: Implications for learning.* Hillsdale, NJ: Erlbaum.

Lepper, M. R. & Greene, D. (1978). Overjustification research and beyond: Toward a means-ends analysis of intrinsic and extrinsic motivation. In M. R. Lepper & D. Greene (Eds.), *The hidden costs of reward: New perspectives on the psychology of human motivation.* New York: Wiley.

Lepper, M. R., Green, D. & Nisbett, R. E. (1973). Undermining children's intrinsic interest with extrinsic rewards: A test of the overjustification hypothesis. *Journal of Personality and Social Psychology, 28,* 129–137.

Lepper, M. R. & Hodell, M. (1989). Intrinsic motivation in the classroom. In C. Ames and R. Ames (Eds.), *Research on motivation in education* (vol. 3). New York: Academic Press.

Licht, B. G. (1983). Cognitive-motivational factors that contribute to the achievement of learning-disabled children. *Journal of Learning Disabilities, 16,* 483–490.

Locke, E., Saari, L. M., Shaw, K. N. & Latham, G. P. (1981). Goal-setting and task performance: 1969-1980. *Psychological Bulletin, 90* (1), 125–52.

Mackey, J. & Appleman, D. (1983). The growth of adolescent apathy. *Educational Leadership, 40*(6), 30–33.

Maehr, M. L. (1984). Meaning and motivation: Toward a theory of personal involvement. In R. E. Ames & C. Ames (Eds.), *Research on motivation in education* (vol. 1). New York: Academic Press.

Malone, F. W. & Lepper, M. R. (1987). Making learning fun: A taxonomy of intrinsic motivations for learning. In R. E. Snow & M. J. Farr (Eds.), *Aptitude, learning and instruction Vol. III. Conative and affective process analyses.* Hillsdale, NJ: Erlbaum.

Mangino, R. A. (1957). *A lab manual for microbiology.* Portland, ME: Walch.

Maslow, A. H. (1954). *Motivation and personality.* New York: Harper & Row.

Maslow. A. H. (1970). *Motivation and personality* (2nd ed.). New York: Harper & Row.

McCall, R. B., Appelbaum, M. I. & Hogarty, P. S. (1973). Developmental changes in mental performance. *Monographs of the Society for Research in Child Development,* Serial No. 150, *38*(3), 1–85.

McDaniel, T. R. (1984). A primer on motivation: Princples old and new. *Phi Delta Kappan, 66* (1), 46–49.

Middleton, J. A., Littlefield, J. & Lehrer, R. (in press). Gifted students' conceptions of academic fun: An examination of a critical construct for gifted education. *The Gifted Child Quarterly.*

Minnick Santa, C. (1988). *Content reading including study systems.* Dubuque, IA: Kendall/Hunt.

Mintzberg, H. (1979). *The structure of organizations.* Englewood Cliffs, NJ: Prentice-Hall

Morgan, M. (1984). Reward-induced decrements and increments in intrinsic motivation. *Review of Educational Research, 54,* 5–30.

Nicholls, J. G. (1989). *The competitive ethos and democratic education.* Cambridge, MA: Harvard University Press.

Oakes, J. (1988). Tracking: Can schools take a different route? *NEA Today, 6*(6), 41–47.

Orgel, A. R. (1983). Haim Ginott's approach to discipline. In D. Dorr, M. Sax, & J. Bonner (Eds.), *Comparative approaches to discipline for children and youth.* New York: International University Press.

Pfeiffer, J. W. & Jones, J. E. (1969). *A handbook of structured experiences for human relations training* (vol. 1). Iowa City, IA: University Associates Press.

Pittman, T. A., Boggiano, A. K. & Ruble, D. R. (1983). Rewards and intrinsic motivation in children: Implications for educational settings. In J. M. Levine and M. Wang (Eds.), *Perceptions of success and failure: New direction in research.* Hillsdale, NJ: Erlbaum.

Pittman, T. S., Emery, J. & Boggiano, A. K. (1982). Intrinsic and extrinsic motivational orientations: Reward-induced changes in preference for complexity. *Journal of Personality and Social Psychology, 42*, 789–797.

Purkey, W. & Novak, J. (1984). *Inviting school success: A self-concept approach to teaching and learning* (2nd ed.). Belmont, CA: Wadsworth.

Raffini, J. P. (1973). Resultant achievement motivation: Does it make a difference in academic success? *College and University, 49* (3), 30–34.

Raffini, J. P. (1980). *Discipline: Negotiating conflicts with today's kids.* Englewood Cliffs, NJ: Prentice-Hall.

Raffini, J. P. (1984). An experimental study of individual goal-setting and competitive performance structures. *Wisconsin State Research Grant #297.*

Raffini, J. P. (1986). Student apathy: A motivational dilemma. *Educational Leadership, 44* (1), 53–55.

Raffini, J. P. (1987). Group dynamics that foster motivation to learn. In W. Roy (Ed.), *Encouraging Student Learning.* Carthage, IL: Good Apple.

Raffini, J. P. (1988). *Apathy: The protection of self-worth.* (What research says to the teacher). Washington, DC: National Educationan Association.

Raffini, J. P. & Rosemier, R. A. (1972). Effects of resultant achievement motivation of post-exam error correcting performance. *Journal of Educational Psychology, 63*, 281–85.

Reasoner, R. (1982). *Building self-esteem: A comprehensive program.* Palo Alto, CA: Counsulting Psychologists Press.

Robertson, D. (1985). *Blast off with book reports.* Carthage, IL: Good Apple.

Rosenholtz, S. J. & Simpson, C. (1984). The formation of ability conceptions: Developmental trend or social construction? *Review of Educational Research, 54*(1), 31–63.

Rosenthal, R. & Jacobson, L. (1968). *Pygmalion in the classroom.* New York: Holt, Rinehart and Winston.

Ryan, R. M. (1991). The nature of the self in automomy and relatedness. In G. R. Goethals & J. Strauss (Eds.), *Multidisciplinary perspective on the self.* New York: Springer-Verlag.

Ryan, R. M., Connell, J. P. & Deci, E. L. (1985). A motivational analysis of self-determination and self-regulation in education. In C. Ames & R. Ames (Eds.), *Research on motivation in education* (vol. 2). New York: Academic Press.

Ryan, R. M., Connell, J. P. & Grolnick, W. S. (In press). When achievement is not intrinsically motivated: A theory and assessment of self-regulation in school. In A. K. Boggiano & T. S. Pittman (Eds.), *Achievement and motivation: A social-developmental perspective.*

Ryan, R. M. & Powelson, C. L. (1991). Autonomy and relatedness as fundamental to motivation in education. Paper presented at the annual meeting of the American Educational Research Association, Chicago. Available from the Department of Psychology, University of Rochester.

Ryan, R. M. & Stiller, J. (1991). The social contexts of internalization: Parent and teacher influences on autonomy, motivation, and learning. In P. R. Pintrich & M. L. Maehr (Eds.), *Advances in motivation and achievement: Volume 7.* Greenwich, CT: JAI Press.

Stanford, G. (1977). *Developing effective classroom groups.* New York: Hart.

Stanford, G. & Roark, A. E. (1974). *Human interaction in education.* Boston: Allyn and Bacon.

Schmuck, R. A. & Schmuck, P. A. (1974). *A humanistic psychology of education: Making the school everybody's house.* Palo Alto: National Press Books.

Shapira, Z. (1976). Expectancy determinants of intrinsically motivated behavior. *Journal of Personality and Social Psychology, 34,* 1235–1244.

Sizer, T. (1984). *Horace's compromise – The dilemma of the American high school.* Boston: Houghton Mifflin.

Skrtic, R. (Nov./Dec. 1987). An organizational analysis of special education reform. *Counterpoint,* 15–19.

Slavin, R. E. (1983). Non-cognitive outcomes of cooperative learning. In J. M. Levin & M. C. Wang (Eds.), *Teacher and student perceptions: Implications for learning.* Hillsdale, NJ: Erlbaum.

Slavin, R. E. (1987). Mastery learning reconsidered. *Review of Educational Research, 57,* 175–213.

Slavin, R. E. (1990a). Mastery learning re-reconsidered. *Review of Educational Research, 60,* 300–302.

Slavin, R. E. (1990b). Research on cooperative learning: Consensus and controversy. *Educational Leadership 47* (4), 52–54.

Slavin, R. E. (1991a). Group rewards make groupwork work. *Educational Leadership, 48* (5), 89–91.

Slavin, R. E. (1991b). Synthesis of research on cooperative learning. *Educational Leadership, 48* (5), 71–82.

Spady, W. G. (1988). Organizing for results: The basis of authentic restructing and reform. *Educational Leadership, 46* (2), 4–8.

Stipek, D. J. (1988). *Motivation to learn: From theory to practice.* Englewood Cliffs, NJ: Prentice-Hall.

Tuckman, B. (1965). Developmental sequences in small groups. *Psychological Bulletin, 63,* 384–399.

Vito, R. C., Connell, J. F. & Bagley-Mengus, J. (1988). *Motivational characteristics of elemetary school students "at-risk" for academic failure and personal maladjustment.* Unpublished manuscript, University of Rochester, Graduate School of Education and Human Development, Rochester, NY.

Vito, R. C., Crichlow, W. & Johnson. L. (1989, March). *Motivational characteristics of academically disaffected and engaged urban junior high and high school students.* Paper presented at the annual meeting of the American Educational Research Association, San Francisco.

Vito, R. C. & Connell, J. P. (1990). *A longitudinal study of at-risk high school students: A theory-based description and intervention.* Unpublished manuscript, University of Rochester, Graduate School of Education and Human Development.

Weiner, B. (1979). A theory of motivation for some classroom experiences. *Journal of Educational Psychology, 71,* 3–25.

Weiner, B. (1980). *Human motivation.* New York: Holt, Rinehart and Winston.

Weiner, B. (1983). Speculations regarding the role of affect in achievement-change programs guided by attributional principles. In J. M. Levin & M. C. Wang (Eds.), *Teacher and student perceptions: Implications for learning.* Hillsdale, NJ: Erlbaum.

Weiner, B. (1986). *An attribution theory of motivation and emotion.* New York: Springer-Verlag.

White, R. W. (1959). Motivation reconsidered: The concept of competence. *Psychological Review, 66,* 297–333.

Wiebe, A., Ecklund, L. & Mercier, S. L. (Eds.). (1981). *Floaters and Sinkers Solutions for math and science.* Fresno, CA: AIMS Educational Foundation.

Wilcox, K. (1982). Differential socialization in the classroom: Implications for equal opportunity. In G. Splindler (Ed.), *Doing the ethnography of schooling*. New York: Holt, Rinehart and Winston.

Wlodkowski, R. J. (1978). *Motivation and teaching: A practical guide*. Washington, DC: National Education Association.

Wlodkowski, R. J. (1986). *Motivation* (rev. ed.). (What research says to the teacher). Washington, DC: National Education Association.

Wlodkowski, R. J. (1989). *Handbook for motivational thinking for educators*. Evanston, IL: Universal Dimensions.

Wood, K. D. (1986). How to improve critical thinking. *Middle School Journal, 18*(1), 24–26. (Reprinted in D. R. Clasen & C. Bonk (1987), *Teachers tackle thinking*. University of Wisconsin-Madison Extension Program.)

Zuckerman, M., Porac, J., Lathin, D., Smith, R. & Deci, E. L. (1978). On the importance of self-determination for intrinsically-motivated behavior. *Personality and Social Psychology Bulletin, 4,* 443–446.

APPENDIX A

Motivational Strategies Classified by TARGET Areas

Task:

Strategy 6-1   Positive Day
Strategy 6-2   Mystery Kid
Strategy 6-5   Five-Year-Old Humor
Strategy 6-6   Family biographer
Strategy 6-7   Identity Cube
Strategy 6-8   Death to Put-Downs
Strategy 7-4   Writer's Block
Strategy 7-5   Celebrity Tea at the White House
Strategy 7-8   Goal Journals
Strategy 7-9   Show Time
Strategy 7-10 Power Notes
Strategy 8-2   Sentence Success
Strategy 8-4   Chain Link
Strategy 8-5   Concept Blocks
Strategy 8-6   Penguin Parents
Strategy 8-7   Reaction Guide
Strategy 8-8   Nonverbal Day
Strategy 8-10 Stingerless Spelling Bee
Strategy 9-1   Jigsaws
Strategy 9-2   Numbered Heads Together
Strategy 9-3   Epidemic
Strategy 9-4   Kids on Camera
Strategy 9-5   Accomplishment Hunt
Strategy 9-6   The Crusher
Strategy 9-8   Belonging Bag
Strategy 9-9   Mystery Problem
Strategy 9-10 Group Consensus
Strategy 10-1 Things Are Not What They Seem
Strategy 10-2 A Dozen Book Bangers

Strategy 10-3   Through the Stomach to the Brain
Strategy 10-4   Mystery Box
Strategy 10-5   Headline News
Strategy 10-6   Geometric-Tac-Toe
Strategy 10-7   How Hot Is It?
Strategy 10-8   Sinkers and Floaters
Strategy 10-9   Word Puzzlers
Strategy 10-10   The Cliffhanger

Authority:

Strategy 6-1   Positive Day
Strategy 6-8   Death to Put-Downs
Strategy 7-1   Control Coupons
Strategy 7-2   The *A* Exchange
Strategy 7-3   You Rule
Strategy 7-4   Writer's Block
Strategy 7-5   Celebrity Tea at the White House
Strategy 7-6   Contract Grading
Strategy 7-7   Grade Grid
Strategy 7-8   Goal Journals
Strategy 7-9   Show Time
Strategy 7-10   Power Notes
Strategy 10-2   A Dozen Book Bangers

Recognition:

Strategy 6-2   Mystery Kid
Strategy 6-3   Celebrity of the Week
Strategy 6-4   PIT Calls
Strategy 6-6   Family Biographer
Strategy 6-7   Identity Cube
Strategy 6-9   Secret Supporter
Strategy 6-10   Success Lifeline
Strategy 7-5   Celebrity Tea at the White House
Strategy 7-9   Show Time
Strategy 8-1   BUG Honor Roll
Strategy 8-2   Sentence Success
Strategy 8-4   Chain Link
Strategy 8-6   Penguin Parents
Strategy 8-10   Stingerless Spelling Bee
Strategy 9-1   Jigsaw

Strategy 9-2   Numbered Heads Together
Strategy 9-4   Kids on Camera
Strategy 9-5   Accomplishment Hunt
Strategy 9-6   The Crusher
Strategy 9-7   New Kid on the Block
Strategy 9-8   Belonging Bag
Strategy 10-10   The Cliffhanger

Grouping:

Strategy 8-5   Concept Blocks
Strategy 8-8   Nonverbal Day
Strategy 8-10   Stingerless Spelling Bee
Strategy 9-1   Jigsaw
Strategy 9-2   Numbered Heads Together
Strategy 9-3   Epidemic
Strategy 9-4   Kids on Camera
Strategy 9-5   Accomplishment Hunt
Strategy 9-6   The Crusher
Strategy 9-7   New Kid on the Block
Strategy 9-8   Belonging Bag
Strategy 9-9   Mystery Problem
Strategy 9-10   Group Consensus

Evaluation:

Strategy 7-2   The *A* Exchange
Strategy 7-6   Contract Grading
Strategy 7-7   Grade Grid
Strategy 7-10   Power Notes
Strategy 8-1   BUG Honor Roll
Strategy 8-3   Criterion Grading
Strategy 8-7   Reaction Guide
Strategy 8-9   Second-Chance Testing
Strategy 8-10   Stingerless Spelling Bee

Time:

Strategy 7-4   Writer's Block
Strategy 7-6   Contract Grading
Strategy 7-7   Grade Grid

Strategy 8-3 Criterion Grading
Strategy 8-9 Second-Chance Testing

Motivational Strategies Classified by Grade Level

All Grade Levels:

Strategy 6-1 Positive Day
Strategy 6-2 Mystery Kid
Strategy 6-4 PIT Calls
Strategy 6-6 Family Biographer
Strategy 6-8 Death to Put-Downs
Strategy 6-9 Secret Supporter
Strategy 6-10 Success Lifeline
Strategy 7-1 Control Coupons
Strategy 7-2 The A Exchange
Strategy 7-3 You Rule
Strategy 7-4 Writer's Block
Strategy 7-6 Contract Grading
Strategy 7-8 Goal Journals
Strategy 8-1 BUG Honor Roll
Strategy 8-2 Sentence Success (Language Arts and English)
Strategy 8-3 Criterion Grading
Strategy 8-4 Chain Link
Strategy 8-5 Concept Blocks
Strategy 8-7 Reaction Guide
Strategy 8-8 Nonverbal Day
Strategy 8-9 Second-Chance Testing
Strategy 9-1 Jigsaw
Strategy 9-2 Numbered Heads Together
Strategy 9-4 Kids on Camera
Strategy 9-5 Accomplishment Hunt
Strategy 9-7 New Kid on the Block
Strategy 9-9 Mystery Problem
Strategy 9-10 Group Consensus
Strategy 10-1 Things Are Not What They Seem (Science)
Strategy 10-2 A Dozen Book Bangers
Strategy 10-3 Through the Stomach to the Brain
Strategy 10-4 Mystery Box
Strategy 10-5 Headline News (Language Arts and English)
Strategy 10-6 Geometric-Tac-Toe
Strategy 10-7 How Hot Is It? (Science)

Strategy 10-8 Sinkers and Floaters (Science)
Strategy 10-9 Word Puzzlers
Strategy 10-10 The Cliffhanger

Elementary and Middle School Level:

Strategy 6-3 Celebrity of the Week
Strategy 6-5 Five-Year-Old Humor
Strategy 6-7 Identity Cube
Strategy 7-5 Celebrity Tea at the White House
Strategy 8-6 Penguin Parents
Strategy 8-10 Stingerless Spelling Bee
Strategy 9-8 Belonging Bag

Middle and Secondary Level:

Strategy 7-7 Grade Grid
Strategy 7-9 Show Time (Music)
Strategy 7-10 Power Notes
Strategy 9-3 Epidemic (Science)
Strategy 9-6 The Crusher (Science and Math)

INDEX

A

Ability
  as learning rate, 45
  and attribution theory, 104–105
  challenge to fixed entity, 40
  confidence in, 38
  differences in, 186
  fixed or malleable, 39–46
  related to effort, 52
Ability grouping, 135–138
Absolute performance standards, 101, 190
Acceptance, 144–45
Accomplishment Hunt, 225–226
Acknowledging conflicting feelings, 92
Adhocracy, 112–113, 118–119
Adlerian psychology, 23–30
  attention seeking, 26
  birth order characteristics, 24
  diagnostic questions, 29
  power seeking, 26–27
  recognition reflex, 29
  revenge seeking, 27–28
  noninvolvement, 28
  social inferiority, 24
  social interest, 23
A Exchange, The, 170–171
Affective goals, 219
Allport, G., 14, 20
Ames, C., 51, 130–131, 137–139
Anarchy, 112–113, 115
Anderson, L., 196
Anderson, V., 172, 178
Antecedents of attributions, 106
Apathy (See Student apathy)
Apollo project, 118
Appelbaum, M., 41–42

Archer, J., 130–131, 138–139
Atkinson, J., 98, 101–104
Attributes, controllability, 105
Attribution retraining, 108
Attribution theory, 104–108
Attributions for success and failure:
  (*illustration*, 104)
  implications for teachers, 107–108
Attention seeking, 26
Authority Structure (A), 132–133
Autonomy, 109–110, 163–164
  in adolescence, 19
  need for, 17–20
  recommendations for enhancing, 167–169
Autonomy orientation, 109

B

Bandura, A., 21, 40, 183, 187
Bangert-Drowns, R., 187–188
Barker, R., 182
Barnstable, J., 224
Baron, T., 174
Beery, R., 50, 52, 57–58, 62, 184
Bell, T., 5
Belonging Bag, 230–231
Belonging, the need for, 21–31
Benevolent dictatorship, 112–113, 116–117
Birth order, 24
Bishop, J., 34–35
Block, J., 187, 196, 205
Bloom, B., 40–42, 44, 50, 186–187, 196, 205
Boggiano, A., 70, 93–94
Book Bangers, A Dozen, 249–252
Borba, M., 144, 146–147, 166

Borchardt, J., 150, 203
Boyer, E., 32–33
Bradway, K., 41
Braun, S., 261
Brophy, J., 61, 67, 98–99, 148, 243
Butt, B., 156, 202

C

California task force on self-esteem,
    142–143
Cannell, J., 47–49
Carlson, K., 153, 174
Carroll, J., 6, 44–45, 51, 98, 186
Carroll's model for learning, 44–45
Celebrity Tea at the White House,
    173–174
Celebrity of the Week, 152–153
Chain Link, 196–197
Challenge, 69
Chandler, T., 187
Choice, 77, 167 (*see also* Autonomy)
Classroom organization patterns,
    111–119
  adhocracy, 112–113, 118–119
  anarchy, 112–113, 115
  benevolent dictatorship, 112–113,
      116–117
  cooperation, 112–113, 117
  dictatorship, 115–116
  individualist, 111–114
  quasi-democracy, 112–113, 117–118
  separatist, 112–115
Classroom personality:
  goal orientations, 129–140
  organizational patterns, 111–129
  teacher beliefs, 95–111
Cohen, A., 188
Cognitive evaluation theory, 74–76,
    109
Communication skills, 121
  phases in skill development,
      214–215
    consciously skilled, 214–215
    consiciously unskilled, 214–215
    unconsciously skilled, 214–215
    unconsciously unskilled, 214–215
Competence

beliefs about, 106
  in all students, 4
  the need for, 20–23
Competition
  debilitating aspects, 56
  forced, 51
Computers and apathy, 33
Concept Blocks, 197–199
Conflicting feelings, acknowledging,
    92, 168
Conflict negotiation strategies,
    122–128
  confronting, 122, 124
    descriptive, 124
    I-message, 124
    inquiry, 124
  consequating, 122, 127
  encouraging, 122, 127–128
  facilitating, 122, 124
  inviting, 122–124
  resolving, 122, 126
Conflict resolution
  helping students use, 218
  helping students use, 218
  skills, 121–122
Confrontation, 124
Connell, J., 30, 74, 77, 79, 81, 83
Consensus information, 106
Contract Grading, 175
Control, 71
  minimally sufficient, 92–94
  orientation, 109
  stage of teacher growth, 134
  versus autonomy, 108–111
Control Coupons, 169–170
Cooperation, 112–113, 117
Cooperative activities, 210
Cooperative learning, 9, 208–217
  activities, 210
  affective goals, 219
  and communication skills, 210–211
  elements, 208–209
    face-to-face interaction, 209
    group processing, 209
    individual accountability, 209
    positive interdependence, 209, 218
  and group goals, 209, 218
  and group rewards, 215–216
  individual accountability, 209, 219

integrating into traditional classrooms, 210
  research, 216–217
  and rewards, 82
  skills, 2112–212
    formenting, 212
    forming, 212
    formulating, 212
    functioning, 212
  structures, 210
  suggestions for effective relationships, 213–214
Cooperative structures, 210
Coopersmith, S., 144
Coping with conflicts, 121–128
Covington, M., 15–17, 50, 52, 57–59, 143, 184, 189–90
Crichlow, W., 30
Criterion Grading, 195–196
Criterion-referenced evaluation, 191
Crooke, S., 256
Crusher, The, 226–229
Csikszentmihalyi, Mihaly, 66–68
Curts, C., 254
Curiosity, 70

D

deCharms, R., 18, 78–81, 90–91, 165–166, 206
Death to Put-Downs, 158
Deci, E., 20, 30, 65, 73–75, 77, 79–84, 86, 90, 109–110
DeRemer, D., 255
Descriptive confrontation, 124
Devil's Advocate, 246
Dewey, J., 241–242
Diagnostic questions, 29
Dictatorship, 112–113, 115
Disilllusionment, 134
Dreikurs, R., 18, 23–29, 56–57, 127
Dropout rates, 1–2
Dweck, C., 36, 130

E

Effort
  and ability, 52

and satisfaction, 55
  double-edged sword, 59
  encouragement of, 52
  relationship to grades, 53
Effectance motivation, 21
Effort, 100, 104–105
Effort-outcome dependence, 100, 182, 192
  requirements for, 101
Effort-outcome feedback, 108
Ego involvement, 39
Ego orientation, 129–130
Emery, J., 70
Empathy:
  listening skills, 217
  required beliefs, 145
  and security, 144
Encouragement:
  defined, 127
  characteristics in teachers, 127–128
  in learning, 239–245
Epidemic, 222–224
Epstein, J., 132, 135, 138
Erickson, E., 19, 146
Escalentes, H., 147
Establishing norms, 121
Esprit de corps, 119
Evaluation, elements, 135
Excellence, 4
Expectancy-value theory, 7, 40, 22, 98–101
Expectation for success, 98–101
Expectations for students, 147
Extrinsic goals, 129

F

Face-to-face interaction, 209
Facilitative listening, 211
Failure:
  avoidance, 103
  avoidance behaviors, 56–62
    ensuring success, 57–58
    student apathy, 61
    withholding effort, 58–59
  effects, 103
Family Biographer, 155
Fantasy, 71–72

Feather, N., 40, 98
Feelings, expressing, 218
Feldhausen, J., 36
Fermenting skills, 212
Firmness, 135
Fisher, R., 122
Five-Year-Old Humor, 155
Flow, 66
Forming skills, 212
Formulating skills, 212
Foster, H., 133
Four-Phase Rites of Passage:
  control, 134
  disillusionment, 134
  humanism, 134
  permissivism, 133
Friedenburg, E., 146
Friends for Education, 47
Fun, 239
Functioning skills, 212

G

Gardner, J., 55
Geometric-Tac-Toe, 256–257
Gifted, 240–241
Gifted and talented programs, 42–43
Gifted and talented, labelling, 43
Ginott, H., 88, 92, 168
Glasser, W., 2, 19, 124, 127, 143, 163, 239
Goal orientation, 129–132
  extrinsic goals, 129
  learning goals, 129
  mastery goals, 130–131
  performance goals, 129–131
  social solidarity goals, 129
Goal Journals, 177–178
Goal setting, 165–157, 182–185
  and competence, 182–185
  goal characteristics, 166–167
Goals for education, 2–5
  effort, 2, 4
  excellence, 2, 4
Goodlad, J., 1
Gordon, T., 121, 124, 210
Grade Grid, 176–177
Grade inflation, 189

Graves, T., 216
Greene, D., 72–74
Gresen, S., 230
Grolnick, W., 81, 83
Group Consensus, 234–237
Group goals, 209
Group processing, 209
Grunwald, B., 127
Guskey, T., 187, 196, 205
Guskin, S., 43

H

Hansen, R., 259
Headline News, 255
History of performance, 106
Hodell, M., 69–71
Hogarty, P., 41–42
Holubec, E., 210–213
Hoppe, F., 182–183
How Hot Is It?, 257
Humanism, 134
Hunter, M., 4, 244

I

Ice-breaking, 120
Identification, 83–87
Identity Cube, 157
I-message, 124
Incentive for success, 102–104
Individual accountability, 209, 219
Individualist, 111–114
Informational limit-setting, 87–90, 154
Inquiry confrontation, 124
Instructional objectivs, 190
Instructional pace, 101
Intelligence (*see also* ability):
  definition, 41
  entity theory, 37–39
  gains in IQ, 41–42
  incremental theory, 37–38
  IQ distributions, 40
Internalization, 83–87
Introjected regulation, 83–87
Intrinsic motivation

and autonomy, 65
and competence, 65
characteristics, 64–65
effects of external rewards, 72–76
fostering, 67–69
flow, 66
sources, 69–72

J

Jacobson, L., 38–39
Jenko, B., 194
Jigsaw, 220–221
Johnson, D., 121, 128, 208–213, 215, 219
Johnson, K., 156
Johnson, L., 30
Johnson, R., 121, 128, 208–213, 215, 219
Joyce, B., 217
Judd, N., 173

K

Kagan, S., 209, 222
Kamali, C., 18
Kangas, J., 41
Kaplan, P., 142
Katz, M., 3–4
Kids on Camera, 224–225
Kiskunas, P., 153
Klausmeier, H., 165
Koestner, R., 88–89, 168
Kohn, A., 82, 94
Kozol, J., 1–2, 35
Krulik, J., 257
Ktulik, D., 257
Kulik, C., 187–188
Kulik, J., 187–188

L

Lake Wobbegon effect, 47
Larson, R., 111–113, 119, 141–142, 181
Law of effect, 72

Leaderless groups, 120
Learning goals, 36, 129–131
Learning rate, 44
Lehrer, R., 240–241
Lepper, M., 69–73, 78–80, 93
Level of aspiration, 103, 183–184
Licht, B., 108
Limit setting, 145
  informational, 88–89
  controlling, 88–89
Littlefield, J., 240–241
Litwin, G., 102
Locke, E., 184
Locus of causality, 104–105
Logical consequences, 91–92, 168
Luck, 104–105

M

McDaniel, T., 128, 217
McKinnon, K., 171
Maehr, M., 129
Magner, D., 258
Maladaptive motivational patterns, 38–39
Mamerow, P., 195
Manke, C., 161
Mangino, R., 224
Marks, L., 225
Marks, S., 155
Maslow, A., 11–13, 17
Maslow's hierarchy of needs, 11–13
  basic needs, 12
  love and belonging, 12–13
  meta-needs, 12
  physiological, 12
  safety and security, 12
  self-actualization, 13
  self-esteem, 13
Mastery goals, 130–131
Mastery learning, 101
  instructional procedures, 186
  and outcome-based education, 188
  research, 187–188
McCally, R., 41–42
Mental imagery, 166
Middleton, J., 240–241
Miley, D., 200

Minimally sufficient control, 92–94, 164–165, 168
Minimal sufficiency principle, 93–94
Minnick, S., 180
Mintzberg, H., 118
Mission, 147
Moe, S., 252
Montessori, M., 77, 108
Morman, C., 154, 159
Motivational patterns:
  ꜰdaptive, 129
  maladaptive, 129
Motivation to learn
  as state, 244
  as trait, 244
Mystery Box, 254–255
Mystery Kid, 151–153
Mystery Problems, 232–234

N

NASA, 118
Nation at Risk, A, 4, 11, 47
New Kid on the Block, 229–230
Nezlek, J., 110
Nicholls, J., 39, 94, 129
Noninvolvement, 28
Nonregulation, 83–87
Nonverbal Day, 203
Norm-referenced evaluation, 3, 46–50, 138, 191
  definition, 46
  labelling, 47
Novak, J., 124
Numbered Heads Together, 221–222

O

Oakes, J., 137
Objectives, clearly defined, 100
Omerlich, C., 17, 59
Organizational patters of classrooms, 121–119
  (*see also* Classroom organizational patterns)
Organizing to develop unity, 119–129

Orientation stage of group development, 120–121
Orientations Scale, 109–110
Outcome-based education, 101, 138, 185–190
  and grades, 189
  and mastery, 188
  and mastery learning, 186
  and teachers, 189

P

Pace, instructional, 101
Paraphrasing ideas, 125
Pavlotos, C., 229
Penguin Parents, 199
Pepper, F., 127
Perceptual field, 13–15
Performance goals, 37, 129–131
Permissivism, 133
Personal construct theory, 240
Peterson, R., 179
Phenomenology, 13
Piaget, J., 18
Pimple, The, 141
PIT Calls, 153–154
Pittman, T., 70
Positive Day, 149–150
Positive information feedback, 147
Positive interdependence, 207, 218
Powelson, C., 207–208
Power Notes, 179–180
Power, the need for, 19–20
Power seeking behaviors, 27–28
Porac, J., 65, 74
Pride of accomplishment, 106
Probability and incentive, 102–104
Productivity stage of group development, 128
Psychologically safe climate, 149, 168
Psychosocial crises, 146
Punishment, 18, 168
Purkey, W., 124

Q

Quasi-democracy, 117–118

R

Raffini, J., 8, 17, 91, 102, 133, 165, 83, 210
Reaction Guide, 200–202
Reasoner, R., 142, 146–147
Recommendations:
  for building student relatedness, 217–220
  for enhancing competence, 190–193
  for enhancing self-esteem, 147–149
  for enhancing student autonomy, 167–169
  for stimulating interest and involvement, 245–248
Recognition reflex, 29
Reflecting feelings, 125
Regulation
  extrinsic, 83–84
  identification, 83–84
  introjected, 83–84
Relatedness, 23–25, 30 (see also belonging)
Relevance, 243
Revenge seeking, 27–28
Rewards
  and activities not intrinsically motivating, 82–83
  controlling aspect, 76
  criteria to be considered, 135
  informational aspect, 76
  Piaget's views, 18
  uses, 76–81
Retesting, 190, 192
Ring toss, 102–104
Risk taking, 211, 168
Roark, A., 237
Robertson, D., 252
Rolheiser-Bennett, C., 217
Rosenholtz, S., 39
Rosemier, R., 102
Rosenthal, R., 38–39
Rossmiller, S., 231
Rudnik, J., 257
Rule enforcement, 145
Rules, purpose for, 148
Ryan, R., 20, 30, 65, 64–75, 77, 79–84, 86, 90, 109–110, 184, 207–208

S

Sadler, E., 177
Sanctions by reciprosity, 18
Schliem, J., 197
Schmuck, R., 23
Secret Supporter, 159
Security, 144–146
  suggestions for fostering, 145–146
Self concept, 14
  defined,d 142
  and self-esteem, 142
Self-determination, 77, 163–164
  (see also autonomy)
Self-efficacy, 21, 183
Self-esteem:
  definition, 142
  and self-concept, 142
Self-evaluation, 149
Self-fulfilling prophecy, 38–39
Selfhood, 146
Self-identity, 146
Self-regulation, 83–87
Self respect, 145
Self-system processes, 30
Self-worth motive, 15–17, 143
Sentence Success, 194–195
Separatist, 112–115
Shapira, Z., 79
Sheinman, L., 110
Showers, B., 217
Show Time, 178–179
Simpson, B., 59
Simpson, C., 39
Sinkers and Floaters, 258–259
Sizer, T., 32
Skrtic, R., 118
Slavin, R., 82, 136, 208–209, 215
Social interest, 23
Social solidarity goals, 129
Spady, W., 138, 185–86
Stability of attributes, 104–105
Stages of group development, 120–129
  coping with conflicts, 121–128
  establishing norms, 121
  orientation, 120–121
  productivity, 128
  termination, 128–129

Stanford, G., 120–129, 234, 237
Stiller, J., 184
Stingerless Spelling Bee, 205
Stipek, D., 106–107, 137
Student apathy
  causes, 34–36
  decreasing, 40
Student effort, 148 (*see also* effort)
Student involvement in learning, 244, 239–345
Success from effort, 99–100
Successful negotiators, beliefs of, 122–123
Success Lifelines, 160–161
Success, personally defined, 191

T

TARGET, 10
  motivational strategies, 139
  structures, 132–140
    authority (A), 132–133
    evaluation (E), 138
    group (G), 135–138
    recognition (R), 135
    task (T), 132
    time (T), 138–140
Task:
  ease and difficulty, 104–105
  involvement, 39
  orientation, 129–130
  structure (T), 132
T-chart, 213
Teacher beliefs, 96–111
Teacher expectations, 39
Teacher enthusiasm:
  criteria defining, 245
  evaluation, 247
Termination stage of group development, 128–129
Testing industry, 181
Tests, formative, 191
Things Are Not What They Seem, 248
Through the Stomach to the Brain, 252

Toffler, A., 118
Tracking, 135–136 (*see also* ability grouping)
Trust, 145–146
Truth in testing, 47
Tuckman, B., 120

U

Unity, developing, 119–129
Ury, M., 122

V

Value of school success, 101–104
Value of success, 98
Vito, R., 30

W

Walberg, H., 136
Wechsler, D., 41
Weiner, B., 40, 104–106, 184
White, R., 21
Wilcox, K., 55
Wlodkowski, R., 5, 40, 99, 241, 244–245
Wolff, R., 249
Wood, K., 200–202
Word Puzzlers, 259–261
Writers Block, 172–173

Y

You Rule, 171–172

Z

Zimmerman, L., 158
Zuckerman, M., 77